Getting the transport right – for what?

Getting the transport right – for what?
What transport policy can tell us about the construction of sustainability

Mathilde Rehnlund

Subject: Environmental Science
Research Area: Environmental Studies
School: Natural Sciences, Technology and Environmental Studies

Södertörns högskola
(Södertörn University)
The Library
SE-141 89 Huddinge

www.sh.se/publications

Cover image: Leopold Rehnlund Magnevill, inspired by Robert Rauschenberg
Mother of God (ca 1950). Map image: Ortofoto raster (c) Lantmäteriet

Cover Layout: Jonathan Robson
Graphic Form: Per Lindblom & Jonathan Robson

Stockholm 2019

Södertörn Doctoral Dissertations 166
ISSN 1652–7399

ISBN 978-91-88663-74-0 (print)
ISBN 978-91-88663-75-7 (digital)

To my children, two of Nature's critical thinkers.

"Get the transportation right. Then let things happen."
Sir Peter Hall (in Kunzig 2011).

Abstract

This thesis studies transport as a governing tool that shapes the physical environment and human society, as well as having environmental impacts. The aim is to learn what policy for transport can say about what sustainability means and does. My focus is Stockholm municipal policy from 2007–2017, a period of sustainability concerns and large transport project agreements. Using the *What's the problem represented to be?* approach (Bacchi 2009), I look at measures proposed for the 'right' transport of people and ask: what kind of 'tool' is transport produced to be, and how is sustainability constructed?

The transport system is one of the most visible parts of the built environment and recognized for its negative impact on environmental and human health. As co-constitutive of social practices, transport is far from a mere technical issue. Despite this, transport policy studies are often technical in approach. Since policy is not a neutral response to pre-existing 'problems', I consider transport policy to be part of a creative process for the whole of society. A main contribution to the field of sustainable transport is a view of transport as a tool for governing and inherently political.

Stockholm is frequently hailed as a 'green' city. I was interested to explore this 'best case' scenario and see what might consolidate the two seemingly opposing aims of greener transport and more car use. I find that Stockholm policy for transport is permeated with technological optimism, reliance on individual choices, and concern for economic growth. Policy measures construct transport as a tool to affirm the commuter paradigm and promote urban expansion. Attention to the sustainability of transport concentrates on emissions from transport work, which is to be addressed by individual consumption choices. Sustainability is associated with efficiency, technological innovation, and above all urbanity. The proposals paradoxically construct the subject as both co-responsible for problem and solution (the conscious or irresponsible consumer), and as a cog in the wheel for economic growth (the commuting worker). This disregards both the *homo ludens* and the citizen: play and the political. These aspects become subordinated while policy enhances the role of work.

Key words, related fields: problem representation, transport policy studies, policy discourse, sustainable transport studies, urban transport studies

Contents

List of Acronyms and Abbreviations.. 13
List of Figures.. 14
Acknowledgements 17
Foreword.. 21

Part 1
Constructing the study 23

1. Introduction 25

1.1 A period of transport project packages.. 27
1.2 Aim and research questions 28
1.3 The structure of the work 31

2. Background 33

2.1 Stockholm as a site of sustainable transport study............................... 33
2.2 Urban transport development in Stockholm 35
2.3 Stockholm transport system... 40

3. Previous research into sustainable transport 41

3.1 Aspects of transport.. 41
3.1.1 Definitions of sustainable transport... 42
3.1.2 Objectives of sustainable transport 43
3.1.3 Posing other kinds of transport questions 46

4. Theoretical and methodological considerations.. 51

4.1 Selecting sources... 53
4.1.1 Selecting the main policy documents 54
4.1.2 Policy documents used as reference points................................... 59
4.1.3 Selecting additional materials – articles, press releases,
letters from readers 62
4.2 Studying policy... 64
4.3 What's the problem represented to be? 67
4.3.1 Critique – an inquiry into the limits of a structure...................... 70
4.3.2 Policy as discourse – making and analysing meaning
through actions and words 71
4.3.3 Six questions about problem representation 73
4.4 Applying the WPR framework... 80

Part 2
Problem representation in Stockholm policy 91

5. The 'fix' and the 'problem': measures for transport 95

5.1 The relative expected potential for greenhouse gas reductions 95
5.2 What the measures address 101
5.3 In what way should the 'problem' be 'fixed' by measures for
non-motorized transport? 102
5.4 In what way should the 'problem' be 'fixed' by measures for public transport? .105
5.5 In what way should the 'problem' be 'fixed' by measures for cars? 111
5.6 What do the measures work to 'fix'? 120
5.7 What is the problem represented to be? 122

6. The problem as emissions caused by 'wrong' technology 127

6.1 Conceptual premises 128
6.1.1 'Smartness' 128
6.1.2 'Green' versus fossil-fuel technology 131
6.2 A technical-rational understanding of the problem 135
6.2.1 Discursive elements 136
6.2.2 The subject 137
6.2.3 Lived effects 138

7. The problem as wrong choices made by individual transport users 141

7.1 Conceptual premises 142
7.1.1 Choice 142
7.1.2 'Necessary' and 'unnecessary' traffic 145
7.2 An individual understanding of the problem 149
7.2.1 Discursive elements 150
7.2.2 The subject 150
7.2.3 Lived effects 153

8. The problem as too little transport work 155

8.1 Conceptual premises 156
8.1.1 Capacity 156
8.1.2 'Framkomlighet' through mobility or accessibility 158
8.1.3 A 'sustainable increase' in transport 160
8.1.4 The growth engine of Sweden 163
8.2 A 'technical' understanding of the problem rooted in narrative 165
8.2.1 Discursive elements 166
8.2.2 The subject 167
8.2.3 Lived effects 168

9. The problem as too little urban space 171

9.1 Conceptual premises 172
9.1.1 The 'walkable city' 173

9.1.2 Urban nodes 175
9.1.3 'Lack of homes' (Swedish: 'bostadsbrist') 175
9.1.4 Space-craving and space-saving modes of transport 178
9.2 A narrative of space 180
9.2.1 Discursive elements 181
9.2.2 The subject 182
9.2.3 Lived effects 183

10. 'Sustainability' in Stockholm policy for transport 187

10.1 Explicit representations of sustainability 187

11. Conclusions and discussion 193

11.1 What kind of 'tool' is produced by policy for transport in
Stockholm municipality? 193
11.2 How is sustainability constructed? 198
11.2.1 Sustainability as urban 201
11.2.2 Sustainability as growth 202
11.2.3 Sustainability as a piece of your life puzzle 204
11.3 Approaching transport as a governing tool 205

12. Populärvetenskaplig sammanfattning (Summary in Swedish) 209
13. References 215
14. Appendix: Measures and the problems they represent 235

List of Acronyms and Abbreviations

IPCC   International Panel on Climate Change
RA   Swedish Road Administration (Vägverket)
SCB   Statistics Sweden (Statistiska centralbyrån)
SEPA   Swedish Environmental Protection Agency
           (Naturvårdsverket)
SIKA   Swedish Institute for Transport and Communications
           Analysis (Statens institut för kommunikationsanalys)
SL   Stockholm Public Transport (Storstockholms lokaltrafik)
SLL   Stockholm County Council (Stockholms läns landsting)
STA   Swedish Transport Agency (Trafikverket)
WPR   *What's the problem represented to be?*

List of Figures

Figure i: My mother's destinations during a workday. (21)

Figure 2.1:   View of Stockholm city centre from Södermalm (south island). (36)

Figure 2.2:   A model of the Vällingby suburb centre, with an early metro train. (38)

Table 4.1:   Main materials. (56)

Table 4.2:   Additional policy documents. (60)

Figure 4.1:   My research questions and the questions of the WPR. (83)

Table 4.3:   The form of the table. (84)

Table 4.4:   Operationalizing the WPR. (89)

Figure ii: Sign on Munsö. (93)

Figure 5.1:   The anticipated potential of measures in the Roadmap. (97)

Table 5.1:   Support for and expected potential of measures for reducing greenhouse gas emissions. (98)

Table 5.2:   Attention given to and expected potential of measures for reducing greenhouse gas emissions. (100)

Table 5.3:   A list of measures addressing non-motorized transport. (105)

Figure 5.2:   Commuter boat at Ekerö centre. (108)

Table 5.4:   A list of measures addressing public transport. (110)

Table 5.5:   Measures and represented problems. (112)

Table 5.6:   Measure combinations and the problems these represent. (113)

Table 5.7:   A list of measures addressing cars. (117)

Table 5.8:   'Problem' representations and measures. (124)

Table 6.1:   Problem representations related to emissions. (127)

Table 7.1.   'Problem' representations related to the lack of sense. (141)

Figure 6.1:   The video screen of a bus. (144)

Figure 6.2:   A more recent campaign. (144)

Table 7.2:   Vehicles charged or not charged under the congestion tax. (146)

Table 8.1:   'Problem' representations related to insufficient transport work. (156)

Figure 8.1:   Construction of the Stockholm Bypass tunnel entry at Lovö, Ekerö municipality. (169)

Table 9.1:   'Problem' representations related to insufficient urban space. (172)

Figure 9.1:   A blunt example of an opinion letter proposing less woodland and more housing. (177)

Figure 9.2:   A schematic of transport modes' relative use of urban space. (179)

Figure 9.3:   A model of a metro train versus the number of cars necessary to carry the same number of passengers. (180)

Figure 11.1:   Homo ludens. Addition to a pavement symbol by unknown artist. (199)

Table 14.1:   Measures and the problems they represent. (233)

Map of Stockholm. Map image: GSD-Översiktskarta © Lantmäteriet 2013. (255)

Acknowledgements

I exaggerate only a little when I say that this section has been the hardest part to write. I did this work on my own, but not alone. Metaphorically and literally, I've had the world around me. Should I thank musicians for the company of their music, writers for the escapism and inspiration, the person who set a baby's lost mitten on a tree branch for the spark of joy it gave me on a tired morning? I could thank the trees lining my walk to work for providing beauty as a happy side effect of their existence, although this would mean little to them. Anyone who's ever inspired me, believed in me, or given me a chance has had a part in getting me this far. There are so many people to thank, so many little kindnesses and great feats to recognize, that this could easily turn into a very long list of names.

First, I must thank the Foundation for Baltic and East European Studies (*Östersjöstiftelsen*) for funding my research through the Baltic and East European Graduate School. Thank you to Södertörn University and the School of Natural Science, Technology and Environmental Studies for giving me a room with a view and administrative support.

E.F. Schumacher once wrote, "Any intelligent fool can make things bigger, more complex, and more violent. It takes a touch of genius – and a lot of courage to move in the opposite direction" (Schumacher 1973a, p. 22). I can certainly not lay claim to genius; rather, to paraphrase Richard Branson (2012-09-03, tweet), complexity has been my enemy, and the hard thing to do has been to keep things simple. My supervisors, Björn Hassler and Fredrika Björklund, know this well. Björn, you helped me navigate between academic ambitions and real-life needs, and reminded me not to overreach. Fredrika, you helped me strengthen my arguments and identify my purpose. Thank you both for sharing your great experience and insights, giving me input, advise, and support, and then letting me figure it out on my own (even when I wanted someone to tell me what to do). I'm so glad that you were my supervisors.

I'm also grateful to the scholars outside my own school who took the time to read, listen, and advice. Thank you, Karolina Isaksson and Karin Borevi, for your valuable and constructive comments at my halftime seminar. You helped me see a way forward when I was still figuring things out. Thank you, Tim Richardson and Hanna Sofia Rehnberg, for being my final seminar readers. You helped me see the last stretch of road ahead and think closer about the destination. Your advice on both content and form, and especially your challenging questions, were invaluable to me. Karolina, you inspired me as an undergraduate, gave me encouragement and advice on the transport field, and generously introduced me to VTI and the KRITS seminars. To researchers at VTI and K2, for excellent comments and interesting discussions: Jacob Witzell, Jens Hylander, Jessica Berg, Malin Henriksson, Alexander Paulsson, Lena Levin, Chiara Vitrano, and Dalia Mukhtar-Landgren: thank you. To Jonathan Feldman, for telling me to go for a PhD when all I wanted was to be done with my master thesis. It took some time, but I did it.

I have often told people that the best part of my job was getting to talk about the Stockholm Bypass for two hours and get paid for it. Of course, this is not true: the best part of my time as a doctoral student has been the people I have worked next to and learned from. Thank you to the crew of incredible people at NMT: teachers, researchers, administrators, and leadership. The members of the School board, and especially Ester Appelgren, taught me what it means to be part of the staff. The teachers I had as a young bachelor's student raised my interest in everything from economics and politics to geology and chemistry: you showed me a much more interesting world than I had imagined. Mats shared my enthusiasm for transport and urban planning and gave me space to teach about it. A big thank you to Andrea, for letting me add to your news archive, for sharing your commitment to good science and good relations, and for all the fun and thought-provoking talks. To everyone with whom I have discussed research and teaching, world issues, and parasites: thank you. Even on hard days, coming to work was good with you around. Thank you also to Göran for the ladder of Getting Things Done, which made what seemed impossible become possible.

Without my doctoral student colleagues this time would have been difficult, lonely, and much less joyful. I may have written this thesis on my own, but you were there to support, commiserate, or just fika. Linn, you got me on this crazy ride and kept me on it with your analytical insight, your encouragement, and your friendship. Josefine, Kajsa-Stina, Erika, Elise, Juliana, Tove: you're fountains of wisdom, jokes, and badass. Thank you to the rest of my fantastic crew: Sophie, Lena, Olena, Igne, Natalya, Sara, Natasja, Falkje, Christian, Anton, Tiina, Emma, Nasim, Kristina, Pernilla, Ola, Nikolina, Thérèse, Mohanad, Naveed, Martin, Ralph, Stefan, Petter. We really are stronger together. I'll miss our group.

Thank you to my friends outside of SH, for making life fun and for being there when it wasn't. Special thanks to Jasmine, Elina, Ivar, Olivia, Kirstin, Lisen, and Leo. You are all incredible.

My family helped me grow into the person that I am. Lars told me to get a proper education and always listened seriously to my arguments, and Hans read my stories and told me to dance the sound of words. They both encouraged me to develop skills that have been important to me, in work as well as in life. One of Lars' favourite stories to tell was one of a Soviet news report after a sports contest: "the Soviet comrade achieved an honourable second-place, while the American finished second-to-last." This was one of my first introductions to discourse: there were only two contestants in this story. The story may or may not have been real, but between fairy tales and debates with my grandfather I learned the significance of weighing and thinking about how things were said as well as what was said.

Mom, you taught me that thinking differently was a good thing, and your unconditional love, support, and faith in me has made everything I do possible. Thank you for always listening, for giving me a place and space to work, and for lending me your power tools when I needed a break. Jens, thank you for your belief in me from my first degree on, for reminding me I could do it even when you had no idea *what* I was doing, and for making me the envy of the lunch room. Most of all: thank you to my children. My *otrolingar*. I am so lucky that you came into my life.

The difficult I'll do right now
The impossible will take a little while

Billie Holiday (1949), *Crazy He Calls Me*

Foreword

I have lived near or in Stockholm all my life, and the various projects and measures have direct impacts on myself and the city around me. My first interest in transport matters, and perhaps the meaning of words as well, stems from my mother's "Ur Tid Är Leden" pin. The slogan, which translates to "The link is out of time", is a play on "The time is out of joint" (Swedish: *"Ur led är tiden"*) from Shakespeare's *Hamlet* and was used by opponents to the Western Link highway (*Västerleden*) in the 1990s. At that time, my mother would often drive for work from our home west of the city to Uppsala north of the city in the morning, and then to Södertälje south of Stockholm while eating for lunch a bar of chocolate she habitually kept stocked in the glove compartment, and so might have benefited from a quicker north–south journey. Yet she wore that pin and opposed the construction of a highway on the far end of the municipality she still calls home. Few Stockholmers are indifferent to the Western Link, reborn as the Stockholm Bypass, and the reader might like to know that I wrote my master's thesis on the environmental impact assessment of the road inquest for the Bypass, out of interest born from personal opposition.

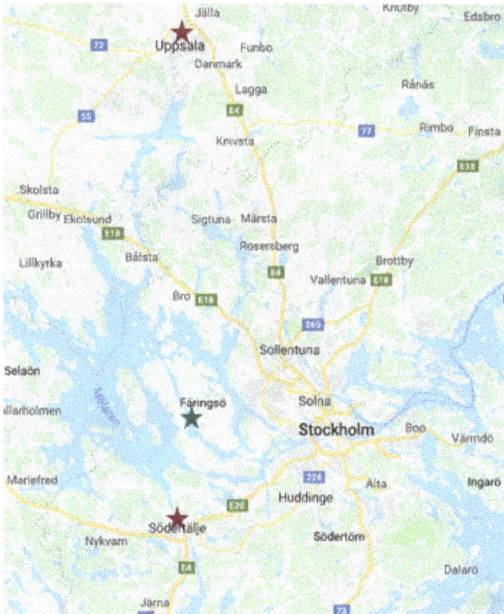

Figure i: My mother's destinations during a workday. Our home (approximately) marked by a green star; Uppsala and Södertälje in red.

Image: GoogleMaps.

While I started out with a fairly simple view of sustainable transport – that it is about ensuring a shift from fossil fuel car to 'greener' modes, and I should study why this isn't happening fast enough – my study has left me with more questions than fit within the scope of the project. During the process of writing this dissertation, I have developed a scepticism towards the city as an ideal image of the sustainable human habitat. The broad political and scientific agreement on the benefits of urbanization seems to continuously disregard the claiming of agricultural land, forests, and green areas, and that for example the sustainable large-scale provision of central heating in Stockholm is currently partially made up of wood chips imported from Brazil and in wintertime the burning of fossil fuels (and it should be noted that few new homes are passive or plus housing, which means that new houses will have no choice but to attach to the single heating provider in Stockholm, coal and all). My enthusiasm for technical solutions has become tempered by curiosity about what kind of society, what forms of life, the 'climate smart city' (for example) enables. Never an early adopter of trends, I have found myself tempted to move out to the countryside, almost out of spite. There seems to me to be a fundamental conflict between the 'dense walkable city' with its inner-city qualities spread out over the whole urban zone on the one hand, and on the other the growing understanding of the importance of trees and green areas for the local and global environment, for health, and for children's development, as well as the qualities which make a 'good' living. I have wondered for whom, exactly, the dense city is built, and for the satisfaction of which needs. These considerations are quite far from the subject of sustainable transport, but at the same time at the very core of it.

Part 1
Constructing the study

1
Introduction

The transport system is probably the most visible part of a city's – or even nation's – infrastructure. Because of its significant presence, it is a crucial component and concern of sustainability efforts. From a human point of view, the transport system is a part of the scenery, a connector of daily activities or important places, and a source of human and environmental health impacts. These impacts are the focus of many studies, reports, and plans aiming to make transport more sustainable.

After the Second World War, car mobility became the norm in large parts of the world. Automobility provides a flexibility that has encouraged not just a shift in transport mode, but a heavy increase in travel as well (Begg 1998, in Rothengatter and Huguenin 2004, p. 460). The flipside of the car's flexibility and speed is that it creates distances and needs only cars can readily satisfy (Urry 2004; Lutz and Lutz Fernandez 2010). Together, cars and efficient public transport have decentralized cities and urban regions and altered the way that we live (Banister 2000, p. 116; Börjesson et al. 2014, p. 145). Transport is also a visible part of the agenda concerning climate change. Scientists, politicians, climate activists, bloggers shaming 'influencers' for their air travel, travel businesses beginning to offer train charter – most seem to agree on the urgency of reducing greenhouse gas emissions to secure a limit of climate change to what we and the ecosystems we rely on can handle, and on the important role of transport. To ensure a more sustainable development (development which enables long-term coexistence of human societies and practices with the biosphere) fossil fuel reduction is agreed on as a main aim.

Stockholm is often held to be an example of a less fossil fuel-intense way of arranging the urban transport system. With an extended public transport system, used for 70% of commutes in the city and 35% in the region (Stockholms stad 2017a), and measures such as the congestion tax in place, Stockholm is factually in a better position for lower CO_2 emissions from the transport system than many other cities in the world. While recent reports for Sweden as a whole show that reaching climate targets for road traffic will require harder work still (cf. Swedish Transport Agency and Swedish Transport Administration 2015; Swedish Environmental Protection Agency

[SEPA] 2019, p. 14; IVA 2019), Stockholm is in line with its own targets (for example, in 2018 the city reached its 2020 targets of 2.2 tons of CO_2 per person and year, and between 2000 and 2017 emissions from transport decreased by 20%; Stockholms stad 2018e). Collective transport is also held to prevent urban sprawl and reduce land use stress (e.g. European Commission 2011). But while Stockholm municipality has set ambitious goals for reducing emissions from transport and increase public transport use, around Stockholm new highways are under construction or proposed. Several have been discussed intermittently since the 1960s. These highways are met positively by the municipality. Given the known contribution of new roads to increased car use, the recognized negative effects of car mobility, and the widespread agreement that these effects should be curbed, I find this curious. Herein lies my interest in scrutinizing the construction (or discursive production)[1] of sustainability in Stockholm policy, to see what this 'best case' scenario is like and what logics or conceptual underpinnings, as one might call them, make sense of it. In this dissertation I study municipal policy measures for personal transport in the years 2007–2017, considering the measures as one proposal and analysing what transport and sustainability are constructed to be through that proposal. If policy measures tell a story, I want to know what transport policy says about sustainability.

In workplaces across Stockholm, three topics are always safe for small talk: the weather, the coffee, and traffic. The 'life puzzle' (in Swedish known as *livspusslet*[2]), the joining of the different aspects of life – home, school or daycare, work, shops, relatives, friends, hobbies, and other obligations and needs – is dependent on a supporting interface. Enoksson (2009, p. 28) briefly mentions the role of mobility for solving one's life puzzle, as well as the high importance ascribed to a 'functioning life puzzle'. Political parties (see textbox next page) hold that smooth transport services are crucial for a functioning society and in solving the problems that arise when work commutes grow longer, housing prices encourage people to live further from their areas of work, shorter-term jobs mean that living close to work is not necessarily a long-term option anyway, and several tasks must be accomplished in shorter time frames (e.g., after work one must pick up children,

---

[1] Construction, in discourse theory and the WPR approach, denotes the way that our understanding of the world is constructed – made – through discourse. When I speak of something as constructed or a construction, I mean that this term, idea, or phenomenon is not 'natural' but a product of discursive practices. Some constructions – such as 'sustainability' – have particular importance in policy rhetoric and practice, and so are particularly interesting to interrogate.
[2] The term "livspusslet" has been used in Sweden since the 1980s but was trademarked by the union Swedish Confederation of Professional Employees (TCO) in 2002 (cf. Röshammar 2013).

sometimes from several different places, shop for groceries, perhaps see to other errands, sometimes take children to after-school activities, go home to make dinner, etc).

Swedish parties on transport: examples from political programmes

Families and businesses should be able to trust that we have good and safe roads and that the trains run on time, regardless of where in the country you live. All transport modes are needed in a Sweden that works. We can't afford to put different transport modes against each other with penalty taxes on distance.

The Moderate Party.
www.moderaterna.se/infrastruktur-och-trafik

A functioning infrastructure is an important part of a stronger society. For us it's a given that the whole country should have the same conditions. No matter if it's about roads, rail, air- or public transport. We don't want to see a Sweden where the gaps between city and country grow."

The Social Democrats.
www.socialdemokraterna.se/var-politik/a-till-o/infrastruktur/

Infrastructure and transport – green environmental investments. For the whole country to live you must have the possibility to choose where you want to live and work. To be able to get between home and work, school and activities in a convenient, environmentally friendly way is a given for us.

The Centre Party.
www.centerpartiet.se/var-politik/politik-a-o/infrastruktur-och-trafik

All translations by author.

1.1 A period of transport project packages

My material spans the time period of 2007 to 2017. This period encompasses the first new large transport packages after the 'fall' of the Dennis Agreement in 1997 (the quotes around 'fall' denote that although one project was found unlawful and the Agreement was officially disbanded, most projects and measures of the Agreement have been implemented). In 2007 the agreement *Traffic Solution for the Stockholm Region* was struck, putting on the agenda several large-scale infrastructure projects such as the Stockholm Bypass and metro extensions. In 2013, the Stockholm Agreement on funding for metro extensions was struck, ensuring a regional agreement on both the necessity of metro extensions and on how they should be paid for – and that the affected municipalities should build housing in exchange. Finally, in 2017 the National Negotiation closed with an agreement for several heavy investments in the Stockholm region.

The time period also covers the advent of new documents for transport policy and sustainability in Stockholm. The *Urban Mobility Strategy*, released in 2012, was written in response to a perceived need to adapt the transport system to a growing population as well as climate change. The *Roadmap for fossil-fuel free Stockholm 2050*, released in 2014, was written in light of a growing concern over climate change. Further, during this time period new projections for population growth in Stockholm instigated in policy debate a significant focus on making room for more. In sum, the period has been an intense moment for transport policy, explicitly reflecting concerns of environment and urban growth.

From a sustainability perspective, large-scale transport packages may provide a 'bigger picture' perspective throughout the transport system, purposely combining measures which have reinforcing, facilitating, or synergetic effects. Gathering projects under one umbrella may prevent "tyranny of small decisions" (Hrelja 2011) and ensure a stricter adherence to sustainability goals. But packages may also hinge one project on another in an 'all or nothing' kind of arrangement, making unsustainable projects required for the implementation of sustainable projects and legitimizing unsustainable projects by the sustainable ones. The tendency towards techno-rational framing of transport packages may also foreclose attention to social or political problematizations (see Isaksson 2001 on the Dennis Agreement). This makes transport policy during this period an interesting unit of observation to see how this 'bigger picture' perspective on transport handles sustainability.

1.2 Aim and research questions

In this study I trace the measures proposed for Stockholm's transport system for people (not goods) in Stockholm municipal policy during the years 2007–2017, to consider what the 'right' transport is set up to do and what this can tell us about how sustainability is constructed. I want to contribute to the study of policy itself and the way that it is written, what assumptions are inherent in that writing, and what effects, beyond emissions, come out of it. In doing this I want to open up the study of sustainable transport policy to questions about what policy for sustainable transport is set up to *do*. I also see a need in transport policy study to consider transport as part of a larger social context, as constitutive of and constituted by social practices (Söderström et al. 2013; see also Shove and Trentmann 2018). This means a step further than the techno-rational approach which is dominant in transport and transport policy study (Marsden and Reardon 2017), into a more complex and sometimes messy view of transport and its interplay with people and the environment. I see within this techno-rational dominance a tendency to discuss the relative usefulness of individual measures for meeting the set goals, rather than what goals are set in policy and what *directionality* (to speak with Howlett and Cashore 2009) policy has. In context of the multiple calls for change under the umbrella of sustainable development – most acutely for transport, mitigating and adapting to climate change – I identify a need to look critically at the building blocks of policy and what future they may build. Rather than ask how 'unsustainable' measures could be promoted *despite* sustainability targets, I assume that the understanding of sustainability is built into policy. I aim to study what Stockholm policy for transport can say about what sustainability means and does. To do this, I must first grasp what is made of transport. Thus, my research questions are:

1) What kind of 'tool' is produced by policy for transport in Stockholm municipality?

   a) How is transport constructed, through proposed measures and discourse of policy concerning transport in Stockholm between 2007 and 2017? If transport is a 'solution', what is it a solution *to*?
   b) What forms of society and subject are produced by this construction of transport, and how does this relate to environmental issues?

2) How is sustainability constructed in Stockholm municipal policy for personal transport between 2007 and 2017?

   a) What is the explicit construction of sustainability in policy, through the way that sustainability is described and discussed?

b) What is the implicit construction of sustainability, through the measures proposed for transport while 'sustainable development' is an agreed aim and ideal?

I ask, that is, what transport *does* in Stockholm municipal policy. And what, to paraphrase Foucault (in Dreyfus and Rabinow 1983, p. 187), does what policy does *do*? When 'sustainable transport' is an agreed aim, the measures proposed for transport will tell us what 'sustainable transport' is by what it *does*. Put another way, if 'sustainability' or 'sustainable transport' is identified as the solution, what kind of a solution is it, and what is it a solution *to*? By this I mean that the precise way that 'sustainability' is represented can be recursively studied through the proposals for sustainable transport. This is not to disregard the many and frequently competing aims in transport policy (and planning). Instead, I do this to highlight the practices which are currently available within the construction of transport. Transport is frequently described as the 'backbone' of society (e.g. Jönköpings kommun 2014; Cox 2015), yet attention to its shaping impact on society (or, the wider socio-economic as well as physical structures of human society) is under-utilized in study.

Through my research questions, I use the on-the-ground components of policy as a starting point to interrogate the goals and logics of policy (to speak with Howlett and Cashore 2009), which are currently less studied than the technical aspects of both the transport system and transport policy. My aim is to understand the construction of sustainability in this particular instance of policy, and to understand transport as a governing 'tool' in the urban environment. In doing this, I contribute to a fairly recent way of studying transport policy: as producing problems, and as co-constituting practices. A close example of this is Hrelja's (2019) article on municipal policy for car reduction in Swedish cities. My study differs from this in that I don't start from an established 'problem' but rather seek to find what problems are represented in policy. I also contribute further to the study of sustainability and sustainability measures as constructions and problematizations, in line with Perman's dissertation on central heating (2008), Olsson's dissertation on climate change adaptation (2018), and Gustavsson and Niklasson's bachelor thesis on carbon neutral cities (2014).

To answer my research questions, I use a series of questions from Carol Bacchi's analytical framework *What's the problem represented to be?* (2009). These questions address what is depicted in policy as something to 'fix', how this makes sense, and the discursive, subjectification, and lived effects. The framework helps me dig into policy and expand on my understanding of the construction of transport and sustainability.

1.3 The structure of the work

This thesis is divided into two parts, and then further into chapters.

Part I holds the roadmap, orienting the reader in what I aim to do and why. In Chapter 1, I set the stage for the work ahead, introducing the research problem and my research questions. In Chapter 2, I present the background for my case, showing that sustainability aims have had little effect on planning practice in Sweden, and that in Stockholm sustainability measures are reconfigured or implemented parallel to conventional measures. In Chapter 3, I situate the study in the research field, presenting different ways of studying transport and considerations for 'sustainable transport' study. In Chapter 4 I present the analytical framework I use to study my material, the *What's the problem represented to be?* framework, and explain how I adapt and use it. This chapter comprises both theoretical and methodological considerations.

Part II holds the analytical chapters of this thesis. In Chapter 5, I address the first question of the WPR (*What's the problem represented to be?*) framework: What is the problem represented to be in the chosen policies? In Chapters 6 through 9 I expand on the analysis of key represented problems identified in Chapter 5: *Emissions caused by 'wrong' technology*; *Wrong choices made by individual transport users*; *Too little transport work*; *Too little urban space*. In these analytical chapters, I direct my attention to the ways that these representations are 'made sense of' (that is, what assumptions underlie them and how they are constructed), what is missing in the representations, and what effects are produced by the ways that the problems are represented. In Chapter 10, I discuss how sustainability is constructed through the problem representations and discourses in the material. In Chapter 11 I discuss what conclusions can be drawn in regard to my research questions.

The Appendix shows the full list of measures and the problem represented by each, with notes on how details and combinations have affected the analysis.

2

Background

In this chapter I situate the material in a historical context, tracing the development of Stockholm urban transport from the early 1900s, through the post-war restructuring, and to the current structure of the transport system.

2.1 Stockholm as a site of sustainable transport study

In Sweden, urban policy and planning have to relate to the path laid down in the post-war period; a path originating not from the wide-sweeping modernistic planning that followed, but from an ad-hoc but inexorable growth of private car ownership. From this development, during which the car went from a marker of (upper) class to every man's[3] possession (and surely the identification of the car as a class marker helped in the enthusiastic adoption of automobility), came many of the most impactful changes to Swedish built environment. In Stockholm, it meant a restructuring of the inner city as a nearly direct result of parking norms (Lundin 2008) and the extension of the urban area far into what had been countryside. The ensuing car dependence, decentralization of the city, and commuter rates have since become the 'normal'.

Today, however, the previously elevated role of the car is questioned, not only by environmental movements (such as Swedish Society for Nature Conservation or *Alternativ stad*) but also by politicians across the spectrum. The car is frequently identified as a climate villain ("klimatbov"), a source of ill health, and a nuisance. But the 'normal' that we know and that policy makers are seeking to navigate by other transport modes is literally – physically – built up around the car. The question remains whether transport can be untangled from the material and social artefacts of automobility. Authors such as Banister (e.g. 2000) as well as policy makers themselves argue for changes to the urban form: the "dense" and "mixed-functions" city

---

[3] It was primarily men who owned cars. As late as 1975, 15% of single women owned cars compared to 43% of single men, while 20% of household cars were owned by married women and 80% by married men (Jansson et al. 1986).

is described as the new ideal urban shape or "the most sustainable urban form" (Banister 2007, p. 104).

By the definition of Statistics Sweden (Statistics Sweden [SCB] 2015), 85% of Sweden's population lived in urban areas in 2015 (by UN definitions, Stockholm is a medium-sized city and in 2015 only 24.2% of the population lived in an urban agglomerate of 300,000 people or more; United Nations 2018). The population of Stockholm is growing, mainly as a result of newborns and immigration from abroad (SCB 2015). Stockholm County Council expects the population of Stockholm County to grow by one million people by 2060, from 2.3 million to 3.3 million people (or an increase by 44%; Stockholm County Council [SLL] 2018). This expectation of growth and Stockholm's reputation for sustainability should make Stockholm a prime area of study for what 'sustainable transport' in 'sustainable cities' might mean as global urbanization exceeds 50%.

Several studies have shown that targets for sustainable transport have so far had little impact on planning practice in Sweden (e.g. Norell Bergendahl 2016:ii), and that sustainable transport measures are implemented parallel to measures which promote car use (Dickinson et al. 2016; Isaksson et al. 2017), while planning documents and impact assessments tend to ignore the "traffic-generating effects" of increased road capacity in urban areas (Næss et al. 2013, p. 485). For example, environmental policy goals are not met, or even included, in two major Swedish infrastructure plans, the Stockholm Bypass and the National Infrastructure Plan 2010–2021 (Finnveden and Åkerman 2014), while sustainable development as a concept is not mentioned at all in targets for the 2010 plans for *Nya Slussen* (New Slussen), a major traffic juncture in Stockholm city (Bjarnestam 2011). Finnveden and Åkerman hold that environmental sustainability policy targets, especially long-term, are clearly missing from the planning process (2014, p. 56), which Bjarnestam also finds to be the case (2011, p. 125).

In a study of three city-regions in Denmark, Norway, and Sweden, Næss et al. (2013, p. 485) found that although "'state-of-the-art' academic knowledge" – in their view, the promotion of dense urban development and improvements of public transport to reduce car use, a combination of *avoid* and *shift* measures – is present in key planning documents, some plans studied emphasize mobility (proximity to public transport) rather than accessibility (proximity to work and services). Even the congestion tax, held to be a "flagship" policy to combat congestion and car dependence, shows an ambivalence towards cars and reducing car use: "Even policies with the strongest potential to control car use, and here we concentrate on urban congestion charging, are not necessarily designed to achieve sustainability goals, and the more radical possibilities of these interventions are often weakened during implementation" (Richardson et al. 2010, p. 54).

Isaksson et al. (2017) focus on framing and objectives in four plans/ strategies for Stockholm transport (Regional Development Plan for the Stockholm Region, 2010; Stockholm Comprehensive Plan, 2010; Stockholm Urban Mobility Strategy, 2012; the most recent round of planning for the Stockholm Bypass, 2005–2011), and conclude that "sustainability emerges strongly in the overall goals) but closer scrutiny of the content of the plan reveals other rationalities that exist alongside the sustainability ambition" (p. 54).

2.2 Urban transport development in Stockholm

Peter Hall writes of Stockholm that the city "deserves its place [in his study of cities], not because it was a great city seeking to solve the problems of giantism, but because it was a small European capital city that ... set a distinctively different course" (Hall 1998, p. 842).

In the first decades of the 20th century, Stockholm was a dense city with narrow streets trafficked mainly by streetcars and horse cars, bicycles, and pedestrians (e.g. Gullberg 2001a). Thomas Hall (1979) categorizes the physical development of Stockholm in three overlapping stages. First, the construction of what in Swedish is known as "City" (the central business district, CBD) around 1860–1930, with brick apartment houses. Second, the development of and expansion into suburbs forming Greater Stockholm, starting in the late 1800s and continuing to this day. Third, the redevelopment of Lower Norrmalm, which took place between ca. 1950 and the late 1970s (Hall 1979, p. 9).

The current shape and structure of the city are to a large extent a result of this third stage, the post-war restructuring. This era was characterized by modernization, where old working-class neighbourhoods in the city centre (which was designated business district; at the time housing newspaper offices as well as workers and poets) were demolished to leave space for the metro and new, modern office buildings. The former residents were usually relocated to the newly built suburbs around the city, where living conditions were politically described as better, healthier, and more modern, especially for families with children. These suburbs were connected to the city centre – and, through this, to each other – by the metro.

While the postwar restructuring was focused on turning the inner city from a mixed-use urban area into a "sanitary" central business district suitable for commerce and banking, it was not only a massive restructuring of the urban environment but also an important factor in developing an auto city – at the time seen as the pinnacle of modern, rational urban planning (Hall 1979; Gullberg 2001a). As such, the Norrmalm redevelopment had impacts on both present and future visions of the city. It was at this point that the Klara tunnel was constructed between Tegelbacken and Svevägen, as well as the new junction at Tegelbacken, and the inner city as a whole was made accessible by car and equipped with car parks (the goal was that there should be a multi-storey carpark – and a metro station – within 250 metres' walking distance from any point in the CBD). The city renewal of the 1960s thus formed the basis for the given position of the car in the city of today.

Figure 2.1: View of Stockholm city centre from Södermalm (south island). The Old Town is on the right side of the image, the CBD between the golden top of the City Hall and the green spire of Klara church. Picture by author, 2017-06-03.

From 1918 to 1930, the number of cars in Stockholm more than quadrupled but was still rather modest, increasing from 4,000 to 17,500 (Hall 1979, p. 12). In the second half of the 1940s, the car shifted from being a novelty – especially discouraged during the preparations for what became World War II – to being an everyday occurrence (Gullberg 2001, p. 200). In 1967 there were 300,000 cars in Stockholm. This put the Stockholm traffic system to a considerable challenge: playing host to pedestrians and bicyclists as well as public transport and the rising number of cars and trucks (Gullberg 2001a, p. 255). Plans began to widen the narrow streets, but this involved changing large sweeps of the city structure, including the demolishing of old buildings (Gullberg 2001a). It was during these years that the Western Link was first conceived; then as Kungshattsleden, now known as the Stockholm Bypass. An inner ring road was planned around the city, complemented by outer roads connecting north and south parts of the region. It was believed that this system would ensure mobility and easy movement through the whole region (Tonell 1997, p. 34).

This is not to say that the car was unanimously seen as problem-free. For example, in 1936 Hakon Ahlberg, architect and alternate member of the Norrmalm Delegacy (Swedish: *Norrmalmsdelegationen;* the group charged with preparing plans for the restructuring), protested the proposed extension of Sveavägen to the royal castle and called it "a cannon, loaded with expansive traffic matter" (in Gullberg 2001a, p. 166). There was also critique of the subordinate position of pedestrians – sometimes quite literal, as in the case of Sergels Torg, a square in the city's centre, where pedestrians were moved underground and cars given the upper level – and of the danger of leading cars straight into the city via the Klara tunnel (Hall 1979).

At the same time, the plans for the metro were made: a system of tunnels for rail transport under the city. The first section, opened in 1950, connected Slussen in the central city and the southern suburb Hökarängen; extensions to suburbs Stureby (south) and Vällingby (west) soon followed (Gullberg 2001a, p. 259). Peter Hall has described this as part of Stockholm's great modernization project. The metro was a crucial factor in the development of the new suburbs, which were to provide residents with housing, leisure and access to work (Hall 1998, p. 562). The metro did not only facilitate mobility in and around the city, but also afforded city leadership with no small mea-sure of control over the lives of city residents. Hall describes the develop-ment at the time as near-draconian, where the state stepped in to regulate the lives of its citizens, pushing them together in the *folkhem* ('the people's home'), the welfare state and its (not to overlook the significant influences of Alva Myrdal) fatherly grip. The metro also allowed for the continued redevelopment of the inner city despite heavy opposition and protests: the tunnels had to be dug from above and then covered, necessitating the demolition of all in its path (Hall 1979; Gullberg 2001a). As such, the metro was a tool of considerable power over both urban structure and citizenry. The now-praised metro of Stockholm was not a project of sustainability, but rather a part of the modernization project of the 1950s, and of the growing welfare state (Hall 1998, p. 562).

Figure 2.2: A model of the Vällingby suburb centre, with an early metro train. Picture taken at the Stockholm Transport Museum by author, 2017-09-08. The museum closed 2017-09-10 and will be relocated to Norra Djurgårdsstaden in 2020.

The Norrmalm restructuring was met with opposition from many directions. Media, architects, poets, and local residents were vehement in their critique. While the plans were supported by the Social Democrats, the Conservatives opposed them for the extensive demolitions (all in all some 450 buildings were targeted for demolition, including the 17th century Preiss House; by 1960 119 had already been torn down and the other 332 was roughly half of the still standing old building stock) and the potential threat to local business (by reducing accessibility to shops and by forcibly relocating shops during construction). The Conservatives finally accepted the plans "with reservations" in 1963; while they opposed the restructuring they had, importantly, no alternative proposal. In this context, the Social Democrats might be seen to represent modernity and – crucial to the post-war world – hope for the future and development for all, while the Conservatives had little to offer at all except seemingly more of the same.

The development continued through the 1960s, with the construction of Essingeleden (planned in the 1950s; Gullberg 2001a, p. 332), and further extensions of the metro. In 1975, the blue line was opened for passengers

(Storstockholms länstrafik, 2011). The metro now connects the city from Mörby in the north to Farsta in the south, and from Ropsten to Hässelby in an east-west direction.

Then in the 1970s, the development sputtered to a halt. A halting economy, the oil crisis, politics (for example the newly awakened environmental movement), and critique of the recent changes in the city (which escalated in the Battle of the Elms, *almstriden*, over the plans to cut down the elm trees in Kungsträdgården park to make way for a metro station) contributed to bringing to a halt the grand plans of the previous decades (Gullberg 2001b, pp. 143-145). In the late 1980s, as population and traffic levels rose again, planning began anew for a great traffic system or roads and rail to solve the city's problems. Former governor of the Swedish National Bank, Bengt Dennis, was assigned to lead negotiations between the parties. But the Dennis package, as it was called, met with fierce resistance from many groups. Some opposed the intrusion into the national park which the northern link would entail; others protested the western road cutting through the culture landscape of Lovön, home of the royal castle and thousand-year-old oaks (Isaksson 2001). Others still criticized the lack of referral procedure and the exclusion of parties strongly opposed to one or several projects (Norberg 2016, p. 23; Tonell 1997). In 1997, the intrusion into the national park was ruled against the law. The package as such deflated, to the relief of politicians caught in a political bind between alliances (Norberg 2016, p. 25), but the task of working out a new proposal was passed on to Minister of Communications Ines Uusman (Norberg 2016, p. 26). Today, many if not all of the projects have been completed (Stockholmsförsöket 2006).

After the Norrmalm renewal of the 1960s, when the "constipation" of the traditional city with its narrow streets (Hasselquist, in Johansson 2011, p. 422) was sought to be remedied, urban traffic planning has largely sought the opposite: to lead traffic around the city, and away from the city, without going so far as to ban cars entirely. This was the case with many of the projects of the Dennis Agreement, and the ring roads (initially conceived as early as the 1930s), and it remains the case today, with the planned Stockholm Bypass, the proposals for an Eastern Link, and the newly finished Northern Link. The expectation of and adaptation to increased car traffic remain, but the aim is now to divert it from the city proper, where it is found to be harmful, out to the greater Stockholm area and suburbs, where it is thought to contribute to job opportunities, retail, and economic growth. This suggests a form of "double-think" where the qualitative impact of car use is interpreted differently depending on where it is performed, allowing a zoning in transport planning: avoid car use in the inner city, enable it in the surrounding areas. Thus, while Stockholm inner city can be said to work towards a modal shift, as it has been praised for, this is not necessarily the case for the Greater Stockholm as a whole. Since the majority of Stockholm residents commute in and out of – and through – the city for employment and errands, separating the city proper from the greater urban area does not contribute to strategic work towards a carbon-neutral Sweden by 2050.

2.3 Stockholm transport system

The public transport system consists of metro, trolleys, commuter rail, buses, and ferries (see Figure 2). It is used by over 800,000 people daily (Stor-stockholms lokaltrafik [SL] 2017, p. 6), or 36–70% of the total number of commutes (depending on if you look at the region or the inner city) (Stockholms stad 2019a). In 2015, approximately 50% of residents said in a survey that they mostly use public transport to get to work or school. Approximately 20% of residents said they always or mostly went to work or school by car, and 16–24% said they mostly go by foot or bicycle (Stockholms stad 2016a; data was collected spring and fall, which has a significant impact on travel choices in Sweden). Stockholm has a much higher public transport use than the Swedish average: the national share of public transport has decreased from 57% in 1950 to 20% from the 1970s and on (Trafikanalys 2012, p. 16; Swedish Association of Local Authorities and Regions 2018, p. 27). In the municipal survey, about half of the (adult) residents responded that they own a car; in addition to using it for work, 46% of respondents said they use it 1–2 days a week outside of work, and 39% use it 3–4 days a week outside of work (Stockholms stad 2016a, p. 37).

3

Previous research into sustainable transport

3.1 Aspects of transport

Transport, sometimes conceptually narrowed down to transport modes and vehicles, is a complex topic which touches upon most of society. The immediate result of transport – mobility or movement – is both *constituted by* paths, velocity, rhythms, spatial scale, meanings, forms of regulation, experience, and competences; and *constitutive of* bodies, subjectivities, materialities, economic resources, social positions and organizational structures (to speak with mobilities studies; Söderström et al. 2013).

To illustrate this, on my last lecture as a doctoral student, I asked the students how they had gotten to university that morning. Then I asked them to trace what was needed for each mode of transport (roads, rail, vehicles, shoes, energy, a public transport access card, keys, driver's license, agreed bus stops, drivers) and what was necessary for those things (asphalt, steel, stone and concrete, plastic, workers, an infrastructure of production and supply, extraction of oil, a banking system, mines). We ended up in space, with the satellites necessary for them to be able to use their credit cards or cell phones to pay for public transport fare.[4] If we had not had other topics to cover, we could probably have spent the full two hours chaining together steps required and the effects along the way. The students pinpointed that nothing we do happens in isolation but requires (through the vast and complex global economic system) a long chain of events, each link with its own story and impact. Something as seemingly simple as scanning one's Access card at the train station can cast a person's shadow across – even beyond – the globe.

Noting aspects such as worker health (domestic and foreign), conflicts around oil and minerals, and the agreed stops and timetables, they pointed not only to the technical and physical aspects and requirements for transport, but the social necessities and consequences as well. A discussion about legs – for walking, but also for cycling or driving a car unless one has made adjustments to the vehicle – and driver's licenses touched upon accessibility

---

[4] It is possible that the internet connection necessary for this is actually on Earth, but the students nonetheless highlighted that distant networks are necessary.

and knowledge. The mention of money to pay for fare brought up equity. Later in the lecture we came to talk about urban growth and the perceived requirement for temporally and spatially long commutes. Together, the students started to map out the far-reaching and closely personal connections between transport and the rest of the world.

'Sustainable transport' could, and should, then be discussed from a wide range of perspectives, perhaps especially as a structuring force of human society. Despite this, many approaches to sustainable transport are closely focused on technology, on transport modes, and on sustainability as a goal: 'produce sustainability by doing X, Y, and Z'. In this chapter I show the most widespread interpretations and objectives of sustainable transport research; then I discuss ways to address other kinds of transport questions.

3.1.1 Definitions of sustainable transport

It is widely understood that transport contributes to a range of negative effects on environmental and human health, through for example particle emissions, noise, and injuries. It is also a widely recognized that carbon dioxide emissions, for example from cars, contribute to climate change which is increasingly understood as a major challenge and potential threat to human society, as well as ecosystems across the globe. Agreeing on this, however, is not the same as agreeing on what the 'problem' is. This is evident when considering the field of sustainable transport.

The Swedish saying "dear child has many names" is highly applicable to the concept of sustainable transport. Alternative terms include sustainable mobility (Banister 2008; Høyer 1999), sustainable accessibility (Bartolini et al. 2005), low carbon mobility (Givoni and Banister 2013), and more. Although there are many definitions and perspective of sustainable transport, Banister's 2008 article "The sustainable mobility paradigm" is frequently cited by scholars (Web of Science notes that it has been cited 632 times as of September 5 2019). Here, Banister proposes a set of changes from the "conventional approach" to transport planning, including looking at transport as a valued activity rather than a derived demand and focusing on accessibility rather than mobility. This paradigm aims to address a range of issues, such as congestion, emissions, and travel costs (such as time).

Greenhouse gas (especially carbon dioxide) emissions is frequently referred to as the major issue to combat. Examples include journal issues dedicated to "the effects of 'fast transport' on future climates" (Urry 2012, p. 533), book titles such as *Moving Towards a Low Carbon Mobility* (Givoni and Banister, 2013), and a number of studies exploring the effect of policy on emissions and the potential of reaching climate targets. To most, this is one of several important environmental factors to consider when planning sustainable transport; concerns such as land use (e.g. loss of green areas and wildlife) and local pollution are also raised. Black and Sato (2007, p. 81) show that the concept of 'sustainable transport' was broadened between 1989 and 2006, from a strict focus on greenhouse gas emissions to a concern with the possibility of peak oil, health effects from injuries or emissions, congestion of streets and roads, and issues of equity (although they argue that the transport system cannot solve poverty; Black and Sato 2007, p. 86). Use of space for transport and decentralization of cities have also become key factors under study (e.g. Banister 2000). 'Sustainable transport' as a concept then relates to social and economic aspects of sustainability, as well as environmental. This broadening of the concept "seems to have made it more palatable to policy makers" (Black and Sato 2007, p. 81) and so may have contributed to its rise on the policy agenda. 'Sustainable transport' is clearly treated as a problem-solving paradigm, and the questions asked in research tend to focus on how to implement this 'solution' or which qualities should take primacy.

Despite this broadening of the concept, much of transport research remains set in the techno-rational model, focused on technical or economic aspects of transport. Even radical proposals, such as the transport reducing measures proposed by Givoni and Banister (2013) or the 'resilient cities' of Newman et al. (2009), tend to treat sustainable transport as a primarily technical issue to be managed by 'good planning' or technological innovation.

3.1.2 Objectives of sustainable transport

In his influential definition of 'sustainable transport' Banister (2008) highlights objectives that Givoni and Banister (2013) term *avoid, shift,* and *improve* to categorize approaches deemed necessary to produce sustainable transport. These objectives will be used below to sum up the types of policy objectives discussed in the literature.

Improve: reducing the harmful impacts of transport. This mainly involves technical solutions, such as exchanging fossil fuel cars ("the literal 'iron cage' of modernity"; Urry 2004, p. 28) for 'green' fuel vehicles, or improving the fuel efficiency of the public transport fleet. While most agree that this is necessary even with a significant reduction of car use (see e.g. Robért and Jonsson 2006), most also agree that it is "a risky strategy to rely heavily on the large-scale introduction of biofuels", largely due to supply issues (a lag between demand and supply, the 'food vs fuels' debate, as well as the probable stress on ecosystems) and the contribution of biofuel production to greenhouse gas emissions (e.g. Åkerman 2011, p. 39).

Improve measures, on their own, address neither the *how* nor the *how much* of transport, but only technical solutions to reduce recognized harmful impacts, and tend to assume sustained levels and patterns of mobility. The issue to solve here is primarily emissions from fuels. As Åkerman points out, improve measures may overlook collateral damage if the focus is kept tightly on one impact.

Regulatory measures could include bans on certain cars within city limits, or on certain fuels (such as leaded gasoline, or more recently diesel). Economic measures could include taxes or bonus/malus incentives. 'Soft' measures could include campaigns on the impacts of different fuels, or visioning of a 'fossil fuel-free' vehicle fleet.

Shift: changing transport patterns. Often this is taken to mean a modal shift, from private car use to public transport or cycling and walking; some, such as Urry (2004, p. 36), argue for a de-privatization of cars, implying that the shift necessary is not one of transport mode but one from private to public, or non-private (Urry sees no return to "19th-century 'public mobility'"). Gullberg (2015) flips the perspective on urban transport space and identifies available capacity (such as unused seats in cars), concluding that higher capacity could be achieved without physical extensions. In Urry's perspective, the negative effects of GHG emissions, pollution, and loss of land can be seen as symptoms of the 'sickness' that is private steel-and-petroleum automobility which cannot be addressed separately.

Economic measures include increased costs for owning, driving, and parking a car, while regulatory measures could mean limited access by car. 'Soft' measures include information, and 'pull' measures such as incentives for flexi-time, or improvements (in e.g. efficiency, safety, comfort, affordability, or availability) of public transport or walking and cycling paths (Stradling et al. 2000, p. 213). Measures relying on costs and restrictions seem to assume mainly rational economic actors striving to avoid unnecessary cost and attain maximum utility. However, for example scholars in behavioural economics argue that "people do sometimes make suboptimal decisions, owing to lack of information or through the influence of habit" (Steg and Tertoolen 1999, p. 63). 'Soft' or 'pull' measures often seek to influence these 'irrational' behaviours and improve the ability and willingness of transport users to make the 'right' choices (using a normative form of power). This is a softer approach, by which car users are to be coaxed and drawn out of their cars, partially for personal emotional reasons. According to Banister, out-and-out regulating against cars "would be both difficult to achieve and it would be seen as being against notions of freedom and choice" (2008, p. 74). Redman et al. argue further that "sustainable urban transport systems do not require complete eradication of private motor vehicles" and that a shift is required in "temporal, price, environmental, social, and affective benefits and costs" (2013, p. 126).

Shift measures address the *how* of mobility, targeting primarily the car as the root of transport's negative impacts on society; they do not directly interfere with the *how much* question of mobility. They can nonetheless be perceived as restricting and uncomfortable to car users, and as placing limitations on citizens' freedom of choice and right to manage their lives as they see fit (e.g. Stradling et al. 2000). Changing patterns and behaviours of transport could then be a 'simple' economic or even technical issue, but could also relate to culture. Sheller (2004) argues that as "automotive emotions" are key in car-based cultures, new cultural articulations are needed if there is to be a transition from car-culture to some other, more sustainable, mobility culture. A move towards sustainable transport can thus not be considered wholly a technical issue to be solved by scholars and civil servants. Not only do many of the approaches described here risk controversy (as for example the congestion tax has been controversial in every setting it has been proposed and/or implemented), but they also compete with the kind of emotional attachment which brings people to name their cars or view their car as an extension of their private home.

As Sheller (2004, p. 236) points out,

> cars will not easily be given up just (!) because they are dangerous to health and life, environmentally destructive, based on unsustainable energy consumption, and damaging to public life and civic space. Too many people find them too comfortable, enjoyable, exciting, even enthralling. They are deeply embedded in ways of life, networks of friends and sociality, and moral commitments to family and care for others.

Avoid: reducing the volumes of transport. Banister (2008, p. 75) argues that this should be done through reducing the "need" to travel and the length of trips (see also Åkerman 2011, p. 39). How this is to be achieved varies greatly: either through more forcible economic measures such as increased costs for owning, driving, and parking a car; or regulatory measures like limited access by car (Stradling et al. 2000, p. 213); or through softer 'pull' measures such as incentives for telecommuting (Stradling et al. 2000, p. 213); or through integration of transport and land-use planning (Bertolini et al. 2005) to change land use patterns and construct denser, more diverse cities that facilitate walking and cycling (Banister 2008, p. 73) according to a kind of "small is beautiful" approach (Schumacher 1973).

Avoid measures do not only target car use. Høyer (1999, p. 170) argues that although busses and trains could allow for a rather high level of mobility despite drastic energy savings, mobility in richer countries would have to be reduced to allow the "environmental space" for an increase in mobility in poorer countries (in accordance with the justice requirements of the 1989 Brundtland Report). This reflects the fact that even 'green' modes require some form of energy, and that paved roads – whether run by busses, cars, or bicycles – have a low albedo (solar reflectance; that is, dark surfaces absorb rather than reflect heat from the sun, heating both local and global climate). It also puts transport in a wider global context, looking beyond CO_2 emissions.

Avoid measures are the most drastic of sustainable transport measures, addressing the core of the present-day mobility: not only *how* people should get around, but *how much*. Mobility itself and its effects on society and the planet are seen as the root of undesirable impacts of transport, which if drawn to its final conclusion implies a near-total remaking of society and its relation to time and space as known today (e.g Bauman 2000). Avoid measures then address mobility culture, whether automobility or some other form. The broader culture of mobility – which has placed value in distance and new sights seen (cf. Ulver 2018 on the journey as a measure of prosperity and development) and conjoined mobility with personal freedom, as well as spread out activities, families, and friends across large areas – may make avoid measures not only controversial but deeply personally upsetting. As society, not only physically but socially and culturally as well, has shaped itself to mobility opportunities, unmaking those opportunities may require rethinking society.

3.1.3 Posing other kinds of transport questions

While the techno-rational approach can provide practical, tangible answers about transport modes and immediate impacts on mobility and environment, or offer suggestions for how best to implement a policy, it might not adequately address what transport does for and to society on a larger scale. This conventional approach to transport research rarely asks about what transport makes of us as humans, or what it says about our visions for society or the world as a whole (including the natural environment). Further, the techno-rational approach may regrettably answer questions asked by policy makers (such as, 'how do we increase mobility while reducing emissions?') without asking questions back (such as, 'why?' or, 'what if you have to choose?'). Put another way, the conventional approach to transport research tends to treat ends and aims as given and focus on the means and tools.

Marsden and Reardon (2017, p. 246) call for "developing a body of knowledge that critiques [policy makers'] practices and also understands why decisions come to be made the way they are" and point to a gap in research regarding the "ends and aims" of policy. Analysing frames, images, or discourse is a way to grasp what the techno-rational approach leaves out, and a perspective which directs attention to those questions frequently fallen to the side under the techno-rational, frequently economistic, approach to transport. Studies may consider equity and 'rights to the city' (e.g. Gössling 2016; Kębłowski et al. 2019), the relation of transport and gender (e.g. Law 1999; Kronsell et al. 2016), or they may question central tenets of transport studies such as travel time saving (Metz 2008). By doing so, these studies work to address the aims of transport, as well as the preconditions for where we currently stand. This can yield answers about how society (as an intangible structure, as a physical build, and as a collection of people) is shaped *through* transport. For example, Hilding-Rydevik et al. (2011) analyse policy discourse on sustainable regional development in Sweden and conclude that the prevalent ecological modernization approach makes "ideologically charged [sustainable development] *politics* redundant" (2011, p. 182; italics in original). Henriksson (2014) analyses municipal planners' images of sustainable transport and the sustainable traveller, as an intentional counter to the prevalent focus on how measures best can be implemented, finding that planners envisage that it is greater to "travel freely" than to "travel correctly" and that sustainable transport must be framed as desirable for personal reasons rather than environmental. In a similar way, tracing development can show the real and lasting impact of seemingly small, as well as more large-scale, policy measures. Lundin (2008) shows how the parking norm – a simple number for how many parking spaces each new home should have – led to the restructuring of not only Stockholm's centre but many cities across Sweden. Hysing (2009) shows the importance of politicizing urban transport for 'green' policy change. Richardson et al. (2010) trace mobility frames in Stockholm over time and argue that despite the introduction of the congestion tax, a frame of automobility remains which muddles the impact of the tax. Isaksson (2001) analyses the power relations during the large-scale transport package of the 1990s, the Dennis Agreement, demonstrating the inherently political nature of spatial issues. Her work, too, shows the impact of the belief in transport as a vehicle of growth and so a necessity for sustainable development; a 'win-win' narrative central to ecological modernization (Isaksson 2006).

To answer my research questions – What kind of 'tool' is produced by policy for transport in Stockholm municipality? and What does sustainability mean in Stockholm municipal policy for personal transport? – this way of thinking about transport and transport policy is valuable. Given my assertion that sustainability, like transport, touches upon all aspects of our lives, I want to build upon this body of research about the shaping force of transport and the ideas behind or within transport policy. While any study on sustainable transport must come up against the normative concerns of most transport research, the recognized physical relations between transport modes and environmental or human health impacts, my intention is not to argue how best to ensure one development or another, but rather to consider policy with an open mind to its qualities and constructions and consider where these might take us.

I propose that the *What's the problem represented to be?* framework is useful for this form of transport study. The WPR framework is set to study the ends (what is to be 'fixed') through study of the means (what 'fixes' are proposed), meaning that 'yet another' study of the measures in policy seeks to understand the goals and motivations. It is a form of poststructuralist analysis which stresses the way that our physical lives are shaped in and through discourse (in the broad sense referring to meaning and meaning-making). Previous studies using the WPR framework have shown the framework useful for analysing the concerns which permeate policy and planning, either explicitly or implicitly. Perman (2008) studies how electric heating was problematized on a national, municipal, and household level, showing that economic arguments influence environmental concerns on all three levels, while the tension between economic and environmental arguments is played down. Mukhtar-Landgren (2016) studies the problem formulations and subject positions preceding the processes of urban regeneration in Malmö, showing that the discourses of progress and problems serve to construct heterogeneity and immigration as threats against the prosperity that unity was constructed to bring, and immigrants as unable to 'keep up' and contribute. Olsson (2018) uses the WPR to analyse problem representations in climate change adaptation politics in Sweden; but also to pose alternative problem representations to question the questions normally asked about adaptation and sustainability. Hrelja (2019) studies explicit problem representation in plans and strategies to reduce car use, concluding that it is the risks cars pose to the 'attractiveness' of cities' which is treated as the 'problem'. Even this small selection of studies shows the breadth of possible uses of the framework.

With this study I contribute to transport research which addresses the aims and goals of transport, by utilising a framework which interrogates the on-the-ground tools of policy. What I aim to do runs closely to the discourse- or framing-oriented studies of Hilding-Rydevik et al. (2011) or Henriksson (2014), and of course parallel to Hrelja (2019). What I do differently is to focus closely on the measures (rather than actors), and to look at the transport system for people as a whole (rather than focus on for example cars). In particular, I collect a significant number of proposed measures to study what problems they represent and what effects they may have as one collective whole, one single proposal. What I have been missing from previous research, and especially from the current political discussion of transport, is this consideration of transport as one *system*. My contribution to sustainable transport studies is a more cohesive view of proposals for the studied time and place, which I hope will be the start of research into the cumulative and conglomerate effects of measures for transport.

The WPR is particularly good for re-politicizing the transport area, which has been depoliticized in both research and politics, through attention to the implications and impacts of measures frequently treated as technical solutions. Rather than treating transport as a system in isolation, the WPR enables us to turn attention to the impacts on society at large as well as consider the ways transport relates to our 'bodies in space' (Ahmed 2006).

In the next chapter, I describe my analytical and methodological considerations for this study and discuss how I use the WPR.

4
Theoretical and methodological considerations

He was determined to discover the underlying logic behind the universe.
Which was going to be hard, because there wasn't one.

–Terry Pratchett, Mort (1987)

In this chapter I present the choices I made to answer my research questions:
What kind of 'tool' is produced by policy for transport in Stockholm municipality? and What does sustainability mean in Stockholm municipal policy
for personal transport? I begin by presenting the material for analysis. Then
I describe my reasons and considerations for analysing policy, and my choice
of the What's the problem represented to be? (WPR) analytical framework.
Finally, I describe in more detail how I used the material and the WPR
framework for policy analysis. Every instance of analysis using the WPR
framework is different, as every case and analyst is different, and I describe
to the reader the choices I made and the specifics of this instance of WPR
analysis.

As I started my doctoral project I knew that I wanted to study policy as a
way to study the 'rules' for transport. Further, I had an idea that I wanted to
know what transport *did*, or what policy was suggesting it should do. I
considered different ways to interrogate and understand the target-decision
discrepancy and grew curious about what could be found out by studying
transport measures together, as one body of policy. After some consideration
I decided to delimit my study to policies released within Stockholm municipality. This way, I would have a body of policy from within the same level
of organization. While it would be interesting to do a multi-level study of
policy to see how different measures are proposed and promoted at different
levels, as well as how the policy levels interact and inform each other, this
would also involve different scales and forms of organizations, working
under slightly different conditions. Taking these differences into account
would make for a different study than the one I wanted to do and have done.
In one way a municipality has the scope to be more radical in its policy than
higher levels of government, as it does not have to take the entire nation into

account; at the same time a municipality may be more pragmatic as municipal funds are limited. This makes municipal policy an interesting site of exploration of how sustainability is constructed in its practical execution.

I chose to focus on the policy documents themselves, studying the measures proposed, the meanings or discourses, and the discursive, subjectification, and lived effects. I paid close attention to the measures, and the way that they construct 'sustainability'.

A brief overview of my process

As my focus was on the empirical case, I started my study by gathering the main body of material for study (that is, the policy documents). I began by reading Stockholm's current (at the time) comprehensive plan (The Walkable City 2010), which sets the overarching aims and priorities for development in Stockholm over time. I reasoned that this plan would inform me about both transport measures and where they fit into the larger picture of urban development. The comprehensive plan, though not binding, also has to relate to sustainability goals and is subject to a strategic environmental impact assessment. This meant that it would also inform me on the more explicit (outright stated) considerations of sustainability in the municipality. From there, I followed references to other documents and sought out documents addressing transport and environmental issues on the official Stockholm municipality website (Stockholm.se). Some documents were not readily available on the website, and these I sought out via google or (if that failed) by e-mailing municipal departments.

I paid particular attention to the use and description of 'sustainability', 'sustainable development' or 'sustainable transport'. I searched in the Swedish PDF files for "hållbar", which covers both 'sustainable' and 'sustainability'. In the table I copied in the paragraphs of text which deal with sustainability, so as not to lose context. I used the mentions and depictions of sustainability in the last part of my analysis, where I bring together the implicit representation of sustainability from my analysis of the problem representations, on the one hand, and the explicit mentions of sustainability on the other. I noted these uses in a Word table, sorted by themes drawn from the material: sustainable growth, a sustainable increase in travel, and sustainable development (for example). Then I set them aside for later analysis. Only after this first read-through of these materials did I start the task of designing the study: choosing my analytical framework and situating the material in a research field. This meant that I chose literature and additional materials which help me address my research aim, questions, and topics in the empirical material. My initial search for the use of 'sustainable'/'sustainability' also helped me reflect as I did my literature study. I considered how the way that 'sustainable transport' was described in previous research related to what I saw in the policy documents, and how well the description in previous research of sustainable transport policy and the implementation of sustainability fit with what I read. My process in analysing this body of material has been inductive, iterative, and grounded in the material itself. I started by reading the documents, making notes in the margins of statements which raised thoughts or questions. Going back to the beginning, I made Word tables of proposals for measures and the details of these (e.g. scope or route).

Following the first read-through and the study of previous research and analytical framework, I went back to the main material. Having chosen Carol Bacchi's *What's the problem represented to be?* framework as suitable for my study, I began to identify the proposed measures. In the following analysis, in which I drew out conceptual premises and effects, my choices of additional material and secondary sources were guided by the questions of the WPR framework. I analysed pictures using the same approach as I did for text, treating both as discursive.

4.1 Selecting sources

I chose to focus on the finished policy documents because they express politically sanctioned proposals for action. By this I mean that while there may still be some disagreement, these proposals were found acceptable and feasible enough to pass through the 'window of opportunity' onto the agenda. As they have been approved as official proposals, I could rely on this material to represent the organizations behind them. That said, these documents come from several different departments within the municipality and so what is proposed by one department may not be promoted by another. My focus, however, is not on actors or intentionality. I have chosen to treat these documents, disparate as they may be in origin, as one proposal to open up a discussion of the overarching directionality of policy proposals.

My interest in policy text has been in both effects and meaning. By *effects*, I mean that which comes out of policy, and by *meaning* I mean the understanding of things which is inherent in or implied by policy: the discursive. These two are interlinked. The discursive has effects on the natural as well as our built and social environment, and the material aspects of society are discursive in their nature, affect the way we view the world, and are altered by the way that we make (new) meaning. Following discourse theory as well as Shove's take on social practice theory (e.g. Shove and Trentmann 2019), the social and the material cannot easily be separated – and doing so may not be meaningful. In this case, it is more meaningful to consider the two together, to acknowledge the interlinkages between the built environment, the practices enabled, and the discursive constructions that make sense of the world for us.

The material (presented below, table 4.1) was chosen to show the overarching direction of transport policy in Stockholm. I found documents covering Stockholm via official web pages, which have all been released by Stockholm municipality (Stockholms stad) but written by different offices within the municipal government. Documents covering Stockholm policy are available in Swedish and often translated into English. Strategies and city plans are translated, while the environmental programmes, budgets, and the agreements are not. Citations will be taken from the English version of each document, where available. Sometimes a quote will be translated from Swedish, as wording or content may differ between versions.

4.1.1 Selecting the main policy documents

Given that a stated objective of Stockholm municipality is 'sustainable transport' and my aim is to understand what this means, my main materials are documents released by Stockholm municipality, addressing transport, environment, and urban development in Stockholm with some prescriptions for what should be done. They are not necessarily binding – most are not – but express proposals or desirable directions for transport in Stockholm. In other words, I have chosen documents proposing regulations and courses of actions, what is to be done, for transport. These policy documents are my main material – that is, the main focus of my analysis and my unit of observation. It is from these documents that I draw out the problem representations and construction of sustainability and transport.

I set three initial criteria for choosing my main body of material: that they were written and released by Stockholm municipality; that they addressed the transport system or transport measures; and that they addressed matters of sustainability. After deliberation, I set the timeframe to the years 2007–2017, allowing for additions of relevant material as it was released (such as the most recent Environmental Programme and the Vision 2040). As I described in the introduction, this was a time of the reintroduction of large-scale infrastructure agreements. I considered extending the timeframe to include the trial period and referendum for the congestion tax (2006). The autumn of 2006, following both a referendum which was positive towards the congestion tax (in Stockholm municipality, at least) and a shift in power in City Hall, marked the beginning of the congestion tax as a source of funding for road construction. In October that year, the Liberal–Conservative Alliance published an opinion article where they agreed on the congestion tax as funding for the Bypass, and proposed stopping the *Citybanan* commuter rail tunnel project (Reinfeldt et al. 2006). After a long debate on the merits and demerits of the congestion tax (with many accusations of 'betrayal'), the Alliance postponed the reintroduction of the congestion tax until August 2007 and installed a negotiator (former Mayor of Stockholm for the Moderate Party, Carl Cederschiöld) to bring about the first broad agreement on Stockholm transport: *Traffic Solution for Stockholm* (2007). The *Traffic Solution* included the congestion tax as a source of funding for road projects (2007, p. 11). Thus, while the congestion tax trial and referendum, as well as the debates, marked the beginning of a 'new' phase, it wasn't until 2007 that this was reflected in policy documents and at that point the purpose of the tax had shifted. For this reason, I treat the pre-2007 congestion tax process as part of its history, rather than part of my policy material.

I came into my project interested in the intersection of transport and sustainability in policy. At first, I set out to study public transport as a 'tool' for sustainability, but it soon became clear that how public transport was used could only be understood in relation to the wider context of all transport modes. That said, I was interested in the more general directions of policy, and the modes in relation to each other, rather than the specificity found in e.g. the bicycle plan or how many vehicles SL requested. For this reason, I focused on policies which addressed traffic flows, modal shares, and the transport system as a whole. I also searched for policies which addressed transport within the context of environmental issues. Realising that I needed to view transport modes in relation to each other and focus on overarching patterns, I selected documents which address transport on a broad level. I found most of the documents on Stockholm municipality's website – www.stockholm.se – by browsing for subjects related to my focus: transport (e.g. *Urban Mobility Strategy*), environment (e.g. the *Environment Programmes* and *Roadmap for Fossil Fuel-Free Stockholm 2050*), and city planning (e.g. *Walkable City*). Some I found by searching on the web or stockholm.se for documents mentioned in other documents (e.g. *Vision 2030* and *Vision 2040*). My main body of materials consists of ten documents, described in Table 4.1.

GETTING THE TRANSPORT RIGHT

Table 4.1: Main materials. Party abbreviations: C = Centre Party, FI = Feminist Party Feministiskt initiativ, FP = Folkpartiet, currently Liberal Party, KD = Christian Democrats, L = Liberal Party, M = Moderate Party, MP = Green Party, S = Social Democrats, SP = Stockholm Party, V = Left Party.

Document	Year	Issued by	Parties in office at City Hall	Description
Vision 2030. A Guide to The Future. *(Vision 2030. Ett Stockholm I världsklass.)* *In-text reference: Vision 2030.*	2007	Stadsledningskontoret/ Executive office	M+FP+KD	A "strategic undertaking" which is to guide the work of all levels of the municipality, including the direction of the budget (which in turn is superordinate to all other documents). 10 pages (Swedish version) 11 pages (English version).
Environment Programme 2008-2011. *(Stockholms, miljöprogram 2008-2011.)* *In-text reference: Environment Programme 2008-2011.*	2007	Miljöförvaltningen/ Environment department	M+FP+KD	This environment programme sets up general aims and guidelines. It is governing for the city as a whole and guiding for each committee or board. This document does not propose measures. 12 pages (Swedish version, no English version).

Action Plan for Climate And Energy 2010–2020. (Stockholms åtgärdsplan för klimat och energi 2010–2020.) In-text reference: Action Plan 2010–2020.	2009	Miljöförvaltningen/ Environment department	M+FP+KD	The Action Plan is part of Stockholm's commitment to the Covenant of Mayors, in which the city promises to reduce CO_2e emissions by more than EU agreements. The plan includes both ongoing or decided measures and possible measures to show how the city can reach targets. 36 pages (Swedish version, no English version).
The Walkable City. Stockholm city plan. (Promenadstaden. Översiktsplan för Stockholm.) In-text reference: Walkable City.	2010	Stadsbyggnadskontoret/City planning office	M+FP+C+KD	This city plan was in effect 2010–2018. The city plan or comprehensive plan (Swedish översiktsplan) is guiding but not binding. It expands on the *Vision 2030* to set the long-term goals and direction for development in the municipality, including the urban structure and the transport system. 92 pages (Swedish version) 83 pages (English version).
Action Plan for Climate And Energy 2012–2015. (Stockholms åtgärdsplan för klimat och energi 2012–2015.) In-text reference: Action Plan 2012–2015.	2011	Miljöförvaltningen/ Environment department	M+FP+C+KD	The Action Plan concretizes aims from the Environment Programme. It is guiding, and "shall be considered" important material for budgets (p. 7). 72 pages (Swedish version, no English version).

Document	Year	Department	Political majority	Description
Environment Programme 2012–2015. (Stockholms miljöprogram 2012–2015.) In-text reference: Environment Programme 2012–2015.	2011	Miljöförvaltningen/ Environment department	M+FP+C+KD	This programme assigns aims to different boards and committees, which are responsible for their success. It proposes measures to reach targets. 59 pages (Swedish version, no English version).
Urban Mobility Strategy. (Framkomlighetsstrategin.) In-text reference: Mobility Strategy.	2012	Trafikkontoret/ Traffic department	M+FP+C+KD	A strategic document outlining how to preserve or promote 'framkomlighet' and increased mobility as well as decreased CO_2 emissions. 72 pages (Swedish and English version).
Roadmap for a Fossil Fuel-Free Stockholm 2050. (Färdplan för ett fossilbränslefritt Stockholm 2050.) In-text reference: Roadmap.	2014	Miljöförvaltningen/ Environment department	M+FP+C+KD (March)	A strategic document outlining how the city can reach its target to be fossil fuel-free by 2050 in order to significantly lower CO_2 emissions. 58 pages (Swedish version) 60 pages (English version).
Environment Programme 2016–2019. (Stockholms stads miljöprogram 2016–2019.) In-text reference: Environment Programme 2016–2019.	2016	Miljöförvaltningen/ Environment department	S+MP+V+FI	The programme formulates aims and indicators, and proposes possible measures. Indicators are confirmed through budgets. Boards and committees are tasked with the success and evaluation of targets. 52 pages (Swedish version, no English version).

Vision 2040. Ett Stockholm för alla. In-text reference: *Vision 2030.*	2017	Stadsledningskontoret / Executive office	S+MP+V+FI	A document staking out long-term targets for Stockholm as a city, which is to run through all municipal work and impact the budget work. 17 pages (Swedish version, no English version).

4.1.2 Policy documents used as reference points

I also selected a few documents to act as reference points or comparisons: City Plan 1999 (1999), Traffic Solution for Stockholm (2007), Budgets of 2010–2017 (2009–2016), The Stockholm Negotiation (2013), Proposal for Revised Vision 2030 (2014), the National Negotiation (2017), and the City Plan 2018.

The 1999 City Plan, which was in effect until it was replaced with *The Walkable City* in 2010, was excluded from my main material because it was falling out of relevance at the time of the large-scale transport agreements. That said, it is a relevant timestamp of city development prior to 2007. In addition, the proposal for a new City Plan was released for consultation with the public late 2016. I debated bringing it into my set of main materials, but ultimately excluded it as it was, at the time, only a proposal and so still subject to change. Reading through the City Plan proposal, I could see that while the power shift in City Hall was reflected in for example a stronger focus on social cohesion and equality and the aim for a "climate smart city" was pushed to the front, measures for transport remained the same. I have used the 1999 or the 2018 City Plans to reflect on past and probable continued developments in 'sustainable transport' in Stockholm. I have also used *Proposal for revised Vision 2030* (2014) as a marker for change in urban development and policymaking, as it expresses the need to alter the original *Vision 2030* (2007). Lastly, I have looked through the Stockholm municipal budgets. These did, to my surprise, not specify which projects were to be funded. I could glean relative funding to the different departments (e.g. Transport or Environment), and occasional mentions of what should be done, but not to reliably say which of the proposed measures were given funding from the municipality. The budgets did, however, describe the direction which the City should go for the budget year, and list overarching priorities. I have used the budgets to seek definitions of keywords from policy. These did not change much within each length of office, and so the budgets show the differences between political blocs in describing goals and aims, and which keywords were used and which meaning they were given. The municipal website only provides budgets from the most recent years (in 2019, the earliest available budget is from 2014). As I realized the budgets would not provide the information I had hoped for, I was satisfied with having the budgets for the years 2010–2017.

As a marker for which measures are given particular support through funding, I have looked to the 2007 *Traffic Solution for Stockholm*, the 2013 report from the Stockholm Negotiation, and the 2017 final report from the National Negotiation on transport and housing. These are also not written by Stockholm municipality, but show national or regional support for certain measures.

Table 4.2: Additional policy documents. Party abbreviations: C = Centre Party, FI = Feminist Party Feministiskt initiativ, FP = Folkpartiet, currently Liberal Party, KD = Christian Democrats, L = Liberal Party, M = Moderate Party, MP = Green Party, S = Social Democrats, SP = Stockholm Party, V = Left Party.

Document	Year	Issued by	Parties in office at City Hall	Description
City Plan 1999. (Stockholms översiktsplan 1999.) In-text reference: City Plan 1999.	1999	Stadsbyggnadskontoret/ City planning office	M+FP+KD+SP	The 1999 City Plan was in effect 1999–2010. Guiding but not binding, this comprehensive plan drew on 14 essays about Stockholm in 2022, published with the county council's office for regional planning and traffic. 161 pages (Swedish version, no English version).

Document	Year	Producer	Governing majority	Description
Traffic Solution for Stockholm. (Trafiklösning för Stockholmsregionen till 2020 med utblick mot 2030.) In-text: *Traffic Solution.*	2007	Stockholmsförhandlingen, Näringsdepartementet/ Stockholm negotiation, Ministry of Enterprise and Innovation	M+FP+KD National government: M+C+FP+KD	The first Stockholm negotiation, led by Carl Cederschiöld, was assigned by the National Government in 2006 to produce a joint traffic solution "for environment and growth" (p. 1). The agreement was supported by M, FP, C and KD, and partially by S. 20 pages (Swedish and English version).
Budgets. In-text reference: *Budget [year].*	2010 (2009) – 2017 (2016)	Kommunfullmäktige/ City Council	M+FP+KD (2006–2010) M+FP+C+KD (2010–2014)	The municipal budgets are the primary steering document for the city. Budgets set up targets and indicators, and divide funding to boards and committees. 384, 415, 369, 422, 413, 484, 519, 482 pages (Swedish version, no English version).
The Stockholm Negotiation. (Överenskommelse om finansiering och medfinansiering av utbyggnad av tunnelbanan samt ökad bostadsbebyggelse i Stockholms län enligt 2013 års Stockholmsförhandli ng.) In-text reference: *Stockholm Negotiation.*	2013	Stockholmsförhandlingen, Näringsdepartementet/ The Stockholm Negotiation, Ministry of Enterprise and Innovation	M+FP+C+KD National government: M+C+FP+KD	The second Stockholm negotiation was led by HG Wessberg. The assignment from National Government in February 2013 was to bring about an agreement on financing for metro extensions and construction of homes. 64 pages (Swedish version, no English version).

Proposal for Revised Vision 2030. (Förslag till reviderad Vision 2030.) In-text reference: Proposal for Revised Vision 2030.	2014	Stadsledningskontoret/ Executive office	M+FP+C+KD (April)	The proposal draft was sent out for referral in April 2014; however, the subsequent shift in City Hall led to the new City Government writing their own Vision. 28 pages (Swedish version, no English version).
Final Report from the National Negotiation, SOU 2017:107. (Slutrapport från Sverigeförhandlingen Infrastruktur och bostäder – ett gemensamt Samhällsbygge.) In-text reference: SOU 2017:107.	2017	Sverigeförhandlingen, Näringsdepartementet/ The Stockholm Negotiation, Ministry of Enterprise and Innovation	S+MP+V+FI National government: S+MP	In 2014, National government assigned HG Wessberg to negotiate for an agreement on "increased housing construction through the development of new infrastructure" (p. 23). Especially the urban regions were targeted for development. 330 pages (Swedish version) 11 pages (English summary).
City Plan 2018. (Översiktsplan för Stockholms stad.) In-text reference: City Plan 2018.	2018	Stadsbyggnadskontoret/ City planning office	S+MP+V+FI	The new City Plan came into effect in March 2018. This non-binding comprehensive plan is based on Vision 2040. 182 pages (Swedish and English version).

4.1.3 Selecting additional materials – articles, press releases, letters from readers

In addition to policy documents, I have looked at how transport and measures for transport are presented or discussed in opinion articles and press releases from political representatives and organizations. I have used press releases and opinion articles from decision makers and organizations to study how proposals have been proposed or opposed, as well as give a broader view of how the problem representations have occurred in the discussion of urban transport.

In Chapter 7, which relates the 'problem' of individual choices, I have used letters from readers (Swedish: *insändare*) and opinion pieces (Swedish: *debattartiklar*) from the broader public as examples of reactions to proposals and measures, in order to draw out both lived effects and subjectification effects as reported by individuals themselves. These letters are of course not fully representative of all effects on all people: they represent only the views of people who chose to write a letter to a newspaper. Some do not refer to their own experiences, but those of other people (e.g. low-income workers or accessibility users). Some seem deliberately provocative. For these reasons, I cannot use them as complete or uncontested material or wholly representtative of effects, but they serve as examples of how some people express their reactions. In addition to looking to the effects, I have used opinion pieces from the public as examples of promotion of or opposition to measures and proposals among Stockholm residents. While they cannot act as a survey, they can, as with effects, give examples of how some people choose to express their views.

I found the material by reading local and national papers, and by searching online for opinions on specific issues by searching archives for "[issue, e.g. parking] + insändare" (English: *letter from reader*) or "[issue] + åsikt" (English: *opinion*). The papers from which I used letters from readers are primarily two local papers, *Stockholm Direkt* and *Mitt i Stockholm*, both of which release separate titles for each part of the city, including to neigh-bouring municipalities (27 and 31 separate titles, respectively). Their material is available online, as well as distributed weekly in paper form (both papers are paid by ads and sponsors). I also used letters from two of Sweden's largest newspapers, *Dagens Nyheter* and *Svenska Dagbladet*, which have online editions as well as daily paper issues, both paid by ads, subscriptions, and single-issue-payments. The local papers focus on local issues large and small and receive letters from local residents involved in local issues, which gave me an idea of how Stockholmers chose to express their opinions. This localized perspective also meant that opinions on more local Stockholm issues were more likely to be published, as opposed to the national news-papers who draw letters from all around the country. However, the letters on local Stockholm issues which were published in national papers were interesting to use, and so I did not limit my scope to only local sources. As the material is used to provide examples or highlight perspectives, I have been quite free in choosing interesting letters rather than trying to read all letters on an issue from a certain source or mapping out every concern and reply (such as the extended conversation on whether cars or motorcycles pay more for parking).

I drew the opinion pieces and press releases from a wider selection of sources, using material both from newspapers, such as *Dagens Nyheter* and *Svenska Dagbladet*, and from websites such as Swedish public television (*Sveriges Television*), *Dagens Samhälle* (a paper and news site, independent but owned by Swedish Association of Local Authorities and Regions; *Sveriges Kommuner och Landsting*), and the websites of organizations. Online material was found by searching for "[issue] + debatt" (English: *opinion*), or as secondary results during other but topically related searches on both news sites or on Google. Press releases are frequently published as opinion pieces or announced in news articles, which then served as a starting point. Here, too, I have focused on interesting key examples.

4.2 Studying policy

In Chapter 3 I presented the field of sustainable transport studies. In this section, I relate to what policy is, how it's studied, and how physical measures can provide explanations. First, I briefly introduce policy, discussing what it is and how it may be studied. I then present the way in which I study policy, and what concepts I use to do so.

> The reality of being a citizen in a modern democratic nation is that everyday life is impacted by the intended and unintended consequences of a whole series of public policies. Some of these policies we may personally be aware of and some we may not be aware of; however, the truth is public policy dictates how we as individuals and society as a whole live and interact, and because of this, the study of public policy has become an increasingly popular academic endeavour (Theodoulou 2013, p. 1).

In other words, policy governs us and shapes us as people and as a society. Despite this, transport policy studies tend to overlook the ends and aims of policy; that is, what policy works to do (e.g. Marsden and Reardon 2017). The broad (if not uniform) agreement on what the components of sustainable transport are (see Chapter 3) seems to focus policy research on how to best bring these about: the means and tools of policy. This type of study treats policy as problem-solving and asks questions about barriers to implementing the agreed solutions to the agreed problems. What these studies do not do, is more broadly consider policy as governing and ask questions about how we as people and as a society are shaped (rather, studies on how to shape us into 'sustainable' subjects who make the right choices abound). The techno-rational approach to transport is then at its core normative, prescribing what ought to be, and because of this techno-rational transport policy studies run the risk of disregarding the impacts of transport as a shaping factor on society and its people.

The simplest definition of public policy is 'anything a government chooses to do or not to do' (Dye 1972, cited in Howlett and Cashore 2014, p. 17). Expanding on that, public policy is intentional action made by governments – legislation, executive orders, rules, and regulations – with end goals as the objective, in the long- as well as short term, ideally involving all levels of government (and not restricted to formal actors). It is an ongoing process involving formulation, implementation, enforcement, and evaluation. Public policy study takes into consideration what governments do, intend to do, and don't do; and is concerned with how issues and problems are defined, constructed, and placed on the political and policy agenda (Theodoulou 2013, p. 3). Policy is the means by which government intervenes "for political, moral, and economic reasons" (Theodoulou 2013, p. 3). Through public policy, government reconciles conflicting claims on scarce resources; establishes incentives for cooperation and collective action that would be irrational without governmental influence; prohibits morally unacceptable behaviour; protects the activity of a group or an individual; promotes activities that are essential or important to government; and provides direct benefits to citizens (Theodoulou 2013, p. 3). All of these definitions construct policy as rational and problem-solving: policy reconciles, it regulates behaviour, it protects and provides for citizens. This is reflected in many transport policy studies which tend towards a techno-rational approach (Marsden and Reardon 2009).

Policy studies broadly tend towards four areas: the policy process, or the policy cycle, (e.g. Lindblom 1979; Kingdon 1995); policy change (e.g. Lindblom 1959; Hall 1993); policy components (e.g. Vedung 1997; Howlett and Cashore 2009; Bemelmans-Videc et al. 2011); and policy evaluation (insofar as this is not considered part of the policy cycle; e.g. Vedung 1997). These approaches address different aspects of policy, but do not address the impacts of policy on society as a whole, or the co-constitutive nature of the social and the material (e.g. Söderström et al. 2013; Shove and Trentmann 2018).

In my literature review, I found that transport policy analysis tends to evaluate policy measures from their efficacy or propose new policy measures to 'better' reach the set targets: what Howlett and Cashore (2009) dub the 'means and tools' of policy. In a similar vein, Marsden and Reardon (2017, p. 245) argue that, "The 'policy' literature is therefore currently drawn to answering questions relating to what is, and making that work more effectively, than on critiquing the assumptions of the status quo, and arguing for what ought to be, or what could be" (Marsden and Reardon 2017, p. 245). My interest in the measures for transport may suggest a focus on the technical or physical aspects, but with Söderström et al.'s (2013) attention to what mobility is constitutive of[5] in mind, I contend that the measures have more to tell us.

Consider the observation, verified through thirty years of application of Kingdon's (1995) multiple streams approach in various fields (Marsden and Reardon 2017, p. 246), that 'solutions' may exist independently of and before 'problems' they are said to address, and think about the rhetorical and conceptual legwork needed to fit the desired 'solution' to the current 'problem' (Sabatier and Weible 2007, p. 195). On the one hand, this makes the focus on the means and tools of policy perfectly reasonable – but on the other hand, it also calls for a different way of looking at 'solutions' or tools. If policy measures are frequently more important in policy making than the issues they are to address, and if – as Givoni et al. (2013) suggest – policy measures can say something about which form of power and governing is being practised, this suggests that policy measures could and should be interrogated as more than technical and neutral 'fixes'. Following these ideas, it is fair to say not just that measures can tell us things about more than the technical or physical aspects of policy – they have something to say about the very way that we are governed, the mechanisms of control and compliance that surround us in our daily lives. They can also, recursively, help us discuss how 'sustainable transport' (as both an aim and a tool) is constructed and understood. Such an interrogation should reach beyond 'measure X is better than measure Y because…' and consider questions such as, *What can we learn of the goals and logics of policy – not from their stated objectives but from the work that the measures do?* We may also consider in what ways transport policies influence our lives, and what people are to do. Phrased in another way: what is the role of people in society, formulated through transport policy? What kind of people are we encouraged or enabled to be, through policy?

---

[5] That is, what mobility shapes, enables, and produces. Söderström et al (2013, p. 3) list bodies, subjectivities, materialities, economic resources, social positions, and organizational structures.

To consider this type of questions requires considering policy as a form of governing – as exertion of political power, not simply 'solving a problem' – and the measures proposed as 'technologies' of governing (Bacchi and Goodwin 2016, p. 44). It also requires regarding policy as discursive, and the proposals for measures as carriers of meaning. One approach which incorporates these two aspects is the *What's the problem represented to be?* or WPR framework.

4.3 What's the problem represented to be?

I have always thought the actions of men [sic] the best interpreters of their thoughts.

– John Locke

In this section I present the analytical framework chosen for this study, the *What's the problem represented to be?* (WPR) approach (Bacchi 2009). The WPR was formulated to 'problematize the problematizations' of policy and address questions of power, silences, and the contingency of meaning and practices. Informed by the WPR approach, I ask: what is policy aiming to change (and so representing as a problem) when addressing urban transport? What effects does this have? To answer my question of how 'sustainable transport' constitutes the understanding of sustainability, I begin by asking: if sustainability is the solution, what is the problem? More precisely, what is the problem which sustainable transport should solve? If sustainability is the solution, then the 'problem' can be assumed to be unsustainability. The problems represented in policy can thus show how sustainability is constituted/constructed. Once these unsustainable problems are out of the way, what should sustainability be?

In the WPR approach, Bacchi (2009) draws upon Foucault to argue that through problematizations, policy has an important function in governing (Bacchi 2009, p. xxi).[6] The way an issue is problematized matters because it dictates and rationalizes the decisions made by politicians on what should

---

[6] It is important to point out that a *What's the problem* analysis does not exclude more direct forms of rule. The approach carries a Foucauldian view of the state, in which there is a 'triangle of rule' – governing or governmentality (both rationalities of different forms of rule, and the specific population-focused form of rule of the past two hundred years), sovereignty (power over territory and its subjects), and discipline (power over individual citizens) (Bacchi 2009, p. 26). However, these forms of power coalesce into hybrid forms of rule, meaning that few, if any, governments are wholly one form or the other, and so different forms of government power can be expected to coexist (Bacchi 2009, p. 29).

be done and how – "the ways in which 'problems' are constituted (or shaped) carry all sorts of implications for how we live our lives on a day-to-day basis" (Bacchi 2009, p. xviii). These problematizations need to be studied, and through analysing the problem representations inherent in policy analysts should scrutinize the "premises and effects" they hold (Bacchi 2009, p. xxi).

The contemporary problem-based reasoning of policy and planning – though a step away from the previous starting assumption that more infrastructure should be built – may contribute to inefficient measures taken (Eliasson 2015). By stating a 'problem' to solve, political and societal pressure may build up to solve the problem, so that even inefficient measures may seem necessary at even very high costs to little benefit (Eliasson 2015, p. 11). One example of this is the proposed high-speed rail from Stockholm to Gothenburg and Malmö in Sweden's southern regions. The rail received a lot of support from municipalities after they were encouraged to envision the many advantages of the rail compared to without it – creating 'problems' only the high-speed rail could solve (Ronnle 2018). Ronnle's study (2018) showed that cost-benefit analysis became less important for decision-making through the narrative about the benefits of the high-speed rail – as Eliasson suggests, the identification of a 'problem' or 'aim' created political pressure to address it which overrode an unfavourable cost-benefit analysis. The narrative of the high-speed rail is "a version of the 'stymied progress story'" (Ronnle 2018, p. 48) – without the high-speed rail, the progress of the municipalities involved, and the whole nation, will suffer. The high-speed rail is shown as the 'solution' for housing shortage, unemployment, environmental degradation from economic growth, and so on. Conversely, not building the high-speed rail would be a 'loss' for the municipalities who have envisioned all the good things to come from the rail and become invested in their realization. Good things come from the new rail, bad things without it. Policy should then be studied not as rational problem-*solving* but as problem-*producing* (Bacchi 2009) – and emotionally charged.

The WPR approach is both a theoretical framework of governmentality and problem representation, and a methodological framework to study the same. It rests on three propositions: that we are governed through problematizations; that we need to study these problematizations rather than 'problems'; and that we need to problematize the problematizations "through scrutinising the premises and effects of the problem representations they contain" (Bacchi 2009, p. 25). These concerns are structured into six questions, influenced by social construction theory, poststructuralism, feminist body theory, and governmentality studies. Together the questions map out the problem representation in policy, what makes it possible, and what some of its effects are.

The WPR approach questions the notion of policy as natural and neutral, and suggests that policy – rather than responsive to pre-existing 'problems' – is *creative*. Rather than a means of 'solving problems' policy can be understood as a way of addressing and making sense of social conditions. In doing so, policy characterizes or creates a 'problem' *as* a problem in the first place (Bacchi 2009), which implies that it can be solved and that there is something policy can and should do (Eliasson 2015). Thus the idea of policy as "neutral, technical and as separate from politics" must be questioned through critical analysis (Bacchi 2009, p. 253).

Policy defines what needs to be 'fixed' – and, indeed, that there is something that needs to be 'fixed' in the first place – and by studying the proposed solutions, the shape of the implicit problem (the problem representation) can be discerned.[7] For example, in a study of Belgium's transport policy, Boussaw and Vanoutrive (2017) found that the construction of a large car park near Ghent railway station, explicitly intended to encourage workers from Ghent's suburbs to park there and continue by train, in fact encouraged people who had previously come by local public transport to instead take their cars. Boussaw and Vanoutrive argue that the "the project design, in particular the large car park, is not consistent with the original problem definition" and that "emphasis [of indicators] was shifted towards maximising the number of station users" (2017, p. 14). From the perspective of the WPR approach, and looking at the project as a whole (sporting the car park, offices, and apartments near the station), it can be said that the problem was represented to be a lack of cars by Ghent rail station. This shows that the explicitly formulated problem is not necessarily the problem *represented* in policy.

The focus of a WPR analysis is on *policy as a creative aspect of governing*: what does it identify as a problem, what allows for this particular representation to happen, what does that representation allow for, and what are the consequences? This study aims to consider the way that urban transport and sustainability are constructed in policy, making problematizations (through problem representations) a highly relevant target.

A WPR analysis is less concerned with problem-solving than with problem-*questioning* (Bacchi 2009, p. 262), and more interested in studying

---

[7] By 'problem', Bacchi means something which, by having been confronted with a solution or a means to 'fix it', has been identified as in need of change (Bacchi 2009, p. xi).

what policy does than in how to make it do what it does better or more efficiently. A relevant example offered comes from Shapiro (1992, in Bacchi 2009, p. xv), who "asks us to think what follows if we broaden our analysis to think about traffic congestion as a middle-class 'problem', produced by people who have enough money to purchase one or more cars, and the funds to fuel them", rather than as a practical or technical 'problem'. The WPR approach studies the qualities and norms of policy itself, not necessarily concerned with intentions of policy makers but rather with the intervention inherent in the problem representation in policy itself (e.g. Bacchi 2014).

4.3.1 Critique – an inquiry into the limits of a structure

The WPR framework is a form of policy critique. 'Critique' in this case is not the same as criticism, or finding fault, but rather akin to literary critique: the practice of drawing out themes and central issues, note approaches used, and consider the significance.

> A critique does not consist in saying that things aren't good the way they are. It consists in seeing on what type of assumptions, of familiar notions, of established, unexamined ways of thinking the accepted practices are based (Foucault 1994, p. 456).

I see two reasons for critical study of policy: one, to ask what is taken for granted and what the limits are of the structure this creates; and two, to question that which is taken for granted, so that decisions can be more reasoned and thought-through. While contestation and resistance exist within organizations at all levels (e.g. Foucault) members of organizations often fear the shame of admitting fault of the organization and reprisals for drawing attention to them (Mosskin 2019). In a joined decision-making, a 'devil's advocate' is necessary as a counter to biases for more reasoned decision-making (Herbert and Estes 1977; Schulz-Hardt and Frey 2002; Bang and Frith 2017). Dissenters (even when wrong!) can change the way an issue is thought about, where those in consensus may consider the down-sides of their own positions as well as the upsides, as well as alternatives or multiple strategies: "the mind opens. And it opens because it is challenged" and "that challenge just changed the nature of discourse" (EconTalk 2018, Nemeth in conversation with Roberts). Critique is one way to ensure that whatever the decision, participants have made it while aware of the implications, limits, and limitations of that particular option, and while aware that they could have made other decisions. For people outside the decision-making organization, critique is a way to make sense of practices by inter-rogating how they came to be, what they do, and how they could be different. As noted by Nemeth, playing the devil's advocate is only effective if one acts with authenticity – one cannot take a 'pretend' position for the sake of the argument. I strive to provide such a voice of authentic dissent with which others can engage, whether they agree or draw different conclusions.

4.3.2 Policy as discourse – making and analysing meaning through actions and words

> Our minds make stories, and stories make our minds. [...] Stories map out the phase space of existence.
>
> – Ian Stewart and Terry Pratchett,
> *The Science of Discworld II: The Globe* (2002)

The WPR approach treats policy as a form of discourse. In Bacchi's take, discourses are "socially produced forms of knowledge" which "set limits upon what is possible to think, write or speak" about an object or practice (Bacchi and Goodwin 2016, p. 35). The WPR framework does then not adhere to the 'linguistic turn' of discourse analysis (where discourse refers only to linguistics or forms of communication). Rather, discourse or dis-courses in WPR relates to the "multifarious practices and relations involved in producing 'knowledge' and 'what is said'" (Bacchi and Goodwin 2016, pp. 37). These may be semiotic or linguistic, or forms of communication (such as policy), but they may also be more material such as plans for physical infrastructure. These in turn accomplish things. Attention to *productivity* is central to the WPR. Power, following Foucault, is productive – that is, it produces 'problems', 'subjects', 'objects', and 'places' (Bacchi and Goodwin 2016, p. 29). In a WPR analysis, policy is regarded as productive of 'prob-lems', which in turn produce discursive, subjectification, and lived effects. Bacchi and Goodwin refer to discourse as "[bridging] a symbolic-material divide" (2016, p. 37) and part of the production of the 'real'[8]. It is important here to note that this attention to the discursive does not preclude the existence of the 'real', or that the 'real' is made up or endlessly relative. It means that our understanding of the world is rooted in discourse, or ways of making meaning of everything around us including each other and ourselves

---

[8] That is, that which exists regardless and independent of our understandings or constructions. This is not Lacan's Real, always out of reach of language and so always the 'lack' or missing part in the symbolic. The WPR approach makes no claims of psychoanalytical influences.

(e.g. Laclau and Mouffe 1985; 1987). The "production of the 'real'" then relates to the production, through discourse, of *our understanding*, or knowledge, of the 'real'. The universe and everything in it exists, but our words and knowledges of it are 'made up' as we try to make sense of it. The suggestion that "the foundations of society are in a crucial sense rhetorical" (Glynos et al. 2014, p. 47) then means that all meaning-making practices (that is, pretty much all practices) are discursive (following post-structuralist discourse theory, e.g. Laclau and Mouffe 1987, p. 83). The discursive offers a way to produce understanding of the world and ourselves, when no meaning is intrinsic or 'natural'.

The human need for meaning is well established in psychology, following the work of psychiatrist and holocaust survivor Viktor Frankl (Frankl 1959). Meaning-making (through narratives) is held to make us more resilient in stress or trauma (although individual experiences may vary; Sales et al. 2013). The human need for making sense of the world more generally can also be seen in mythology worldwide (see e.g. May 1991), as well as the many branches of science. The emotional need for making sense and meaning of life and the world is then strong. However, this also means that that which is discursive may come to be taken as 'natural', and the emotional anchor it provides may make us resistant to questioning it (e.g. Glynos et al. 2014, p. 48; Gunder 2014, p. 3). This forecloses attention to – or even awareness of – alternatives, which may produce or prolong harmful or undesirable effects, or prevent preferable practices. Discourse analysis within the WPR approach involves attention to the "unexamined ways of thinking" (Bacchi and Goodwin 2016, p. 36), to make the implicit explicit. Bringing attention to the way that social practices are discursively founded may open up for considerations of other practices, if such a thing is desired.

If we humans understand everything through discourse/s (knowledges, constructions), we cannot expect or assume an underlying logic of the 'real' (the universe) – but there are underlying logics within every human social practice, because these are discursive.[9] The contingency of these practices and the meanings we assign to them might to some seem like a dismal mire of pointless relativity – but to me they provide hope, that we're not bound by some universal law to hurtful or harmful practices. After all, if no meaning is necessary, why not strive for that which does good? What exactly 'good' means is of course contextual and rooted in discourses, and all living beings (humans and otherwise) need different things depending on their

---

[9] Whether the social practices of for example bees and crows are discursive is a study for ethologists.

experiences and situations, but discourse analysis enables us to at least discuss the questions.

When I speak of something as discursive, I mean the meaning-making and meaning-carrying inherent in words and practices. A discursive effect, via the WPR approach, is the way that a particular meaning-making can shape and limit our way of thinking and acting in regard to what it makes meaning of (such as transport). Discursive elements are those elements of a problem representation which carry or make meaning.

4.3.3 Six questions about problem representation

I now describe the six questions formulating the concerns of a WPR analysis, drawing on a range of theoretical influences, which the WPR analyst should apply to their material. As each analyst, case, and instance is different, the relative focus on each question may differ between uses. In Section 4.6 I show how I used the WPR framework and discuss which questions and considerations have been more and less central in my analysis.

Question one – What is the problem represented to be in a specific policy?

The first question is a "clarification exercise" (Bacchi 2009, p. 2) to provide the starting point. By studying the concrete proposals of policy, the approach entails "working backwards" to show what the problem is represented to be in policy (Bacchi 2009, p. 3). The presentation of solutions provides a sort of negative space in which the shape of problem representation can be seen. Problem representations can also be read from stated aims, or objectives: if the objective is sustainability, this suggests that there is *unsustainability* which must be remedied. It may seem like stating the obvious, but that can be necessary to do in order to begin questioning that which is taken for granted and making explicit that which has been implicit. In this study, where I include proposals from several different policy documents in the same analysis, this will be a little less straightforward.

This question relates directly to a sub-question to my first research question, How is transport constructed, through proposed measures and discourse of policy concerning transport in Stockholm between 2007 and 2017? If transport is a 'solution', what is it a solution to? By posing this question, I take the first step to answer my research question, What kind of 'tool' is produced by policy for transport in Stockholm municipality? I also use this question to relate my findings to my second research question, in

73

particular the sub-question, What is the implicit construction of sustainability, through the measures proposed for transport while 'sustainable development' is an agreed aim and ideal?

The WPR approach holds no assumptions of intentionality, hence it would be erroneous to speak of problems as represented *by someone*. Instead, problems are held to be represented through the policy – this is, of course, written by real life people, but the way that problems are represented may not be due to a strategic decision to make it so. The actors and process involved in policy making are thus secondary targets of study in the WPR approach, and the main focus is on the discourse.

When I say that a problem is represented to be 'X', I mean that the measures proposed imply that 'X' needs to be addressed. Proposing that there could or should *be* a 'fix' in the first place constructs a condition as a problem. The problem representation I discuss is thus primarily implicit, rather than explicit.

Question two – What presuppositions or assumptions underlie this representation of the problem?

This question aims to "identify the conceptual premises … that underpin specific problem representations" (Bacchi 2009, p. 5). It reveals the influence on the WPR approach of post-structuralism, which "draws attention to the politics involved in the process of assigning meaning to key terms, picturing contents and categories as contested and malleable" (Bacchi 2009, p. 265). In the WPR approach this is not about what individual policy makers believe, but rather about what is lodged within problem representations, what makes the particular representation possible – that is, what "meanings much be in place for a particular problem representation to cohere or make sense" (Bacchi 2009, p. 5). The analyst is to ask themself: What is assumed? What is taken for granted? What is not questioned? This question addresses premises and assumptions behind the representation of a problem. These are not in any way guaranteed to be conscious values of individual policy makers, and as stated, the beliefs of those making policy are not the study object. To study the way that a problem representation is constructed, Bacchi recommends looking in policy for *binaries*, *key concepts*, and *categories*.

Binaries, or dichotomies, are common and/or important in public debate, often shaping the understanding of an issue in simplifying juxtapositions and hierarchies – for example nature/culture, public/private, responsible/

irresponsible (Bacchi 2009, p 7). In discourse theory, *signifiers*[10] are understood as defined always in opposition to something else – the discursive outside. An 'us' can never be wholly inclusive because without a 'them' the defining limits will disappear, and 'we' will no longer be a whole. In discourse theory this is understood as a *logic of equivalence*. Simply put, all things on *this* side, articulated (joined together) into a chain of equivalence, are the same (Culture, for instance); while all things on *that* side (in this example, Nature) are also the same as each other, but completely different to everything on *this* side. As in an equivalential logic, there is an implicit hierarchy in binaries: 'we' are a little bit better than 'you', 'culture' takes precedence over 'nature'. The binaries, or dichotomies, are then hierarchizing aspects of policy.

Key concepts or *keywords* are "abstract labels that are relatively open-ended" (Bacchi 2009, p. 8). Another way of putting it is that keywords, or buzzwords, "are useful in policy statements because they are fuzz-words" (Cornwall and Brock 2005, p. 1056). The meaning put into these concepts can differ between political visions, which is the cause for much debate. Indeed, Bacchi is careful to point out that even seemingly 'obvious' concepts can hold uncertain or conflicting meanings when studied more carefully. This is because keyword "evoke, and come to carry, the cultural and political values of the time" (Cornwall and Brock 2005, p. 1047). Within contemporary urban transport, examples of common key words may be accessibility and sustainability/sustainable development.

Categories are a way to organize behaviours, people, and other objects of study, through measurement (e.g. censuses and surveys). In policy and projects, calculations, as pointed out by e.g. Ronnle (2018, p. 61) are "tools for political actors to frame their decisions and actions". So what are these calculations based on, *what* is counted in order to justify a given policy proposal? What – or who – is given particular attention as something to be addressed, or as a reason for action? In transport, categories may include passengers, drivers, cyclists, workers, but also commutes, passages through a section, and demand. Categories are used to give meaning to problem representations: how, for example, does the category 'work commute' give meaning to the problem representation in transport policy? Further, different meanings can be given to categories in different times and across the world, as with the category 'youth' (Bacchi 2009, p. 58). The contingent

---

[10] That is, the semiotic element – such as a name, term or concept – used to signify something and form the *sign* (the total name+thing).

character of categories and the power inherent in using them, particularly in policy, means that they cannot be accepted as neutral but must be interrogated for their content. *Who* is included, and what does it mean to be included/excluded? Bacchi's example suggests that logics of equivalence come to play – 'us' the adult population and 'them' the youth, for example – but this is not a given. However, as categories are "created by measurement", so people are "made up" by categories (as when 'homosexuality' became the label for sexual activities between people of the same sex, and so 'heterosexuality' 'came to be'; Bacchi 2009, p. 9, after Hacking 1986). This will have effects on those reached by the policy, and it is important to consider what those may be.

These considerations help me answer my research questions: What kind of 'tool' is produced by policy for transport in Stockholm municipality? And What does sustainability mean in Stockholm municipal policy for personal transport?

Question three – How has this representation of the problem come about?

The WPR approach further prompts creating a genealogy, a history over when, how, and why decisions came to be. This will highlight that the problem representation is not given or 'natural', that there are other ways of thinking about a 'problem', other decisions that were *not* made. Discourse is always rooted in history and context, and must be understood in relation to it. There are chains of events and power relations (that is, differences in the *power to*) involved which may become apparent in a genealogy (Bacchi 2009, p. 11). This draws on social construction theory, from which "a WPR approach accepts that things we often take for granted as forms of 'fixed' reality are products of particular times and places" (Bacchi 2009, p. 264), and on governmentality studies. At all times, a meaning, practice, or regime could have been understood or constructed some other way and could still be so.

The critical power of mapping out a genealogy could perhaps best be illustrated by the discouragement of time travel films – which "disrespect history" – made in 2011 by the Chinese General Bureau of Radio, Film and Television. Film critic and journalist Raymond Zhou notes that time travel plots in Chinese film are often "an excuse to comment on current affairs" and Landreth argues that time travel "potentially gives the individual the freedom to reorder reality" (Landreth 2011). Time travel plots show that through little changes, history could be different (as in *Back to the Future*) – or simply that it is possible to be happy in some other context than the present one (see for example the *Outlander* series by Diana Gabaldon, or the Chinese *Shen Hua [Myth]*). A genealogy taps into that potential to highlight the non-necessity of the current way of things.

This question does not directly relate to either of my research questions, as I focus on a 'snapshot' of policy rather than the way that it came to be.

Question four – What is left unproblematic in this problem representation? Where are the silences? Can the problem be thought about differently?

This question addresses the limits to a certain problem representation – what fails to be problematized? Attention should be paid to missed observations, distortions caused by simplifications (e.g. when binaries are used), and other ways of perceiving the issue. Similar to discourse and assumptions of Question 2, we should note "the tendency for actors to relate to the world through a set of perceptual filters composed of pre-existing beliefs that are difficult to alter" (Sabatier and Weible 2007, p. 194; see also Jenkins-Smith et al. 2014, p. 191). These filters can be expected to shine through in policy, and providing alternative perspectives can highlight that they're there. The WPR approach calls for attention to other contexts (whether in time, place, or culture), as having something with which to compare the identified problem representation may open up one's eyes to new questions and issues on which the existing policy is silent.

This question relates to my research questions in the sense that it highlights the edges of the construction of transport and sustainability, showing the limitations, but it does not directly satisfy my research questions.

Question five – What effects are produced by this representation of the problem?

This is not the same as 'outcomes' in policy evaluation. Rather, the WPR approach calls for the consideration of *discursive, subjectification,* and *lived* effects.

- In a WPR approach, discourses "are socially produced forms of knowledge that set limits upon what it is possible to think, write or speak about a 'given social object or practice'" (McHoul and Grace 1993, quoted in Bacchi 2009, p. 35). The term *discursive effects* refers to the way that a problem representation will close off other venues, or that "identified problem representations and the discourses which frame them make it difficult to think differently, limiting the kinds of social analysis that can be produced" (Bacchi 2009, p. 16). In each given context, some topics, issues, and problems will simply be (or be regarded as) more meaningful than others (Bacchi and Goodwin 2016, p. 65). A certain discourse may this way limit what options are perceived to be on offer (e.g. Soneryd and Uggla 2011). Discourses of 'mutual obligation' may make it difficult to talk about 'rights' (Bacchi 2009, p. 69). As discourse guides not only how we think about something but also what is possible to think (or, in what ways it is possible to make sense of things). Under a dominant discourse of rationality, for example, critique against the status quo based on other values or perspectives may be interpreted as 'irrational' and so automatically discarded. But there is also the way that a particular kind of thinking or talking about issues makes one 'blind' to other perspectives: Bacchi (2009, p. 67; after Eveline 1994) uses an example where a discourse of women's disadvantages foreclosed attention to men's advantages.

Subjectification effects refers to the subject positions made available through a problem representation – which kind of subjects a representation (and its resultant policy) opens up for. In this, it also entails the matter of who is made responsible for the 'problem' and who is responsible for its 'solution' – particularly interesting when viewed against the recognition of private cars as an important contributor to carbon dioxide emissions and the argument that liberal modernization pushes the responsibility for environmental issues onto individual citizens (see e.g. Uggla on the individualization of responsibility; HumUs 2013). Often groups are set in opposition to each other; for example, when costs of public transport are held to be too high because of 'free-riders' (e.g. Bråstedt 2017). Subjectification thus deals both with the pragmatics of who is held responsible (e.g. car users, 'free-riders'), and with "the ways in which they influence how we feel about ourselves and others" (Bacchi 2009, p. 17) (e.g. ashamed or victimised for using a car, or angry at people who do not buy tickets). In the sense that subjectification effects help support the status quo – Bacchi mentions the example of affirmative action reforms, where targeted groups may be deterred from supporting the reform when 'dependence', and being a dependent subject, is seen as undesirable – they can also tangent logics of fantasy. The subject imagines herself, with encouragement from policy, to be the type of subject that the policy supports, and so can ignore the nonnecessity of the way that policy is shaped. An example of how policy creates or makes available subject positions can be seen in a statement from Stockholm Vice Mayor and head of transport, Daniel Helldén, who said of the new parking rules that, "The main principle is that the parking issue shouldn't be solved collectively. They who own a car should take the cost," said Helldén in 2016 (Majlard 2016). This statement suggests that car users looking to park are to be seen as a minority of individuals separate from the collective, that the collective (the 'we') has interests separate from or even counter to those of car users. The subject position granted to car users here is one of responsibilization – the individual is responsible for her own parking costs – and one where they are depicted as people who have hitherto been a financial burden upon the collective. The collective, meanwhile – the 'we' – is constructed as better served by other allocations of funding, and as hitherto victimized by having to 'take the cost' for unpaying car users.

Lived effects, finally, concern the material impacts of the way a problem is represented. This addresses resource allocation (Bacchi 2009, p. 17), such as whether a person is eligible for access to the zero-fare public transport system. This draws on feminist body theory and directs attention to 'lived materiality' – that is, the real-life consequences of the problem representations and perceptions in policy (Bacchi 2009, p. 265). These may follow from the problem representation and measures themselves, but also from the subjectification and discursive effects. The post-war view of the bicycle as in the way of cars and a health hazard for unprotected cyclists (Emanuel 2011) had the effect that bicycle passages were not included in the new traffic routes of the 1960s – a very direct effect for the then-many bicycle commuters. Contrary to the commonly received idea that demand is a given (and quite similar to the way Bacchi notes that 'problems' are constituted in policy), Elizabeth Shove and colleagues argue that "infrastructural provision co-constitutes 'needs' and practices" (Shove et al. 2018, p. 4). Technology and infrastructures facilitate specific habits and customs, and structure our rhythm of life, temporally and spatially, in specific ways (Coutard and Shove 2018, p. 18). The distances and speeds we can travel impact what is considered 'normal' to do in a day, and this perception of 'normal' in turn impacts demand or perceived need. New tech, then, brings about different rhythms and scales of life. An electric car (as pointed out by Shove et al. 2018, p. 211) may require a different kind of planning than a fossil fuel car. Time saving technologies "co-develop with more exacting standards", meaning that faster transport may lead to more tasks expected to be performed in a day, or longer daily trips (Coutard and Shove 2018, p. 14). So which practices are made possible or suppressed by the proposed measures impacting infrastructure and the uses of it?

These considerations relate to a sub-question of my first research question: What forms of society and subject are produced by this construction of transport, and how does this relate to environmental issues?

Question six – How/where has this representation of the problem been pro-duced, disseminated and defended? How could it be questioned, disrupted and replaced?

This question is a continuation of the genealogy, and poses quite practical topics for consideration: who has access to shape the discourse, how does a problem representation "reach its target audience and achieve legitimacy" (Bacchi 2009, p. 19) and what is the "relationship between the discourse, speakers and its destined audience" (Foucault 1991, in Bacchi 2009, p. 19)? In this, it concerns the role of the media and which representations are seen there. The second part of the question does not necessarily imply a complete 'end' to the current problem representation, but rather directs attention to how its non-necessity can be revealed through counter-discourses and alternative problem representations, as well as forms of resistance. As power, in the WPR framework, is understood as *power to* rather than *power over*, forms of resis-tance may be enacted at all points and levels ("everywhere in the power net-work"; Foucault 1990, p. 95, in Bacchi and Goodwin 2016, p. 31).

Another way of thinking about this question is to consider stability and tensions. A certain representation of the problem may result in or come from lock-in and path dependence, as well as resistance to change by some actors (see again the co-constitutive nature of practices and infrastructure), and logics may be more or less stable over time in the face of competing priorities (Wells et al. 2012; Sheller 2012; Marsden and Reardon 2017, p. 259). This would bring attention to the measures and their effects, to their history, and to the discourses constituting and surrounding them, as well as to changes or trends in practices.

These considerations do not reflect my research questions.

In sum, the WPR poses six questions addressing construction, context, and contingencies, as well as some effects that may come from the repre-sentation of a problem. These considerations draw out different aspects of the way that an issue is treated in policy, and as I have shown some relate more closely to my research questions than others. I now go on to discuss how I use the WPR framework for this particular study in order to answer my research questions.

4.4 Applying the WPR framework

In this section I expand on the methodological justifications for choosing the WPR framework to study the construction of sustainability in transport policy. The WPR framework provides a hands-on and multifaceted approach to study policy. With questions addressing discursive, political, and more pragmatic ('lived') aspects of policy, I find that the WPR framework lets me study not only the cumulative direction or general aim of policy measures, but also what makes sense of this direction and what it might lead to. The WPR framework offers a pragmatic and hands-on way of addressing my research question and aim.

For my research question and aim, questions one, two, and five are the most relevant: What's the problem represented to be?; What presuppositions or assumptions underlie this representation of the problem?; and What effects are produced by this representation of the problem? These questions relate closely to my research questions by directing attention to what policy addresses, which I take as a starting point for a discussion of what sustainability should fix or what sustainability is (or is not). I use the analysis of what allows this representation to make sense for a discussion of the conceptual premises and ideas underpinning the construction of sustainability. I use the analysis of what policy does for my discussion of the effects of this particular construction of sustainability. To a smaller degree, I also address question four – What is left unproblematic in this problem representation? Where are the silences? Can the problem be thought about differently? – to highlight the non-necessity of the way that the problem is presently represented and show what options it obscures, or the 'alternative costs' to speak with economists. The results I got from asking these questions were woven into the text, whereas the questions I paid particular attention to have formed the structure of my chapters. Questions three and six are less relevant for answering my research question, and so I chose to exclude these from this study in order to focus more closely on my main aim.

Figure 4.1 (below) shows how my research questions relate to the questions of the WPR, and how they may answer what transport policy has to say about the construction of sustainability. I split my initial aim – understanding what transport policy can tell us about what sustainability means – into two research questions: (1) What kind of 'tool' is produced by policy for transport in Stockholm municipality? and (2) How is sustainability constructed in municipal policy for transport? Question 1 was further split into two questions. "If transport is a 'solution', what is it a solution to?" was operationalized into "What is the problem represented to be [in Stockholm municipal policy measures for transport of people in 2007–2017]?" and "What conceptual premises underlie this problem representation?" The other subquestion, "What forms of society and subject are produced by this construction of transport, and how does this relate to environmental questions?" was operationalized into "What discursive, subjectification, and lived effects are produced by this problem representation?"

Question 2 was also split into two subquestions. The first, "What is the explicit construction of sustainability in policy, through the way that sustainability is described and discussed?" was operationalized into attention to the explicit descriptions in text, and used to answer the second subquestion. The second subquestion, "What is the implicit construction of sustainability, through the measures proposed for transport while 'sustainable development' is an agreed aim and ideal?" was operationalized into "What is the problem represented to be?" and "What conceptual premises underlie this representation of the problem?"

I relate the answers to these questions to my initial inquiry, summing up by contemplating what policy for transport *can* tell us about the construction of sustainability.

I now present the way that I addressed the different questions and the materials I used for each part of my analysis.

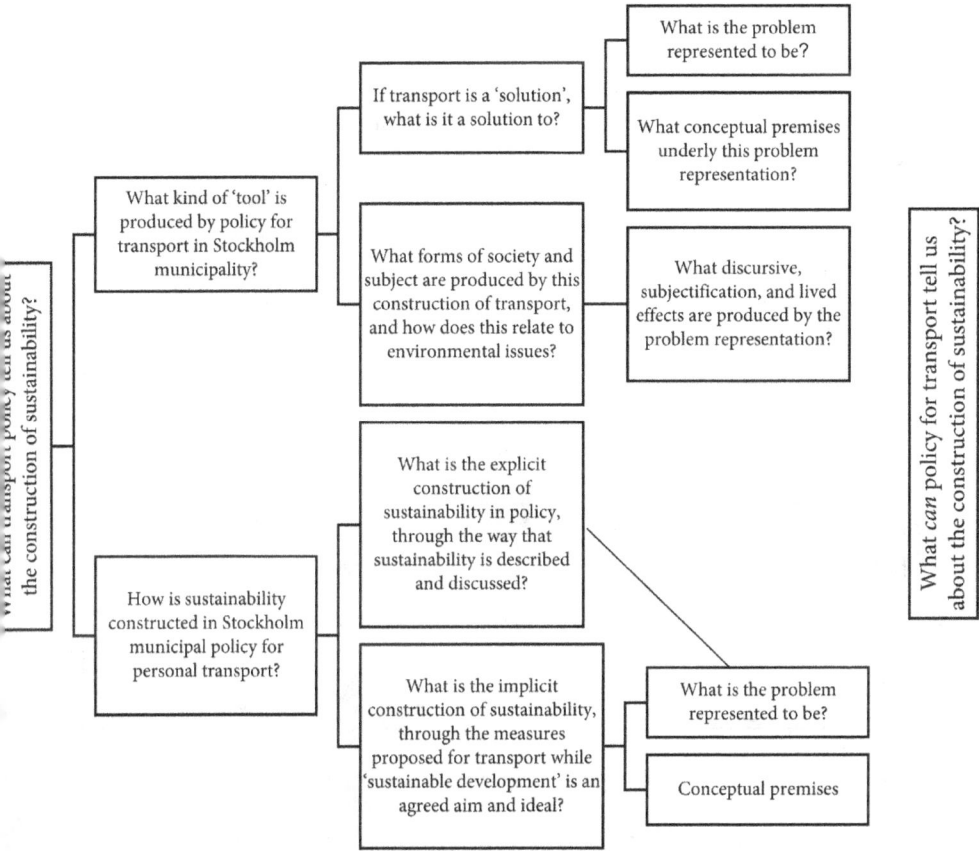

Figure 4.1: My research questions and the questions of the WPR.

Question one – what is the problem represented to be?

This question requires the analyst to look at what is proposed to see what is represented as in need of 'fixing', or a 'problem'. Because my material includes many proposals from several different documents, my analysis is a little less straightforward than studies of one proposed measure. For the first step in my analysis I turned to my main material and looked for measures promoted, proposals for action, which I wrote into a Word table. I focused on those which were practical in nature – that is, I disregarded proposals such as 'dense city' or 'smart choices', because the details of what was to be done remained unspecified. These I considered to be keywords rather than proposals for measures. I used policy and materials related to the main body of materials to draw out as much detail about each measure as possible: what

Howlett and Cashore (2014) call *settings* and *calibrations*. I let these details influence my reading of problem representations, as they altered what each measure was set to do, and what it was expected to do. I added these details into a column to the right of the measures in my Word table. Then I considered each measure on its own, and what it implied was a 'problem'. I wrote these 'problems' into another column to the right of the details. I then had three columns: Measure; Detail; and Represented problem (see Table 4.5, below; the completed table can be found in the Appendix). This first list was quite simple. If the 'fix' proposed was to raise parking charges, for example, the first-level 'problem' represented was too low parking charges. This implies that parking should not be 'too cheap' – that is, it should be costlier to park.

Table 4.3: The form of the table.

Measure	Detail	Represented problem
Non-motorized transport		
Public transport		
Cars to be purchased or discarded		
Parked cars		
Cars in motion		

In Chapter 5, I have sorted these problem representations according to what they aim to affect (car traffic, public transport, or cycle/pedestrian traffic) to map out what the 'problem' is represented to be for each transport mode (important, since the different modes are frequently ascribed different sustainability potential). In this way, I have worked to show how this body of policy texts works as a cohesive unit, rather than a collection of separate but related texts.

Following this, I considered the measures together as a single proposal and how they interacted (for example with the congestion tax and new infrastructure projects). These interactions I listed on a whiteboard before drafting chapter 5. Finally, I drew from this chapter the four main problem representations which I use for later analysis. These main 'problems' I found by listing all the represented problems from this part and bundling together similar problem representations. For example, I bundled 'insufficient supply of rail transport/cycleways' and 'insufficient number of passengers' with 'insufficient land capacity' into a main problem representation of 'too low use of public transport and cycling'. For another example, I bundled 'people are ill- or misinformed' with 'parking was too cheap' into a main problem representation of 'wrong choices made by individuals.'

Already at this stage of the analysis, I go partially into question two (below) and consider conceptual premises and assumptions – what it *means* that these problems are represented in policy. The entangled nature of representation and assumptions made this the most meaningful way to address these particular parts of the analysis; however, most of the analysis for question two was addressed in Chapters 6–9.

After some thought, I returned to the documents to list in which documents each measure was proposed. I did this to get an understanding of the 'weight' each measure holds – assuming that measures proposed in many documents and/or approved in e.g. transport agreements should be attributed more 'weight' than measures proposed in only one document and not approved in any agreement. These 'weightier' measures are more likely to be implemented into material form, whereas the less-supported measures may turn to nothing. It was also interesting to see the timeline over measures proposed, although the policy process as such is outside the scope of my study.

As I made this analysis, I found four overarching 'problems' represented. I let these four problem representations form the basis for the following chapters (Chapters 6–9). Taking each problem representation in turn, I continued my analysis by applying questions two through five. The overarching problem representation themes which I used for my continued analysis are: emissions caused by 'wrong' technology; wrong choices made by individual transport users; too little transport work; and too little urban space.

Question two – What presuppositions or assumptions underlie this representation of the problem?

This question calls the analyst to examine the underlying conceptual premises which let the representation of the problem cohere: that is, what must be taken as 'true' for the problem representation to make sense. The example problem representation of 'too cheap' parking may imply a series of assumptions, such as the notion that street space should be paid for, that people use space 'wrong' if they do not pay, or that car use is too cheap. The WPR framework lists *binaries, keywords,* and *categories* as types of words of phrases to pay attention to.

To answer this question, I took as my starting point the main problem representations I found through question one. Then I went back to the policy material and read the texts with a focus on alongside which words, phrases, or types of argument the measures were presented: that is, what was used to support the problem representation. I also looked wider for keywords in the materials, whether in direct relation to measures or not, which could help me analyse what assumptions ran through policy and so supported the problem representations.

Binaries I discerned through reading for instances in the material where things or ideas were situated as opposites, often hierarchized as *better – lesser.* These may be explicit and semiotic, but they may also be constructed, represented, or implied. In the material I have looked particularly close to descriptions or identified phenomena that set a 'good-bad' relationship between stated or implicit opposites. An example of this is the 'necessary' versus the 'unnecessary' transport which several texts deal with.

To find *keywords* or *key concepts* I assumed that keywords or buzzwords are "fuzzwords" (Cornwall and Brock 2005, p. 1056). I searched, that is, for words which may seem to have some built-in meaning, but which upon closer scrutiny are vaguely and loosely defined, and whose meaning may shift depending on who uses them. Many of these words or phrases were used in headlines and I often found them in more visionary aspects of policy, where the material depicted what should *be,* rather than what should be *done.* I have paid particular attention to words that may seem simply descriptive but are loaded with emotional or ideological content (such as 'choice' or 'a sustainable increase in transport'). I have identified words – primarily used positively – that sum up or lend a certain weight to a problem category.

To study *categories* – the ways that people, behaviours, and things are organized and "created by measurement" (Bacchi 2009, p. 9) – I paid attention to descriptors and things counted. I considered the way that people and actions were given labels that made them easier to follow, and that made it easier to describe in what ways they should be influenced (such as modes of transport, which allow for discussions of which forms of mobility should be promoted or discouraged). Categories in the WPR framework are ways of sorting or organizing people and their behaviour, using numbers to support and justify given proposals. In my material, categories have been largely technical justifications for policy proposals: things being counted, such as emissions, vehicle passages, and modal shares.

In my analysis, I found different proportions of binaries, categories and keywords/concepts. I have taken these differences not as errors in method, but as another facet for analysis, considering what it implies that one problem representation is supported more, for example, by "fuzzwords" than by 'things counted'.

Question five – What effects are produced by this representation of the problem?

The WPR framework addresses three types of effects. The first are discursive effects, where the conceptual premises of the problem representation limit what is meaningful to say. The second are subjectification effects, where the problem representation and its conceptual premises construct a specific type of subject and incites people to feel a certain way about themselves and others, as a form of self-governing. The third are lived effects, which deal with the pragmatic and practical effects on people's lives and surroundings of both the problem representation itself and the discursive and subjectification effects.

To study the discursive effects, I used the conceptual premises as my starting point for considering the discursive elements in policy. I also looked to the silences and non-problematizations (question four) to consider what was not said within this discursive frame. "which topics, issues, and problems are regarded as meaningful in the context" (Bacchi and Goodwin 2016, p. 65) and "What can legitimately be thought, said, and done?" (Poulsen 2006, p. 76).

The subjectification effects were studied in two ways. One was through the discourse of policy material: how subjects were described and what actions were possible or encouraged for people. The other was through letters and opinion pieces from readers in newspapers, especially local news. I chose to study these letters as an expression of people's reactions to policy. While not all policy measures merited letters, and certainly not all people affected were represented by letters, those who did write letters did so because they felt one way or another about policy measures and wanted to express that. The letters could then show me on the one hand how policy incited them to feel about themselves (and policy makers), and on the other hand what their responses and reactions were to this feeling. The nature of letters from readers tend to be that those who write them are those most opposed to the topical measure; this is one of the reasons they are not representative in the way that a survey or poll might be.

The lived effects were also drawn out through a few different ways. One was through the letters from readers, where they expressed their own experiences with policy measures. Another was through reasoned analysis of available options in modes, routes, and behaviours. Using the idea that infrastructure and practices are co-evolutionary, I considered what effects transport measures would have on people's behaviour and choices and vice versa. A third and final was through secondary sources, for example studies on the effects of commutes or assessments of environmental effects. It was important to me to include environmental effects under this rubric. Our lives are impacted on by the environment we're in, and the environment in itself is a key factor in sustainability and life on earth, as well as worthy of protection in its own right. That said, the main focus is on the construction of transport and sustainability, and so I have used secondary sources to make brief mentions of possible or likely environmental effects.

Table 4.4: Operationalizing the WPR.

Questions	Operationalization	Material	Chapter
What's the problem represented to be?	List measures, with details (calibrations). List what measures address. Attention to support – number of documents, amount of space. Relation between measures. Is the development cumulative or a variation?	Main policy material.	5, 10
Assumptions and presuppositions	Hierarchies Keywords Categories	Main policy material, opinion pieces.	5, 6–9
Effects	Discursive: discourse analysis of problem representations and silences/alternatives Subjectification: Lived: draw out practical effects of measures and problem representations; consider impacts on lives and environment. Consider the practices enabled or disabled by the problem representation; consider their potential impact on future decisions.	Discursive: use main material. Subjectification: use main and additional policy materials, and letters from readers. Lived: letters from readers, secondary sources (studies and reports).	6–9

In Chapter 11, I use the analyses made in Chapters 5–10 and return to my research questions to round up and expand on the findings. What can be said of the problem representation in municipal transport policy in Stockholm? What does it tell us about the construction of sustainability?

Part 2
Problem representation in Stockholm policy

Welcome to the congestion world!

The woman is in her sixties, her hair white and her eyes bright. She is originally from the region but has dragged her heavy suitcase by train, metro, and now bus from the Swedish midland to this island municipality west of Stockholm in anticipation of her second grandchild, whom she hopes will be given a nice, solid name. As we get to talk about the traffic, as people in Stockholm inevitably do, she voices a complaint I've often heard from those who do not live in the city regions: that the legislation and taxes designed to lower car use are unfair to those living where alternatives are few and unsuited to a working life. "We don't have any options," says this woman from Dalarna, like residents of Nacka, Värmdö, and indeed, this municipality so close to Stockholm: Ekerö, which will be home to the Stockholm Bypass in ten years. During the morning rush from Ekerö (and it is from as most people work outside the municipality), some 1,200 vehicles per hour roll along the one road leading off the islands (Swedish Transport Administration [STA] 2011, p. 6; this number may have increased since 2010).[11] Busses are similarly full. There is no rail transport. There are commuter boats for those heading to the city, with a capacity for 200 and 340 passengers respectively and five additional departures daily announced in August 2018 (bringing the total up to eight departures on weekdays, with an average capacity of 810 passengers for the three departures of the morning rush; Månsson 2018). But for many, the car seems the only option.

And for many of those, the Bypass seems like the answer to all their prayers (see e.g. Cannervik 2015). Designed to "make life easier" (STA 2011a) and "create opportunities for continued development in a growing region" (STA 2012, p. 1), the Stockholm Bypass has also been lauded as an environmental project. In a joint press release on the admissibility of the Bypass according to the Environmental Law of Sweden, the Ministers for Environment and Enterprise argued that the Bypass was part of a "complex whole" and would be trafficked by the green cars of the future (Regeringskansliet 2009-09-03). Similarly, the Swedish Transport Administration argues that the smoother traffic flow would decrease greenhouse gas emissions (STA 2017), rejecting claims by the Environmental Protection Agency, Swedish Society for Nature Conservation, and others that the Bypass would increase car use and thus increase greenhouse gas emissions and so ruin the

---

[11] For comparison, in 2010 some 450 vehicles per hour drove *to* the municipality. In the afternoons, the flow is reversed (Traffic Agency 2011, p. 6).

efforts to reach climate targets (e.g. SEPA 2007; Swedish Institute for Transport and Communications Analysis [SIKA] 2007; Swedish Society for Nature Conservation 2009).

During the launch of the plans the Bypass was described as a way to decrease congestion in the city and improve traffic flow along the current main routes. The inquest itself contradicts the promises this implies – that Stockholm will be released from some of its traffic burden and that the heavy congestion on the main roads will be eased. As with any comparison to the do-nothing alternative (Swedish: nollalternativet), made as a matter of course for every infrastructure project, the inquest predicts an improvement over what would be the future situation if nothing were to be done. Traffic and congestion in the city are expected to increase even with the Bypass, but to be lower than was expected without the Bypass. Yet around the city, car users grit their teeth and say to themselves, "oh, if only they'd built that road in the nineties!"

Figure ii: Sign on Munsö, the first island of Ekerö municipality, which reads "Welcome to the island world of culture!" However, the addition of a single letter has altered the meaning into "Welcome to the congestion world of culture!" Picture by author, 2018-08-11. The sign has since been cleaned up.

5
The 'fix' and the 'problem': measures for transport

This chapter deals with the first question from the WPR framework: What is the problem represented to be in Stockholm policy for transport? I study the collected policy documents? of Stockholm to find out what measures are proposed and what these aim to 'fix', and what this suggests of the 'problem' which should be 'solved' through transport. Throughout the chapter, I use the term *explicit* for that which is outright stated in policy or by policy-makers, and the term *implicit* for that which is not stated but necessitated or suggested by the policy proposals. Problems or aims can then be *explicitly* represented, or they can be *implied* by the measures proposed.

I start out by sorting the measures into 'non-motorized transport', 'public transport', and 'cars'. I categorize measures by what they aim to influence to reflect my focus on measures ('fixes') and explicit as well as implicit 'problems'. Another starting point might have been the measures/power/governance framework (following Givoni et al. 2013), sorting the proposals by what class of measure they are. This would serve well for tracing forms of power and governing in policy, but would have shifted the focus away from the implied 'problems' and might have complicated a discussion of underlying assumptions. My aim is to maintain a focus close to the material transport system and how people's lives are affected; hence, my starting point is the different modes of getting around.

5.1 The relative expected potential
for greenhouse gas reductions

Although the aim of this dissertation is to study the measures on their own merit, rather than what they are believed to do, it is interesting to see which measures are promoted in relation to which measures are believed to yield the highest potential when it comes to reaching the declared aims. One of the primary sustainability aims explicitly stated for transport is that of reducing greenhouse gas emissions (CO_2 or CO_2e, where e stands for equivalents). The *Roadmap for a Fossil Fuel-Free Stockholm 2050* (2014; henceforth referenced to as *Roadmap*)[12] ascertains the effectiveness of four groups of measures believed to reduce greenhouse gas emissions from transport, compared to the estimates for 2050 if no measures are taken to reduce emissions, shown in Figure 5.1. The length of each arrow indicates the scope of the expected potential. The yellow box to the right reads "LCA trace to be offset": it represents the emissions caused throughout production, transport, use, and disposal (identified through a life-cycle analysis) which can't be avoided but must be compensated for in other ways.

More efficient vehicles and non-fossil fuels (the longest, red arrow) are believed to hold the most potential; 30% of the total emissions from road transport (Roadmap, p. 44). This is followed by a switch from car to public transport, expected to give a 25% decrease of total emissions (anticipated from the public transport extensions and improvements, congestion tax, and parking strategy) (Roadmap, p. 39). The potential for emissions reduction via more efficient goods transport (not further discussed in this study) is shown by an arrow as long as that of a modal shift to public transport, but in text this potential is written out as 5–10% (Roadmap, p. 41). Least potential, going by length of arrows, is ascribed to measures such as reduced travel (something which is expected from e.g. the dense city and improved internet access facilitating work from home) or switching from car use to cycling or walking. These measures are expected to give a decrease in emissions of 12–22%. If adding "City planning" to the mix, however, the total expected reduction goes up to 22%, only just below the expected efficacy of "Switch to public transport". Left out of the chart is "City planning", which is expected to give a decrease of 5–7% of total emissions from road transport through shorter journeys and access to service, as well as a shift to walking and cycling (Roadmap, p. 41). In text, it is located under the header "Reducing the use of private cars" (p. 41); if included in the arrow labelled "Reduced travel + switch car to cycling/walking", that arrow would represent a reduction of emissions by some 22%, making it almost as efficient as a switch from car to public transport.

---

[12] To make the text easier to follow and references easier to trace, I have chosen to reference the material directly by titles, rather than to authors and year. This applies only to the documents in my list of materials (see Section 4.1, where the in-text references are listed).

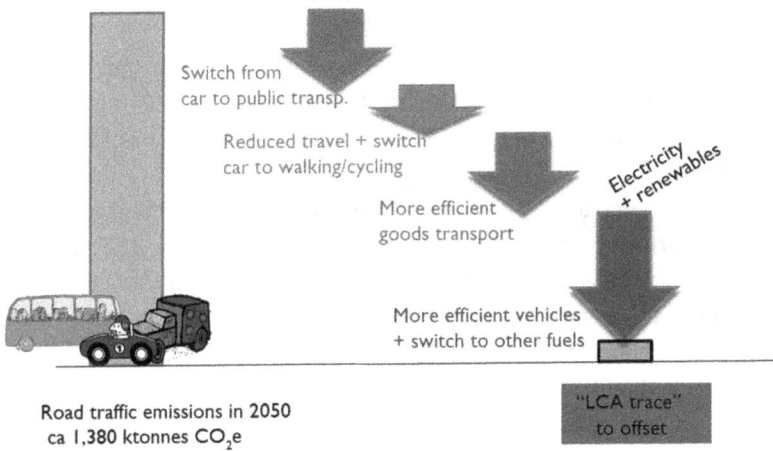

Switch from
car to public transp.

Reduced travel + switch
car to walking/cycling

More efficient
goods transport

Electricity
+ renewables

More efficient vehicles
+ switch to other fuels

Road traffic emissions in 2050
ca 1,380 ktonnes CO_2e

"LCA trace"
to offset

Figure 5.1: The anticipated potential of measures in the Roadmap (p. 39).

This must be taken into account when considering the solutions proposed. For the assumed least-efficient measures (reduced travel, switch to walking or cycling), solutions include the strongly pushed for dense urban planning with access to services and important functions that can be seen in budgets, policies and plans, and political rhetoric of the urban future; encouraging reduced commutes by introducing travel-free meetings and the possibility to work from home for employees of the municipality; good internet capacity throughout the city; local job cafés; and an extended and child-safe infrastructure for cycling and walking. Most of these measures target white-collar workers whose jobs can be done anywhere or offer some flexibility in time. Further, they target those who live within biking or walking distance from work (while it has long been agreed that housing costs in Stockholm are quite high).

For a switch from car use to public transport, improvements in supply and efficiency of public transport are proposed: more busses and bus depots; more departures along the red line; quicker stops through "more efficient" ticketing; better information and connections; and either extended rail or rapid bus transport. Further, public transport should be given signal priority and bus lanes, while car parking spaces should be removed or priced higher, and the congestion tax should be extended or developed.

For the efficiency measures that are expected to be most efficient, switching fuels and/or vehicles, a few different 'solutions' are proposed. Ultimately, no fossil fuels should be sold within city limits after 2050, and no contractor hired by Stockholm municipality should use fossil fuel vehicles after 2030. A system to provide financial incentives for the 'best' green cars should be put in place, including a zoning system based on greenhouse gas emissions (Stockholm authorities have announced a future ban on diesel cars from parts of the city). Biogas should be produced more locally, encouraged by land reserved for the purpose and an increased collection of organic material. Lastly, car buyers should be informed of available 'green' vehicles via a website. The measure expected to yield the greatest result is then reliant on personal choice, largely to be influenced by positive and negative reinforcements. The 'problem' then becomes people choosing the wrong vehicles.

The expected efficiency is particularly interesting to consider when placed side-by-side with the measures receiving the most support (i.e. proposed as measures in the higher number of policy texts), which is done in table 5.1. Then it becomes clear that the support for a measure is not necessarily related to its expected efficiency for reducing greenhouse gas emissions. For example, extending the infrastructure for cycling – a measure aiming at a shift from car to bicycle, in the 'low potential' group – receives very high support, while measures for promoting car pools, junking old cars, and other incentives to choose 'green' cars are proposed in very few texts.

Table 5.1: Support for and expected potential of measures for reducing greenhouse gas emissions.

Support received in policy texts ↓	Expected potential for greenhouse gas reduction (Roadmap 2014)		
	Least expected potential (reduced travel; shift from car to walking and cycling)	Medium expected potential (shift from car to public transport)	Highest expected potential ('better' fuels and vehicles)
Least support (in 1–2 documents)	Teleworking: job cafés, video meetings etc	- Citybanan - More bus lanes - Modernizing local rail - Closer departures - More efficient ticketing - Easier multi-modal use	- Incentives for 'green' cars over 'bad' cars - Ban on sale of fossil fuels after 2050 - Traffic management (to promote efficiency) - Lower speed limits

		- Information to promote a shift from car use to other modes	- Activities to promote car pools - Offering rewards for junking old cars
Medium support (in 3-4 documents	- Dense city (aim: lower transport demand, walking and cycling) - Safer, better, or more attractive infrastructure for cyclists and pedestrians - Bicycle parking	- Increased public transport supply - Higher parking costs - Turning over street space from cars to other modes - Removed parking spaces	- Environmental zoning for private cars - Higher production of biogas
Most support (in 5-6 documents)	Extended and improved infrastructure for cycling	- Congestion tax (if there is a shift from car use to public transport) - Public transport by water (if there is a shift from car use to public transport)	

Another way to look at it is to place side-by-side the expectations for efficacy for greenhouse gas reductions (where technological measures such as fuel conversion are given most faith) and the measures most put in the spotlight (that is, with the most text devoted to them, rather than those supported in the highest number of policies). It is a way to juxtapose the stated aims of policy with the expected outcomes of it, by considering the attention given to each group of measures. The outcome of this is shown in table 5.2. The table shows that measures perceived to have high potential for reducing greenhouse gas emissions – a shift in technology – are given quite little attention in policy, while a lot of attention is given to the 'walkable' city, which is centred on a shift to walking and cycling perceived to have lower potential for reducing greenhouse gas emissions, and public transport measures.

Table 5.2: Attention given to and expected potential of measures for reducing greenhouse gas emissions.

Attention received in policy texts ↓	Expected potential for greenhouse gas reduction (Roadmap 2014)		
	Least expected potential (reduced travel; shift from car to walking and cycling)	Medium expected potential (shift from car to public transport)	Highest expected potential ('better' fuels and vehicles)
Least attention			- Improvement of fuels - Green cars - Information to encourage "smart choices" - Ban on sale of fossil fuels after 2050 - Emission zoning for vehicles
Medium attention	- Increased reach, accessibility and safety of walkways and cycle paths - Better bicycle parking and supply	- Public transport by water (if there is a shift from car use to public transport) - Congestion tax (if there is a shift from car use to public transport)	
Most attention	- Dense city (aim: lower transport demand, walking and cycling) - Parking strategy (if there is reduced car ownership in the city, increased walking or cycling)	- Extended public transport supply (if there is a shift from car to public transport) - Parking strategy (if there is reduced car use in the city, increased public transport use)	

The combination of these two tables is further interesting when considered in line with slogans such as "Chase emissions, not drivers" (from the Centre Party election campaign of 2010 and current political platform; Centre Party 2018) and other assurances from policymakers that with better technology, car use can be separated from negative effects and the current mobility patterns can be made sustainable (e.g. Brinck 2018; Social Democrats 2018). The tables show that measures deemed the most promising, both by the *Roadmap* and by politicians, are given less widespread support and less attention in policy documents. That said, a bonus/malus system to promote 'green' cars was introduced in July 2018 (Transport Agency 2018a), suggesting that the degree of support and attention given to a measure does not predict its eventual status as implemented or discarded.

The potential of the road extensions, such as the Stockholm Bypass (which receives high support though given little attention) is not evaluated in the *Roadmap*. This is not surprising; the aim of the *Roadmap* is to identify ways to reach the zero-emission targets, and the highway is evidently not designed as a measure to reduce greenhouse gas emissions. The Stockholm Bypass was chosen over an alternative which would have reduced emissions rather than increasing them, with a difference of 290,000 tons of CO_2 (compared to the do-nothing alternative; Road Administration [RA] 2005, p. 106). The Transport Administration estimates that the Stockholm Bypass will contribute "less than one percent" of Sweden's greenhouse gas emissions from road transport by 2020 (based on the current vehicle fleet) and make it "neither easier nor harder to reach the climate targets" (STA 2018a).

In sum, there is a lack of a clear correlation between categories of measures estimated to have a high potential for the main sustainability goal of reducing greenhouse gas emissions from transport, and the measures receiving the most support and attention. In the next section I expand on these measures and delve into which problems they represent.

5.2 What the measures address

This section will display the measures proposed in the policy documents, organized by what they aim to influence: *non-motorized transport*; *public transport*; or *cars*. These categories draw on the reading of the material and collect the measures in anticipation of extracting the problem representation: in what way is policy aiming to influence these modes of transport, and what does that say about what the 'problem' is represented to be in policy? I begin with the measures for non-motorized modes of transport, frequently hailed as the 'greenest' option and shown in tables 5.1 and 5.2 to be disproportionally supported in relation to their expected potential to reduce emissions, and end with the measures for cars, often pointed out as a source of negative effects.

5.3 In what way should the 'problem' be 'fixed' by measures for non-motorized transport?

Non-motorized transport has of late been increasingly hailed as hallmarks of a 'green' transport system, and both walking and cycling are portrayed as 'good' modes of transport. Measures in policy largely address extending the infrastructure supporting cycling (cycle lanes and parking), but there are also measures addressing pedestrian infrastructure (primarily ensuring the safety of pedestrians), as well as information and projects to influence the transport choices of workers. In the material, *non-motorized transport* means bicycles and pedestrians, but could also include for example scooters. It should be noted that 'non-motorized' is a slight misnomer on my part, since electric bicycles and low-power mopeds may also use bicycle lanes and so are also served by extensions of cycle paths.

The proposed measures (see Table 5.3, below) serve primarily to give cycling more new space, which typically also promotes an increase in use. The extended, wider, and new bicycle lanes serve to make bicycle use easier; and in the cases where parking spaces for cars are to be removed from streets to make room for cycle lanes, bicycle use is made easier at the expense of car use. Cycling is the most strongly explicitly supported and invested-in of the non-motorized transport modes; see for example the existence of the *Cycle Plan* (2013). While the city plan is called *The Walkable City* and walking is described as something to be made more attractive and safer, possibly enabled by signal priority at intersections with a lot of pedestrian traffic (Mobility Strategy, p. 42), there are no real proposals for extending walkways, as there are for cycling. *The Walkable City* (p. 25), the *Mobility strategy* (p. 3) and *Roadmap* (p. 41) do propose promoting teleworking (e.g. video conferences, local job cafés, ensuring good internet capacity[13]) as a way to remove the need to travel entirely; the *Roadmap* (p. 39), however, simultaneously identifies this as a measure with comparatively lower potential for reducing traffic emissions (section 5.1).

Most of the proposed measures concern facilitating bicycle use, largely through extending infrastructure, safety, and maintenance of infrastructure for cyclists. The agreement of the National Negotiation (SOU 2017:107) includes 30 "bicycle objects" (some of these are bicycle lanes and paths, but no further explanation is given in SOU 2017:107) for just over half a billion SEK in proximity to the planned rail projects in Stockholm, mostly paid by

---

[13] This is also mentioned in *Vision 2030* (2007, p. 4), but there as a means to support businesses.

the municipalities, but no walkways. These bicycle projects appear to be intended to connect homes with public transport, and possibly to centres as well; perhaps to encourage bicycle use across longer distances and make public transport more attractive. Without seeing the routes, however, it is hard to be certain of anything beyond a connection of cycling and public transport. The new metro routes to neighbouring municipalities with large populations, Järfälla, Solna, and Nacka, are not currently attached to any requirements for bicycle investments, despite the large number of homes agreed on in the 2013 Stockholm Negotiation (see textbox).

New metro municipalities

Järfälla
Population: 76,460 people in 2017 (Järfälla 2019-04-15).
Getting metro to Barkarby.
Building 14,000 homes (Stockholmsförhandlingen 2013).

Solna
Population: 79,000 people in 2017 (Solna 2019-05-22).
Getting metro to Arenastaden.
Building 4,500 homes (Stockholmsförhandlingen 2013).

Nacka
Population: over 101,230 people in 2017 Nacka (Nacka 2019-09-18).
Getting metro to central Nacka.
Building 13,500 homes (Stockholmsförhandlingen 2013).

Extending the loan cycle system and adding more bicycles is a way to make bicycle use easier for visitors and those who do not own bicycles but wish to use one occasionally. It could be viewed as the bicycle equivalent of the car pool: a way to avoid purchasing and storing one's own bicycle, while still having access to the advantages the bicycle affords. In the *Mobility Strategy* the extension of the system to the outer city and near suburbs was to be pushed into the future (Mobility Strategy, p. 60), which would make this type of having-without-owning of bicycles an inner-city privilege. However, bicycles within the City Bikes system can be found as far out as the areas Bromma (west of the city), Hallonbergen (north), and Lidingö (an island just east of the city). Bicycles are aided as a vehicle for longer distances through the loan cycle system as well as the extensions of bicycle infrastructure.[14]

The much larger support given to cycling over walking implies a pre-occupation with *distance*; that is, an assumption that although the city should ideally be 'walkable', in practice most will travel longer distances between destinations; distances for which one's own feet are inadequate. The few who are truly flexible in where their work gets done may stay at home or in nearby job cafés; the rest have a journey ahead of them. It may justly be pointed out that an extended network of sidewalks has been around for as long as the city, making investments in cycle paths seem more necessary. However, given that new residential areas are often placed a little ways outside the city proper, and given the critique from organization Yimby[15] that for example Årstafältet south of Stockholm is planned with insufficient pedestrian infrastructure connecting the area to other parts of the city (Gardebring 2015; Thörnqvist 2016), and further given the strong focus on a regional labour market (see Chapter 8), it is clear that the walkability is not necessarily connected to work journeys.

The strong support for cycling in Stockholm may also coincide with the rise of the middle-class cyclist. Cycling in Stockholm has increased greatly between 2000 and 2018 (Stockholms stad 2019b), and while in the post-war era cycling may have been the blue collar worker's commute (cf Emanuel 2015, p. 103), now business suits, air resistance-reducing lycra bodysuits, and expensive bicycles are common on Stockholm's streets (that last certainly being an explanation for the stress in policy on secure bicycle parking). Emanuel (2010, p. 12) notes that the revival of the bicycle is connected to its "re-interpretation" as a 'rational' and 'modern' choice. It is interesting to note that whereas during the post-war period the bicycle was a 'nuisance' crowding the streets and getting in the way of the 'modern' automobile, and a health hazard due to the risk for accidents (Emanuel 2010, pp. 2, 8), the tables have now turned. The car is now the 'space-craving' nuisance while the bicycle is seen as a 'space-saving' mode of transport (Mobility Strategy, p. 8; more on this in Chapter 9), and furthermore good for the health of

---

[14] However, the removal of the loan cycles in the gap between one contract ending and the next being negotiated implies that cycling is not *that* important. As a side note, in the absence of the loan cycles a supply of electric scooters have taken their place.

[15] Yimby stands for 'Yes in my backyard', a play on the pejorative 'Nimbyism' or 'not in my backyard' mentality; Yimby gathers those interested in urban development and expresses opinions on everything from City Plans to infrastructure projects and single house projects.

oneself (as a means of exercise), others (as it emits no particles or other harmful emissions), and the environment.

Table 5.3: A list of measures addressing non-motorized transport.

Measures	Details
More bicycle lanes and – parking	– Extended, wider, and new bicycle lanes – Extending the loan cycle system and adding more bicycles – Thirty new "bicycle projects" are connected to the metro and rail extensions in Stockholm – Shifting space from cars (parking) to bikes
More attractive and safer walkways for pedestrians	Possibly signal priority in high-traffic intersections
Promote teleworking	e.g. by good internet access, job cafés
Information	– Traffic information to travellers – Information on laws and regulations for cyclists – Improve information on bicycle lanes
Signal priority to bicycles, in some cases pedestrians (in heavily-used crossings)	

5.4 In what way should the 'problem' be 'fixed' by measures for public transport?

Public transport is explicitly portrayed as a 'green' mode of transport – for example, the potential for providing people with a public transport system capable of carrying large numbers of passengers is one of the things claimed to make cities more sustainable than other types of settlements – and as a necessity for making life (and the 'life puzzle' of work, child care, activities, and access to services) work in cities. Measures in policy address large extensions of the public transport system and propose giving signal priority to public transport and yielding street space to public transport from cars. Information to travellers is proposed, explicitly to influence choices and increase satisfaction with the system.

The central focus implied by these measures (see Table 5.4, below) is to increase the transport work done by public transport, and mobility for public transport in the city. There is also an implied and explicit focus on urban growth. The main proposed measures serve to increase public transport supply to nearby neighbouring municipalities and in the city, with a probable increase in public transport use. In particular the metro extensions, largely funded by the 2016 extension of the congestion tax to the inner ringroad Essingeleden (introduced before the opening of the Stockholm Bypass, contrary to earlier promises), are high-capacity transport investments in near-central locations to be developed for an increasing population, likely to carry a high number of passengers. Contrary to frequent calls for cross-directional connections (e.g. Vision 2030; The Walkable City), the larger metro extensions connect nearby Solna and eastern Nacka municipality with the inner-city metro system. The shorter metro extension connecting northern Barkarby commuter stops to the Akalla metro line partially does the same, but it primarily forms a cross-connection for the northern suburbs and gives the newly-formed residential areas of Barkarby more public transport options and residents along the blue metro line easier access to Barkarby shopping area (which includes an Ikea and a large number of stores currently easiest accessed by car). On a surface level, the increase in metro capacity through new metro routes represents a problem of too little public transport work. On a second level, the extensions may represent a problem of a needed modal shift. On a third level, the municipalities in the agreement have also committed to constructing a large number of homes, which represents the problem as one of insufficient or inadequate urban growth to be alleviated by new residential areas and high-capacity transport. The extensions may also represent the problem as one of emissions or limited road space, by providing metro to people who would perhaps otherwise take the car.

The sole explicit purpose of the new central commuter rail tunnel City-banan was to increase capacity through the so-called 'wasp-waist' (or bottleneck) for both commuter and regional rail through the inner city. All in all, Citybanan is six kilometres long and includes a dedicated commuter rail bridge just south of the city and a new tunnel from Södra station (the stop south of the city centre) to the underground Odenplan station. Odenplan, also a metro station, replaced the previous Karlberg station as the next stop north of the Central station, and the Central station was moved to new underground platforms placed under the metro lines of T-centralen. These changes and constructions represent the problem as one of competing uses between regional and commuter rail, and insufficient capacity through the inner city. The replacement of stations with ones adjoining the metro also represents the problem as one of inadequate connections between metro and commuter rail.

The light rail extensions (*tvärbanan* stretching from Sickla in the southeast to Solna in the northwest, and the future *Spårväg syd* connecting southern commuter rail and metro suburbs in a westwards loop) are to carry passengers on cross-directional journeys. These lines connect metro and commuter rail lines and local rail lines around the city. The extensions of the *tvärbanan* and the future *Spårväg syd* serve to carry people between destinations and lines around the city without passing through the inner city. They represent the problem as one of inadequate cross-connections, and possibly also as one of too high pressure on the inner-city systems. They also take some focus off the inner-city as a – or *the* – destination, connecting the suburbs and establishing them as more independent from the inner-city system.

The public transport measure with the widest support (counted as 'proposed in the highest number of policy documents'), public transport on water, has so far yielded relatively few results: the commuter boats to nearby municipalities Nacka (east of the city) and Ekerö (west of the city) have been successful and made permanent, but the inner-city line (*Riddarfjärdslinjen*) was cancelled as of January 1 2019, with the County Council citing low passenger numbers (Ejneberg 2018). Commuter boats are particularly interesting as they are a break with the perception that lake Mälaren is a problem for transport, and rather a return to the earliest forms of 'public transport' in the city which were largely made up of rower women taking passengers to the many islands and islets of the city (not to mention Stockholm's attraction as a trade city prior to rail transport). The commuter boats, like most of these measures but more so than any other, serve to seek out new space for public transport, stepping off dry land to use the one place where transport is not in conflict with homes or green areas: the water. They are also a form of cross-directional transport, called for in many documents. Public transport on water thus represents two interlinked problems: one of inadequate cross-connections, and one of too little space for transport on land.

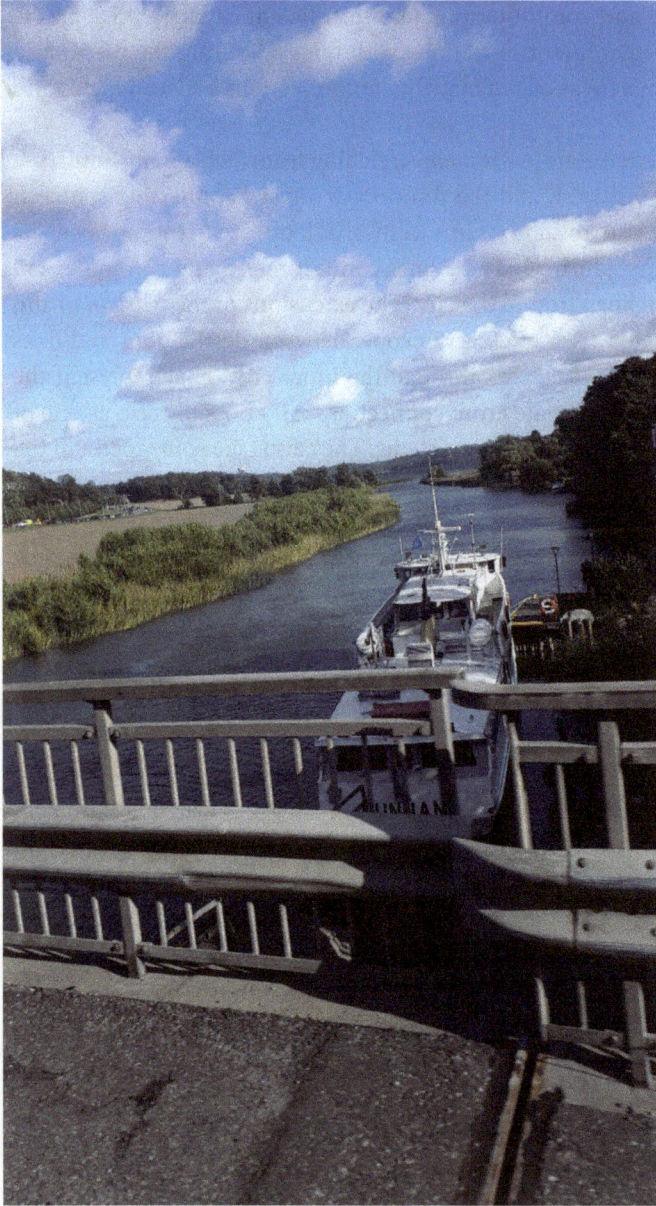

Figure 5.2: Commuter boat at Ekerö centre, bound for Stockholm city centre. Picture taken by author, 2019-09-15.

The *Roadmap* also proposes measures for a more intense use of the existing public transport system, such as closer departure times and more vehicles, which serve to fit more people into the public transport system. This represents the problem as too little transport work done, and as an inefficient use of the current system.

Information campaigns to get more people to choose public transport, aimed particularly at new residents and businesses, represents the problem as one of people making the wrong choice due to too little or bad information. The proposal in the *Mobility Strategy* to inform people about what they can expect from the transport system and about their responsibility for the system to function well reinforces the representation of the problem as one of people's choices.

Another related 'fix' is getting cars out of the way. Signal priority to public transport in high-traffic intersections and removing street parking for cars to make public transport lanes are both measures that can be expected to increase mobility for public transport (and bicycles) and put up obstacles for car use in the city. They can be said to reward transport modes held as 'good' and put into question the previously accepted view of the car as the natural master of the road. As will be discussed in Chapter 9, it also clearly prioritizes modes perceived as 'space saving' over modes seen as 'space craving' (Mobility Strategy, p. 7), aiming to permit modes carrying a lot of people on relatively small surfaces a quicker journey. These measures suggest that journeys which need to be on time – such as work commutes – should be done by public or non-motorized transport. This represents the problem as one of cars getting in the way of public transport, and of hinders for public transport.

Thus far policy for public transport reads like the 'fix' is to increase public transport use in and near the city, especially through rail investments. But the demand for construction of homes (for example, negotiator for the state HG Wessberg told municipalities, "the more homes you build, the more metro you get"; Stockholm Negotiation 2013a, my translation) and the choice of routes by their superior capacity for making many homes possible (Stockholm Negotiation 2013b, p. 24), changes the meaning of the rail investments for public transport, showing them to be less about promoting sustainable transport and much more about enabling and promoting urban population growth, and providing a space-efficient transport option for the growing population. Both of these foci – an increase in transport work and a growing population – will be further discussed in Chapters 8 and 9 respectively.

Table 5.4: A list of measures addressing public transport.

Measures	Details
Rail extensions	Metro from Odenplan to KI and Solna
	Metro to Älvsjö (from Hagsätra or from Fridhemsplan)
	Metro from Kungsträdgården to Nacka and Tyresö (or to Nacka and Gullmarsplan)
	Rail to Barkarby (connecting with Hjulsta and Akalla)
	Extended light rail/tvärbanan Hammarby to Slussen
	Extended light rail/tvärbanan Alvik to Solna and Kista
	Spårväg syd (new light rail)
	Increased capacity on regional and commuter tracks
	Citybanan (new commuter rail tracks through the city: 6 kilometres, 2 new stations, 17 billion SEK)
More intensely used public transport	Closer departures
	More vehicles
	Shorter stops (for example by more efficient ticket controls)
	To encourage businesses to promote public transport use for employees
	Target people moving to or within the city with information on advantages of public transport
	Targeted information and 'tester' campaigns, handled by SL
	Information to travellers (to increase satisfaction): on the targets of the Mobility strategy on reasonable expectations on mobility on personal responsibility for the quality of the transport system on options, "making the right decision at the right time."

Information to promote public transport use	
Supporting a change in the public transport fleet	This is beyond the control of the City, but the City can participate in demonstrations and work to secure infrastructure and fuel access.
Signal priority to public transport or bicycles	
Public transport by water	

5.5 In what way should the 'problem' be 'fixed' by measures for cars?

Cars are both hailed as useful and necessary modes of transport, providing users with freedom and efficient journeys, and denigrated as literal vehicles of unsustainability. Measures address *moving cars*, proposing ways to remove them from the inner city and/or ensure that they use 'green' tech-nology (both by coercion and by easier access to e.g. biogas), as well as extending infrastructure: *parked cars*, almost uniformly by proposing higher fees for parking, but also by proposing making parking car pool and electric cars easier and cheaper; and *cars to be purchased or discarded,* by promoting 'green' choices in fuels and vehicles through information and regulation (in combination with the measures addressing moving cars).

Analysis shows that measures addressing car use work to 'fix' issues such as the 'wrong' technology used by individuals, car users not paying for using urban space, and insufficient or not easy enough car use between the north and south parts of the region. Measures addressing cars work largely to ensure that the presence of cars – whether in motion or parked on the street – is paid for. Through adjustments to the congestion tax and higher parking charges, 'necessary' transport is distinguished from the 'unnecessary' (see Mobility Strategy, p. 5) – implicitly asserting that the 'necessity' of any given journey can be measured by the willingness or ability of the user to pay (further discussed in Chapter 7). The problem might even be said to be represented as one of too many car users in the city with too little money.

Other measures, such as applying environmental zones to private vehicles and extending the bans on spiked tires, work to exclude 'bad' technologies (that is, technologies which emit carbon dioxide or particles hazardous to human health) from the city proper. These measures identify bad technology as the cause of harmful emissions and seek to exclude them from the inner city, representing the inner-city as particularly important to protect. This is also an obstacle which can be overcome with money – either by investing in a 'green' car or by paying the fine if caught with illicit technology – and car ownership and -use are typically expected to increase with economic growth (see e.g. Trivector 2018, p. 16). The combination of the congestion tax and higher parking costs represent the problem as one of cars taking up too much urban space, but they also represent a problem of too high car use by people who do not pay (or do not pay enough). The proposal for environmental zones on its own represents a problem of too high emissions from cars in the city (and one of greenhouse gasses as 'worse' when emitted in the city centre, contrary to scientific facts), but together with the other measures largely reinforce the problem representation as cars taking up too much urban space for too little money. Using a car in the city is to cost, either through charges and fines or through the purchase of a new 'green' car. Tables 5.5 and 5.6 show measures and represented problems, and measure combinations and combined representations, respectively.

Table 5.5: Measures and represented problems.

Measure	Problems represented
Higher parking charges	• Parking was too cheap • People didn't pay for street space • Not paying encouraged people to use street space 'wrong'
Fewer parking spaces	• There are too many parking spaces – there are too many parked cars – there are too many cars • Cars use up space needed for public transport or cycling • Cars are habitually planned for in new areas; this is 'bad' and encourages unnecessary car use • People will use cars out of habit unless prompted to change

Congestion tax	• Unfair or suboptimal charge; 'green' cars are a service to society which should be promoted/rewarded; insufficient incentives to switch cars • Suboptimal use of the tax risks the targets not being reached = too lenient congestion tax risks too high emissions • The charge is not covering all the times and places it should (connected to the Negotiations, it doesn't rake in as much revenue as it should)
Environmental zoning for private vehicles	• Emissions are a problem; some cars should be banned from parts of the city – 'wrong' technology is a problem
Spiked tire ban or tax, local or city-wide	• Spike tire use is a problem, at least in some places • Unpaid-for spike tire use is a problem
Signal priority to public transport and non-motorized transport, limiting mobility of cars	• Cars hamper the mobility of public transport and non-motorized transport; these modes should be promoted (at the expense of cars)
Road extensions	• Insufficient road capacity around the city • Insufficient transport work (by car) through/across the region

Table 5.6: Measure combinations and the problems these represent.

Measures combined	Combined problem representation
Higher parking charges + fewer parking spaces	Too many cars parked in the city, and too cheaply
Higher parking charges + congestion tax	Car users don't pay enough to move in the city
Parking charges + parking spaces + congestion tax	Too many cars in the city (too cheaply)
Environmental zoning + spike tire ban	Wrong technology used
Charges + spaces + tax + zoning + ban	Too many cars using the wrong technology in the city

The proposal for a city-wide ban on the sale of fossil fuels after 2050 (Road-map) is interesting to consider. While it ties in with the explicitly stated problem of fossil fuels as a source of carbon dioxide emissions, and the objective of removing fossil fuels from the city, as a 'fix' representing a problem it is more curious. It implies either that measures to discourage fossil fuel use in the city will not succeed (at least sufficiently) and that demand will remain high (representing measures for a fossil-fuel free Stockholm as inadequate), or that the lack of demand will not have sufficient impact on the supply (representing the supply, or presence of fossil fuels, itself as a problem). It reads as a symbol to emphasise the aim, rather than a measure intended to make a change.

The represented aim to remove 'bad' or unpaid for cars from the inner city is not the same as to say that cars are to be removed from the transport system completely. Rather, policy measures work to move them off the inner-city streets and place them outside the city. The *Action plan for climate and energy 2012–2015* (henceforth *Action Plan 2012–2015*) proposes to reward those choosing to scrap their older cars (e.g. by a bonus, one month's SL fare, or a subsidy for a new bicycle), but this is the only measure aimed specifically at taking cars off the streets entirely (and even then, only older cars – that is, 'bad' technology – are targeted, and there is no guarantee the scrapper won't just buy a new car). One 'solution' often proposed as a way of clearing inner-city streets is the Stockholm Bypass, a six-lane, 21 kilometres, 27 billion SEK[16] highway connecting the southern and western suburbs of Stockholm. This measure alone, and the continuous support it receives in policy, shows that Stockholm policy for cars is not aimed at removing cars; the car in and of itself is not represented as a problem, only specific cars in in specific locations. The refusal of the County Council in 2014 to redirect the revenue from the first step of the congestion tax to public transport (from the Stockholm Bypass) shows a preference given to the Bypass over public transport. Between 2008 and 2013, the congestion tax was used wholly for roads; about 50% of it went to the Bypass, the rest to maintenance and new construction of other roads. Prior to the recent raise of charges, some 80% were destined for the Bypass project between 2013 and 2024, with the rest funding other road projects. The revenue from the Stage

---

[16] This is the number stated by the Transport Administration on the official webpage for the Stockholm Bypass (STA 2018b). The sum is in price level of 2009; at 2019 values that sum is a little over 32 billion SEK. Including costs for rent over time, as well as inflation, the final cost was in 2013 estimated at 44-61 billion SEK (by independent investigation for parliament, ordered by the Green Party; see for example Helldén et al. 2013). A broken contract with a subcontractor is expected to cause delays and increase costs (e.g. Lindholm 2019).

1 toll line (the inner city excluding Essingeleden) is devoted to pay off the loans for the Bypass until sometime after 2050 (Permell 2013).

The use of the revenue from the congestion tax to fund the Stockholm Bypass, and the linking of these two seemingly contradictory measures (one aimed at placing a penalty on car use and one aimed at facilitating it), shows the car as treated with a high degree of ambivalence – or perhaps it is the environmental targets which are. In terms of environmental health, measures for cars address inner-city air quality and space (e.g. by environmental zones and information to promote 'green' cars), but do not to the same degree aim to reduce emissions outside the city. This represents the sustainability concerns as largely limited to the city.

At the same time, much of the responsibility to reduce emissions from remaining traffic is placed on individuals, who are to be prompted into action by information and pricing. The *Roadmap* (p. 44) for example states that, "Mobility management is based on the conclusions of studies into a mix of information measures that encourage smarter travel and more public transport". The *Walkable City* notes:

> Sustainable travel is, to a large extent, a case of locating destinations in a way that does not generate unnecessary travel. Metropolitan regions also have great scope to use financial instruments to influence traffic and travel patterns. In Stockholm, the congestion tax has proven to be a successful method of reducing congestion and encouraging more people to choose public transport. Access to car parking also has a major impact on car use, so a considered parking policy is one way of encouraging a trend towards sustainable travel. There are therefore good grounds to study different financial instruments in more detail and carefully assess how they affect accessibility in the region and how good alternatives to car travel can be offered (The Walkable City, p. 22).

These measures address lack of knowledge (with information) or lack of concern (with charges and taxes), implying that transport users are ignorant of environmental issues or simply selfish.

The city's responsibility for 'green' technology is visible in measures creating a supportive infrastructure, e.g. by promoting biogas production through collection of household waste and the construction of production facilities, or by providing parking spaces with chargers for electric cars. The environmental targets addressed with some degree of force through measures are primarily local air quality, i.e. ensuring a low concentration of harmful particles (see the Environmental Programmes, especially that covering 2012–2015). While several measures explicitly aim at lowering CO_2

emissions in the city, the Stockholm Bypass – and the possibility of the Eastern Link in the future, as well as other smaller road extensions currently underway – works to contradict a general decrease in CO_2.

Again, the close ties between the Bypass and the congestion tax alter the significance of pricing as a measure, reducing its potential as an environmental measure, as well as raising the question of what is an 'optimal' charge when the aim is to *both* reduce traffic *and* fund other projects (see also Richardson et al. 2010 for a more in-depth study of how the congestion tax came to fund further car use). The second step of the congestion tax, a charge on Essingeleden introduced in 2016 despite previous promises not to do so until the Bypass was constructed, is dedicated to fund the new metro extensions (2013/14:SkU24).

This second step of the charge is even closer tied to the funding of a project, and it cannot be read as primarily aimed at reducing traffic. The measures for the congestion tax presented by the National Negotiation especially negates such a reading; the agreement is that if revenue from the congestion tax appears to sink under the level necessary for funding the investments, for example due to decreased car use, the tax is to be raised to ensure funding (SOU 2017:107, p. 214). It is not stated which is the right balance between 'prohibitive' and 'lucrative'. The adjustments of the congestion tax are expected to decrease congestion and improve mobility on the roads, as well as increase public transport use by 1% (SOU 2017:107, p. 214). That is: 1) about 30 % of the infrastructure investments in the region are to be paid through the congestion tax (SOU 2017:107, p. 210); 2) for this reason the tax is extended and raised during the times of heaviest road use, which is expected to decrease car use on the roads in the zone, which is in turn held to be 'good' (reducing congestion and improving mobility); 3) but if revenue drops below necessary levels (i.e., if transport work decreases too much), the congestion tax is to be raised, which should be expected to further decrease transport work, as per the original intent of the congestion tax (SOU 2017:107, p. 214). This double work of the congestion tax can be expected to lead in one of three directions: A) the tax serves its original purpose and decreases transport use to the point that infrastructure investments are no longer securely funded; B) those who still have no other choice but to drive their cars across the toll lines are heavily taxed to ensure funding; or C) the congestion tax zone is expanded to encompass an even wider area in order to compensate for revenue loss, putting at risk the principle that those who pay should also benefit.

By design, the Stockholm Bypass affects transport patterns throughout the greater Stockholm region. The key arguments for promoting the Bypass over other alternatives were its capacity to link the northern and southern parts of the region across (or, as it were, under) lake Mälaren, its capacity to connect places difficult to provide with high-frequency public transport (RA 2005, p. 216), and the fact that many municipalities were already prepared for a highway in the area (RA 2006, p. 3). That is, the Bypass is to further support sparsely populated and remote areas, which is likely to promote further urban sprawl (cf. SIKA 2007, p. 6). Via the congestion tax and rhetoric about 'unburdening' the inner-city, the 'walkable' inner-city is in this way made contingent on regional development in the opposite direction, through continuation of automobility.

In conclusion, measures for cars put responsibility for emissions on individuals, and for congestion on neighbouring municipalities; while several measures do work to reduce and/or charge for car use in the city, the linking of measures ostensibly intended to meet environmental targets to car use, together with the reliance on the Stockholm Bypass to reduce car use in the city, makes the 'fix' to Stockholm's transport 'problem' one based on car use and urban expansion.

Table 5.7: A list of measures addressing cars.

Cars to be purchased or discarded	
Measures	**Details**
Promoting 'green' fuels and vehicles	Information to prospective buyers of new vehicles; individuals and businesses
	Participate in or run demonstrations on vehicles and fuel handling
	Municipal procurement of 1,000 electric cars as a way to push prices down.
	Procurement policy for municipal operations, e.g. home care services
	Work for a long-term keeping and development of tax incentives for bio fuels
	Harder environmental regulations for cars

	Promote incentives to benefit and remove obstacles for 'green' vehicles and renewable fuels
	Increased mix-in of alternative fuels in petroleum fuels; biogas in gas fuels
Junking bonus for older cars	This is beyond the control of the City

Parked cars:

Measures	Details
Higher parking charges, charges where before parking was free	
Fewer parking spaces	• Removed entirely • Turned into public transport- or bicycle lanes or bicycle parking Reconsider the parking norm (requiring minimum of cars for each new home)
Tax on free or discount employee parking	
Allowing car pool cars to use residential parking (requires a change in law)	

Cars in motion:

Measures	Details
Road extensions	Stockholm Bypass 21 kilometers 27 billion SEK; 80% funded through congestion tax
	Eastern Link?? kilometers 18–21 billion SEK; no funding at the time of writing
	Extensions of existing roads
	Improvements to existing roads (tune-ups, widenings; re-routings; smaller extensions or new constructions of roads and bridges)
Fuels and vehicles	Supporting infrastructure for biogas and electricity

	• Increasing the collection of food waste in the municipality* • Setting aside land for a biogas facility • Constructing a new biogas facility* • Parking spaces for car pool vehicles • Parking space for electric cars, with chargers and possibly lower cost (requires a change in law, because it is currently not legal to differentiate parking charges based on type of car) • Build a foundation for an infrastructure for fuels and charging stations
Congestion tax	• Differentiated, lower charge for 'green' cars • "Optimize" the use to reach targets • Extend the toll or time zone

Information	• To travellers on current traffic for smoother traffic flow and 'smart' choices
	• To businesses on more efficient business journeys
	  – Recommend economic driving to businesses; give subsidies to businesses to establish routines and follow-up
	• To businesses on economic (fuel-saving) driving
	• To businesses on how to promote change in travel behaviour among employees
	• On fuel use and economic driving
	• To encourage a shift from private car to car pool
	• Information to travellers (to increase satisfaction)
	  – on the targets of the Mobility Strategy
	  – on reasonable expectations on mobility
	  – on personal responsibility for the quality of the transport system
	  – on options, "making the right decision at the right time."

City-wide ban on fossil fuel sale after 2050	
Climate tax	In addition to the congestion tax. Rate? Operating at all times of the day and differentiating between how much carbon dioxide cars emit.
Spiked tire ban or tax	Local or city-wide. At the moment of writing: Hornsgatan
Signal priority to public transport and non-motorized	

transport, limiting mobility of cars	
Environmental zoning for private vehicles	

5.6 What do the measures work to 'fix'?

To sum up the findings in the material and explain in what way transport should be 'fixed', the combined body of the measures work to 1) remove cars from the inner city; 2) ensure room for a growing population; 3) extend the urban region and increase commutes (in several texts deemed a positive development as this is held to improve economic growth); 4) encourage changes in technology; and 5) encourage a change in transport behaviour. Policy for transport in Stockholm works to limit car use in the city proper, through a range of proposed measures such as extending the congestion tax, applying environmental zones to private vehicles, and placing higher costs on parking. The extensions of rail for public transport do encourage an increase in public transport use but cannot with certainty be read as a measure to reduce car use. There are two important aspects that alter the meaning of these measures: 1) the rail extensions are almost all predicated on the municipalities constructing a large number of new homes in near-urban locations; and 2) none of the measures – save that of the scrapping bonus (where a car owner receives a bonus for leaving their car at the scrapyard to be demolished), mentioned in only one document – work to remove cars from the transport system entirely; rather, they work to shift car use out from the city, aided by the Stockholm Bypass.

The continued strong support for the Stockholm Bypass, deemed incompatible with environmental targets by the Swedish Environmental Protection Agency and based on calculations that SIKA found deficient in several significant ways, further alters the meaning of the measures. The effect of the Bypass which can be relied on are that 1) it will connect the northern and southern parts of the near-urban region through a high-capacity highway; and 2) it will expand the region into places deemed difficult to provide with good public transport (RA 2005, p. 216). This will extend the range for commutes in the region and increase car use.

Excluding the Stockholm Bypass, the measures form a different kind of 'fix'. The congestion tax would be a measure to limit car use in the city and, if all of the revenue was used to fund public transport, encourage a shift from car to public transport. The measures for limiting car use in the city (signal priority, shifts in use of space, pricing, and bans) would limit car use in the city without purposely shifting it to other municipalities, and could potentially encourage lower car use around the city as well. The public transport extensions would still encourage an increase in transport work and facilitate an urban expansion that may or may not encourage an increase in car use; however, the strong urban expansion into low-density areas, based on car mobility and by design difficult to supply with public transport, would be halted, and the urban growth might be concentrated to the Stockholm urban area rather than a continuation of the 1960s' expansive model.

The measures for public transport, especially when read together with the measures aimed at preserving inner-city street space, are aimed at making room for "a new Malmö" (Säll 2018), or some 300,000 people, by 2026 – a higher demand on urban space that is clearly not perceived to leave much room for cars parked 95% of the time (Mobility Strategy 2012, p. 37). The requirement of new homes for new public transport routes shows this measure to be not so much as 'better transport' as 'bigger city'– although public transport facilitates this, a modal shift reads as a secondary concern. With an increasing population and most of the rail extensions placed in locations to be further developed as residential areas, the new rail might be primarily used by new travellers. The public transport investments are a way to ensure that *future* residents will choose public transport over cars – a conclusion explicitly supported by the *Mobility Strategy*, which states that the aim for a modal shift applies primarily to those who will move to or be born in the city, rather than those using the car now (Mobility Strategy, p. 26). This may very well be an attempt at easing critique from motorists of Stockholm, of course, but it also raises the question if the same 'sustainable transport' measures would be perceived as reasonable if population growth were to halt.

The measures proposed in policy for transport imply a technocratic view on both the transport system and sustainable transport. The 'solutions' presented are focused on improving efficiency in use of energy and space, as well as steering people towards 'green' technology. Sustainable transport is represented as an aim reached through technological improvements. Crucially, transport is represented as a 'solution' to many problems, but primarily as a matter of movement (of people, to 'opportunities'), surface area, and emissions.

5.7 What is the problem represented to be?

With so many measures from a range of different documents, there is more than one 'problem' represented. First, each measure represents one problem, as discussed in this chapter. Second, when considered together as part of a whole, the measures combine to represent different problems.

Measures for extending the public transport system, extending cycle paths, and turning car space over to public transport and cyclists represent the problem as a too low use of public transport, cycling and walking, compared to car use. This representation rests on the understanding of these transport modes as 'greener', or as emitting lower rates of greenhouse gasses, than cars. Similarly, a representation of the problem as too low use of alternative fuels and -vehicles, and too high use of petroleum fuel vehicles can be read from measures such as information campaigns (on green cars), financial incentives (to promote green cars and demote petroleum fuel cars), environmental zones for private cars, the ban on sales of fossil fuels after 2050, and (although these proposals seem to have been discarded) the climate tax and scrap bonus. Information campaigns on alternatives to cars, the congestion tax, and parking charges together represent the problem as too high car use (although, as Richardson et al. 2010 showed, the congestion tax is ambiguous on car use). Finally, there is a secondary 'problem', more explicitly stated than represented, as one of unnecessary journeys, constructed through proposals for job cafés, good internet access (for work and business purposes), the congestion tax, and higher parking charges.

A common theme in policy is also the aim of changing how people act. Measures such as the congestion tax and raised parking charges represent the problem as unnecessary car use in the city, while measures for information campaigns (to promote both alternatives to car use and green vehicles), financial incentives (for people to choose green vehicles), and environmental zones (prohibiting use of certain vehicles within areas of the city) represent the problem as too low use of alternative fuels and -vehicles. The reliance of these problem representations on financial incentives – primarily punitive in nature – and information to change the way that people act represents a shared problem as one of people making the wrong choices due to misinformation or plain selfishness, and that people must be coerced or even forced to act right.

Measures aim to make room for more passengers within the transport system. The problem as too low transport use is represented by the measures for extensions of rail, a more intense use of the public transport system, and information campaigns to encourage people to choose public transport over cars. Similarly, problems of too low bicycle use and too low car use are represented through measures for extending these respective infrastructures. The use of congestion tax revenue and the extensions of the tax, as well as the assurance that the tax should be raised to make up for lower car use, represent the problem as one of too little funding for transport infrastructure, both for cars and for public transport.

Measures for extensions of public transport infrastructure on land and public transport in water represent the problem as one of insufficient space for transport infrastructure on land. The demands for large-scale construction of homes in exchange for the new metro lines represent a problem of too few homes and municipalities who do not construct enough homes. Finally, there is a 'problem' as one of cars getting in the way of cyclists and public transport, represented through measures for turning car parking or car lanes into public transport or bicycle lanes, and for giving signal priority to public transport and bicycles.

In sum, these problem representations can be bundled into four main problems:

- Emissions caused by the wrong technology;
- Wrong choices made by individual transport users;
- Too little transport work;
- Too little urban space.

I stated in the start of this chapter that there are inherent tensions in transport policy, between different targets and aims. The problem themes and problem representations I have identified both converge, as with 'emissions caused by wrong technology' and 'wrong choices by individual transport users', and conflict, as with 'too little transport work' and problem representations of 'unnecessary journeys' causing emissions, as well as the theme of 'too little space'. The different representations of the problems show an ambiguity towards the private car (it is 'bad' because it uses fossil fuels, but this can be solved by a shift in technology; but it is still 'bad' because it takes up space, but this can be solved by weeding out the 'unnecessary' car journeys through charges; but at the same time car use is too difficult, so new roads are planned outside the city with the use of revenue from the congestion tax) and the role of the transport system in creating the green city. This ambiguity will be studied closer in the next four chapters, in which the problems will be analysed for the conceptual premises that they house and rely on to 'make sense'.

Table 5.8: 'Problem' representations and measures.

'Problem' theme	Problems represented within this theme	Measures representing problems
Emissions caused by 'wrong' technology	Too low use of public transport, cycling, and walking	Extending public transport system Extending cycle paths Turning car space over to public transport and cyclists
	Too low use of alternative fuels and –vehicles / Too high use of petroleum fuel vehicles	Information campaigns Financial incentives Environmental zones (Climate tax) (Junking bonus) Ban on sales of fossil fuels after 2050
	Too high car use	Information campaigns Congestion tax Parking charges
Wrong choices made by individual transport users	Unnecessary car use in the city	Congestion tax Raised parking charges
	Too low use of alternative fuels and vehicles	Information campaigns Financial incentives Environmental zones
Too little transport work	Too low use of public transport	Rail extensions More intense use of public transport system Information campaigns
	Too low use of cycling	Extensions of bicycle paths Bicycle lanes on streets Information campaigns
	Too low use of car	Stockholm Bypass, other road extensions
	Insufficient funding for new infrastructure	Congestion tax (used for infrastructure investments and extended to cover more investments)

Too little space	Insufficient space for transport on land	Extensions of transport Public transport on water
	Too few homes (and recalcitrant municipalities)	Demanding homes for metro extensions
	Cars get in the way of public transport and cyclists	Turning car parking or car lanes into public transport or bicycle lanes Signal priority to public transport and bicycles

6
The problem as emissions caused by 'wrong' technology

To answer my research question of *what kind of 'tool' is produced by policy for transport in Stockholm municipality* I continue my analysis of what transport *does*. In the previous chapter I showed my analysis of what the transport 'problem' is represented to be in Stockholm municipal policy. I showed that Stockholm transport for policy represented several problems, and now I begin to discuss the central problem representations in more depth, beginning with the representation of the problem as *emissions caused by the wrong technology*, or too low use of alternative fuels and vehicles. In doing this, I address the questions from the WPR framework: What conceptual premises underlie this representation and What effects (discursive, subjectification, and lived) follow from this representation of the problem?

A problem represented in all ten policies is that of wrong technology, namely fossil fuel vehicles, and insufficient use of public transport and bicycles. These representations are surrounded by expressed concern for greenhouse gas emissions (primarily carbon dioxide) and climate change (see for example the *Roadmap*). This chapter will show that the depiction of sustainability in policy for transport is largely a narrow focus on greenhouse gas emissions. Further, the understanding of sustainability is tied closely to the urban setting through the construction of the 'climate smart city'.

Table 6.1: Problem representations related to emissions.

'Problem' category	Problems represented within this category	Measures representing this 'problem'
Emissions caused by 'wrong' technology	Too low use of public transport and cycling (and to some degree walking)	Extending public transport system (especially rail) Extending cycle paths Turning car space over to public transport and cyclists
	Too low use of alternative fuels and –vehicles / Too high use of fossil fuel vehicles	Information campaigns promoting alternative technology

		Financial incentives to subsidize alternative technology and charge for fossil fuel use Environmental zones to remove less 'green' cars from the inner city Ban on sales of fossil fuels after 2050 Climate tax to incur costs on higher-emission cars Junking bonus for older cars turned in
	Too high car use	Information campaigns promoting alternatives to car use, discouraging from car use Congestion tax incurring costs on car use Parking charges incurring costs on car use

6.1 Conceptual premises

In this section I discuss the conceptual premises, drawing on identified keywords or concepts, hierarchies, and categories from the material. I have sorted these premises into subsections, titled by what sets each apart and distinguishes it as a premise. To recap, *keywords* or *concepts* are what may be called 'buzzwords' – frequently used and seemingly meaningful words or phrases the meaning of which nonetheless may be difficult to exactly pin down and define; *hierarchies* are explicit or implicit relations between things, such as the binary 'nature'–'culture', often implying a 'better'–'lesser' or 'either-or' relation; *categories* are things sorted and classified, labelled and separated, which may imply opposites.

6.1.1 'Smartness'

Policy frequently refers to smart solutions and choices, without further specifying what 'smart' means. It is usually mentioned together with technological solutions, such as information technology, as in *Vision 2030* (p. 6), where "smart traffic solutions and modern information technology" is predicted to improve mobility and reduce emissions under the headline "Ecologically sustainable city". Since Stockholm is proposed to be "the city in the world where residents use public transport the most" and reference is made to cycling (Vision 2030, p. 6), 'smart' presumably involves public transport and cycling, modes held to use less energy per unit, with lower CO_2 emissions than cars, and recognized as capable of transporting many people on a small surface area (see Chapter 8). 'Smart' then seems to refer to efficiency of space, energy, and atmosphere. For example, the *Mobility Strategy* (p. 6), states that,

> For Stockholm's transport system to function efficiently, and for car traffic to function efficiently, the proportion of journeys undertaken by car must be reduced. More people need to choose to walk, cycle and use public transport. To achieve this, the street environment must make the step-by-step transition to more dedicated lanes for public transport, more cycle lanes, fewer parking places and an enhanced street environment for pedestrians. This will not happen overnight, but it is a strategic aim for 2030. If the city steers towards these goals, the traffic situation will become sustainable given time.

The *Mobility Strategy* (p. 17) also points out the connection between high-capacity transport modes, energy efficiency, and low climate- and environmental impact (further discussed in Chapter 6).

In *Vision 2040* (p. 13), as well as the *Roadmap* and the municipal budgets (2012–2017), sustainability work is equated to 'climate smart' solutions, or the 'climate smart city': "A climate smart Stockholm" is the header for a section on environmental sustainability and living an urban life close to nature. 'Climate smart' also became one of the four central development goals for Stockholm in budgets 2015–2018, and clearly the rubric for environmental sustainability (previous budgets, written by the liberal-conservative Alliance municipal government, had a different tack on both sustainability issues and the presentation of aims). The 'climate smart city' includes integrated planning of housing, infrastructure, and services: the dense, or walkable, city. In addition to this, there are measures to reduce local environmental effects, mostly out of concern for human health: dust binding (Environmental Programme 2012–2015), noise-cancelling architecture or planning, and changing road surface (Environmental programme 2012–2015; Environmental Programme 2016–2019).

It is clear that several aspects of environmental sustainability have become bundled together under the umbrella of climate concerns (see textbox for aims from the 2017 budget). Whether or not indoor environment is 'sound' or parks are 'maintained' is unlikely to have significant impact on the global climate, yet here they are listed as factors for a *climate* smart city.

This demonstrates the use of 'climate' as a buzzword without necessary logical linkage to the contents of 'climate strategies', and as conceptually superordinate over other environmental concerns – why, for example, is the headline not an 'environmentally sustainable' city?

Content of climate smartness; Stockholm municipal budget 2017

In the introduction to Stockholm budget 2017, 'climate smart' involves:

- "sustainable energy use" aiming to decrease climate impact, more efficient use of energy, and a shift to more sustainable energy), reduce climate emissions, and become fossil fuel free by 2040 (through a "complex structural change"; p. 8);
- priority to public transport, commercial traffic, walking and cycling; reducing car use;
- working for greatly increased investments in public transport; and becoming a "leading cycling city" (p. 9);
- improved air quality through more greenery, reduced car use, reduced use of spiked tires, and monitoring speed;
- work for a non-toxic environment, and sound indoor environment (p. 10);
- sustainable use of land and water (showing "great consideration" for 'green and blue' values, ensuring better maintenance of parks and reserves; p. 9, and protecting the water, p. 10);
- "resource efficient cycle/flow" (p. 10).

The term 'climate smart city' is not just a descriptor for what the city should be, but for 'climate smartness' as well. These two parts of the phrase become interdependent: the city must be climate smart to be green and modern, and climate smartness is automatically urban given the way it is constructed as a matter of technology and large-scale solutions based on aggregations of people and resources. The city is constructed as more important in achieving sustainability. This interlinking of 'climate smart' with 'urban' also serves to gloss over the fact that the less climate smart measures which serve to increase car use are shifted out of the city. The extra-urban is in this way constructed as irrelevant or uninteresting to sustainability work: there is nothing which is recognized as something the non-urban can teach the urban. On the one hand, urban areas have the high concentration of residents which allows for efficient high-capacity transport, but there is also a representation that the same vehicle emits more CO_2 within the city than outside of it. Consider the 'walkable city', in part designed to achieve climate targets, next to the Stockholm Bypass running just 250 meters from homes in Akalla – also, according to the Stockholm Chamber of Commerce and the Swedish Transport Administration, beneficial for climate targets by moving cars out from the congested city. The same car, then, is represented to be less harmful to the environment outside of city borders than within them. In this way, policy represents CO_2 emissions from urban sources and car use in the city to be more harmful and so more urgent to remove – but since they are represented to be less harmful outside of the city, it becomes enough to move that traffic to a peri-urban location to achieve a positive effect on CO_2 emissions. The way that the 'smart city' is constructed then both leads to a concentration of funding for sustainable transport to urban areas and reroutes car traffic to peri-urban or non-urban areas; areas where a sprawl effect is more likely to occur (see e.g. critique of the Stockholm Bypass, which is designed to serve and connect areas seen as unattractive to public transport – that is, areas of low population density). It is also worth reasserting that the effects of CO_2 emissions are not local; they rise into the atmosphere and trap heat regardless of where they occur. This representation of CO_2 as more harmful in the city is then not in agreement with scientific facts about climate change.

6.1.2 'Green' versus fossil-fuel technology

Policy presents a desire to reduce emissions of greenhouse gasses from urban transport, primarily carbon dioxide. The focus in policy is on green technology, as opposed to fossil-fuel based technology (which then reads as 'not-green'). The *Roadmap* (pp. 43–44) cites a "great potential" for 'greener' technology to reduce emissions from transport by as much as 30%. Under the rubric 'green technology' fall vehicles run on alternative fuels such as biogas, ethanol, or electricity, as well as public transport (ideally run on alternative fuels), and non-motorized modes such as bicycles and on-foot transportation. Not-green technology is a private vehicle run on fossil fuels. Public busses run on fossil fuels are represented as problems through the proposal for supporting SL's shift to biofuels, but given the priority to public transport overall (e.g. the fact that public busses are not charged via the congestion tax, and were not proposed to be charged via the climate tax regardless of fuel type) this problem is represented as a lesser evil, mitigated by high passenger numbers. As shown in Chapter 5, transport measures for environmental sustainability largely include better fuels or vehicles; a modal shift from car to public or non-motorized transport; and to some extent reducing the need to travel at all (through for example e-meetings or local job cafés, supported by 'good' internet services) – all measures with the stated aim of reducing fossil fuel use and greenhouse gas emissions.

By not differentiating between fuels the congestion tax represents private cars in the inner city as a problem overall, constructing public transport as greener than for example an electric car. This relates to the focus on high-capacity modes of transport: vehicles which can carry a large number of people while taking up a relatively small amount of space (e.g. Mobility Strategy, p. 17; further discussed in Chapter 9). Included in this category are public transport, cycling, and pedestrian traffic. High-capacity solutions carry are held to be more sustainable than especially the private car, by virtue of efficiency of energy and space. Another type of wrong technology is then the mode of transport which is inefficient in use of space. The representation of the private car as less green than other modes draws heavily on this, constructing the demand for urban space as a strong indicator for sustainability. The *Roadmap*, listing the hinders for a complete switch to green fuels, states that, "The biggest problem, however, is that the 40-percent increase in the number of vehicles would significantly impede throughput and would encumber the traffic system to such an extent that the slightest disruption would bring the entire flow of traffic to a halt" (Roadmap, p. 16).

The switch to fuels itself is otherwise contingent on biofuel production, and whether *sustainable* biofuel production can keep up with demands of the future green fleet. The sustainability of the *Roadmap* itself is not discussed; rather it is taken as a given that lower emissions will yield sustainability (provided biofuels are produced in the right way), and beyond that there is no need to discuss it.

Counting 'green' vehicles

Policy pays particular attention to the modal share of different transport types: the private car (run on fossil- or alternative fuels), public transport, cycling, and walking. The Mobility Strategy states the aims for 2030 to be 80% modal share for public transport (of motorized journeys during rush hour; p. 25); 60% share of local inner-city journeys (and 50% of the local outer city journeys) to be made on foot by 2030 (Mobility Strategy, p. 42); 15% modal share for cycling (of total rush hour traffic; p. 27); limiting through-traffic to 5% (regional journeys without destinations in the city; p. 48), and the total driven distance by car or truck on the city's roads to 2008 levels (p. 49). This collection of numbers and percentages and the focus on modal *share* over *numbers* of for example cars distracts from the fact, stated in policy, that transport use is expected (and encouraged, as will be discussed in Chapter 7) to increase, and that commuting remains a requirement for most.

Which cars are considered green changes over time? As of January 1 2013, the national definition of a green car (applicable to private cars) is based in part of the weight of the vehicle – heavier vehicles may emit more CO_2 per kilometre than lighter cars. Cars run on diesel or patrol may emit up to 95 grams of CO_2/km. Cars run on ethanol or gas (methane, natural gas or biogas; frequently a mix is used) may release up to 150 grams of CO_2/km, as "emissions from these cars are from renewable sources".[17] New cars taken into use between 2013 and 2018 were exempt from vehicle tax for five years; this rule ended July 1 2018 (SFS 2006:227). Definitions of green vehicles are continuously updated, as development of cars with lower emissions rates progresses – and as national and local government seek to increase the pressure on those buying new cars to choose green and lower the harmful impact of vehicles. As late as 2015 the diesel car was hailed as an environmentally friendly choice thanks to low rates of CO_2 emissions, but by the end of September 2015 it had become known that the local emissions of nitrogen oxide, harmful to human health, were far higher than information from car manufacturers had let on (e.g. Fröberg 2018).

Several documents list emissions of CO_2, in weight measurement per kilometre or per year, as important focus of policy. Emissions per kilometre are typically measured in grams and relate to the relative 'greenness' of different car types. Emissions per year are typically measured in tons and relate to the relative potential of different measures to reduce emissions. Likewise, other harmful emissions from transport are listed with limits, although not as frequently as carbon dioxide (which is the main or sole focus of several documents). This reinforces the focus on fuel and technology.

The municipal site *Miljöbarometern* (the Environment Barometer) tracks the share of green cars in Stockholm traffic, as well as the share of biofuels sold, and the share of "heavy strong" versus "light weak" cars (these two categories relate to fuel consumption, where "heavy strong" requires more fuel than "light weak"; Stockholms stad 2018c). In 2016 the share of new

---

[17] If the result of the equation <the weight of the car, minus 1372, multiplied by 0.0457, plus 95 for fossil fuel cars or 150 for cars run on renewable fuels> is higher than the CO_2 emissions rate data from the manufacturer, the car is a 'green' car. Stockholms stad 2018g.

green cars sold was 22%, reported to meet the "target for Stockholm's environment programme 2015, which was 20%" (Stockholms stad 2018a). Where this target comes from is unclear. The 2016 *Environment programme 2016-2019* does not set a number, only an aim of higher use of alternative fuels to reduce use of fossil energy (Environment Programme 2016–2019, p. 23). The 2011 *Environment Programme 2012–2015* sets the target for new private cars sold to be 50% green, and the share of alternative fuels to be 16% (Environment programme 2012–2015, p. 9). Whatever the number and source, I have found no aims for decreased car ownership. Car *use* should be reduced in the city and the share of public transport, cycling, and walking should increase, while the share of green fuels should increase – but only one measure proposes taking cars off the streets for good (by rewarding those who scrap old cars; Action Plan 2012–2015).

The environmental measures are tied to physical zones in the municipality (the congestion tax zone, the streets where spiked tires are banned, and the environmental zones proposed for private cars), the efforts to decouple transport from its harmful effects bound – by law, in the case of the congestion tax – to constructed borders. Figures 6.2 and 6.3 show the borders of the congestion tax and the environmental zone for heavy transport. The proposal for environmental zones for private cars (as of December 2018) does not change the outer border of the zone, only adds stricter zones within it (Stadsledningskontoret 2018). The combined zones construct the inner-city (and by extension the people in it) as more harmed by the negative effects of transport, or more worthy of protecting. As stated in Chapter 5, if the environmental zones are based on greenhouse gas emissions, as proposed, *where* the emissions are released does not matter to the global climate system. This is obscured by the environmental zoning system, which addresses only emissions stemming from the inner city – although it could be argued that it will also not matter to the global climate system if a certain reduction occurs within a smaller geographical area or is spread out over a larger one.

The Chamber of Commerce argued in 2010 that the Stockholm Bypass would reduce CO_2 emissions by reducing congestion. The *Mobility Strategy* (p. 17) is on somewhat the same track when it states that by 2030, "smart transport solutions and modern information technology have increased accessibility [Swedish: *framkomligheten*] and thereby reduced emissions" from the city's car fleet. This view suggests that in part, the city's problems with emissions can be mitigated by improving traffic flow. The *Mobility Strategy* recognizes car use in general as a source of emissions as well as of congestion, noise, and injuries, but aims to mitigate the harmful effects of car use by "encouraging the use of vehicles for journeys where cars can create the most public benefit" (Mobility Strategy, p. 45). Measures such as zoning to move cars from the inner-city to outside of the city represent car use outside of the city as creators of more public benefit, and cars within the city as more damaging to global environmental health.

6.2 A technical-rational understanding of the problem

The problem representation of emissions caused by the wrong sort of technology in the wrong place is conceptually underpinned by technical-rational premises, counted and visualized in tables and graphs: types of vehicles and transport modes, physical zones, the vision of a climate smart city created through technical measures. This representation of the problem can be traced back to scientific research on air quality and emissions, which has previously given rise to measures such as the catalytic converter and the ban on lead in fuel; both of which have drastically improved health of humans living near cars. Svante Arrhenius used previous research to calculate effects of decreased and increased levels of CO_2 in the atmosphere as early as 1896 and Charles Keeling showed in 1960 that anthropogenic emissions were substantial enough to cause significant climactic change, but the 'greenhouse effect' was effectively brought onto the global political agenda through the 1987 Brundtland Report and again in 1997 through the Kyoto Protocol. The Brundtland Report, also known as the genesis of the modern understanding of sustainable development, established the three-legged image of environmental, social, and ecological sustainability, all required to achieve sustainable development. Whatever its other aims and achievements, the Report set up technological innovation and economic growth as the most important tools of sustainability politics. Ecological modernization, the understanding of sustainability work as win-win scenarios driven by technological advancements, market powers, and adaptations of material systems rather than radical change of social systems (Isaksson 2006), came to be the practical application of sustainable development ambitions. Against this background, it is easy to understand the focus on technology in transport as both 'problem' and 'solution'. Further, while the Brundtland Report stresses sustainability as a communal concern and effort, under ecological modernization the focus is rather on industrial efficiency. Within the framework of ecological modernization, the individual has the (lonely) task of making environmentally sound choices: "considerable efforts are required from the city and from everyone who lives and works in Stockholm to reach the ambitious aim of a fossil fuel-free city by 2050" (Walkable City, p. 7). The measures addressing the use of 'wrong' technology rest on changing the behaviour of individuals (as will be discussed in Chapter 7).

At the same time, the average fill rate in Stockholm is only 1.2 people in each car (Lundin and Gullberg, in Gullberg 2015 p. 5) on the main roads during rush hours. Another way of looking at the problem could then be that the individualism of car use, supported by a level of affluence that allows one or two people to carry the costs for each car themselves, underutilizes seats and overuses roadspace. The problem could be viewed as rooted in a per-ception of the 'normal' as the 1960s ideal of one car per household, with the car being considered a private sphere almost like a second home or one's purse (UT 2010).

What is missing is a clear, unambiguous stance on the car: while measures represent some cars as problems, car use outside of the city is still repre-sented as desirable. There are also no hard aims to reduce car use. The *Action Plan 2012–2015* states the need to reduce car use by half to achieve the 2030 climate targets even with the proposed measures for emissions reductions – but this is not a proposal, nor echoed anywhere else in policy. By contrast, Vancouver set as a definite target to reduce car use by one-third until 2030, and declines new highway projects (Dickinson et al. 2016).

6.2.1 Discursive elements

The representation of the problem as one of emissions caused by the wrong sort of technology takes place in a discourse of modernization, where sustainability becomes intrinsically linked to technological innovations and marketized solutions. This precludes attention to social and societal patterns behind transport habits and choices: for example, the high costs of homes near the city in combination with a concentration of workplaces may keep some people from living close to their workplaces and 'force' them to com-mute; frequent changes in workplace (becoming more common, especially for people under 25; SCB 2015) might also mean that moving with the job becomes untenable, especially if one has children in school or daycare. Additionally, in some professions, changing workplace is the surest way to get a pay raise (for example teachers, Lärarförbundet 2019; and engineers, Virgin 2018). Attention to technology over other issues also draws attention away from the effects of the freedom of choice which has become a central tenet in Sweden's welfare system, allowing citizens to choose schools, health-care, and other necessities beyond walking distance from their homes.

Lastly, the focus on technology as both 'problem' and 'solution' and the discursive frame of modernization which articulates 'sustainability' with 'growth' preclude critique against the perceived need for continuous economic and urban growth and its effects.

The rhetorical and material focus on reinforcing the present-day status quo and standard of living bars from discussion alternatives that bring about faster and more radical reductions of energy use and greenhouse gas emissions; such as *not* extending transport supply but rather reducing current levels of transport work, or addressing the locations of workplaces and levels of consumption. In combination with the focus on individuals as the responsible partner for sustainability work, more collective solutions for accessibility – in contrast to car pools and public transport, which are collective solutions for mobility – fail to be considered. The possibility of a 'small is beautiful' kind of development is also not evident in policy; the continued focus on growth extends to all aspects of life.

6.2.2 The subject

The focus on measurement of different transport modes and vehicles as indicators for sustainability reduces residents and visitors to the vehicle they use: they become travellers or transport users rather than people. The *Mobility Strategy* (p. 5) states that "traffic comprises people and goods – not cars", and policy pays attention to people mostly as they move about: as travellers, or subjects in traffic. These travellers, in turn, are more 'sustainable' (walking, cycling, public transport), or less (car use, further hierarchized by type of technology). Given the emphasis on choice and personal responsibility, these travellers are also more or less morally upright, where the moral subject is the one who chooses the greenest vehicle. Users of fossil fuel cars are constructed as the least moral, while cyclists are at the very top (along with pedestrians, but few measures actively address walking) followed by public transport users. Being a 'good' car user is tied to economic capacity – and being a 'green' transport user is tied to being an urbanite, as most public transport modes require a concentration of residents for frequent departures, and as walking or cycling to work tends to require living centrally (which in the city is usually quite expensive). The subjectification inherent in the representation of the problem as one of emissions caused by 'wrong' technology, which premiers non-motorized modes and public transport (especially rail) over cars then also premiers urbanization of the subject.

6.2.3 Lived effects

The representation of the problem as one of the wrong technology in the wrong place – and of the solution as the *right* technology in the right place and time – proposes some change to the transport fleet, in that some private cars are to be moved out of the city and more space is to be given to public transport and bicycles in the city. Car users with limited financial margins may find it harder to get to, through, or around the city, while cyclists and public transport users – primarily bus passengers, through public transport lanes on roads – may find it easier.

The focus on getting car users to switch out fossil fuel cars to green vehicles, and the frequent updates of what is considered green (e.g. permissible within the future environmental zones or eligible for green car bonuses) may encourage car users with financial means to replace their cars more often than they would otherwise. While the CO_2 emissions from their journeys may decrease, the production of new cars also contributes to greenhouse gas emissions and resource extraction. It also reinforces 'sustainability' as a state of consumption. The rebound effect, or the observed relationship between higher energy efficiency and increasing use which negates the positive effects of that efficiency (Caro 1975; Duranton and Turner 2011; Santarius 2012), further suggests that although 'green' vehicles may be an energy-saving solution on paper, the reductions in energy or resource use may not be as great as expected.

The discourse of sustainable transport as a matter of technology focused on climate aspects and continued growth, coupled with the consumerization and urbanization of the subject, and especially the absence of a discussion of alternatives in terms of social structure, serve to lock society and subjects into continued urbanization and focus on (primarily economic) growth. The focus on technical solutions as opposed to structural change requires increasing production and access to electricity and biofuels (acknowledged in the Roadmap 2014, p. 37 to be uncertain, even before recognizing the future use of biofuels for aviation, as well as biological resources for everything from medicine to plastics to fabrics). It also risks a continued disfavouring of rural Sweden (as both collective transport solutions and distribution of alternative car fuel is difficult in sparsely-populated areas). The construction of a battery factory in Skellefteå suggests the focus on technology may provide work in rural areas, but at the cost of 50 hectares of land and at least 40,000 trees (in the future, this might increase to 200 hectares of land; Öbrink 2019) – news presented just after the IPCC report on the importance of uncultivated land and vegetation for climate change mitigation (IPCC 2019). Batteries for cars also require rare metals often produced under conditions dangerous for humans and the environment. Even with 'green' energy, continued or increasing mobility has very tangible effects for humans and the environment. Further, the reliance on continued large-scale technological development, as well as biofuels (possibly imported) and electricity for public transport and batteries, may make the transport system – and with it, society as a whole – vulnerable to future disturbances in global trade and climate.

The representation of the problem as emissions caused by the wrong technology then has very real and sometimes very bodily effects on the lives of humans and the environment here and elsewhere. By presenting technology as the first and most important 'solution', it creates pressure for continued expansion of resource use and covers over the negative aspects with technological optimism. The silence regarding alternative transport systems (e.g. not extending the transport system, working for localized accessibility) constructs a false lack of alternatives for solving the 'problem' and so enhances that pressure: if we do not do *this* then we can do nothing, and then we fail. The urbanization and moralization of the subject puts a significant portion of that responsibility in the hands of the individual, while the constructed lack of alternatives takes or hides choices away from the individual and from citizens as a collective.

7
The problem as wrong choices made
by individual transport users

To answer my research question of *what kind of 'tool' is produced by policy for transport in Stockholm municipality* I continue my analysis of what transport *does*. In this chapter I discuss in more depth the representation of the problem as *wrong choices made by individual transport users*. As in Chapter 6, I address the questions from the WPR framework: What conceptual premises underlie this representation and What effects (discursive, subjectification, and lived) follow from this representation of the problem?

In Chapter 6 I showed that the 'problem' of emissions, via technology, is largely constructed as a problem of choice and individual responsibility. The representation of the problem as people making the wrong choices, or irresponsible individuals, comes up in relation to both emissions and space (both discussed later in this chapter). It is a key point in policy, and many 'problems' are to be solved by making individuals make better choices. So what are the assumptions and presuppositions which make sense of this problem representation? The material shows a concern for 'unnecessary' traffic, and for the mobility of 'necessary' traffic; the categories of behaviour or people are travellers, types of vehicle, and passages into and through the city; *choice* is a keyword for this problem representation.

Table 7.1: 'Problem' representations related to the lack of sense.

'Problem' category	Problems represented within this category	Measures
Too little sense	Unnecessary car use in the city	Congestion tax Raised parking charges
	Too low use of alternative fuels and -vehicles	Information campaigns Economic incentives Environmental zones

7.1 Conceptual premises

In this section I discuss the conceptual premises, drawing on identified key-words or concepts, binaries, and categories from the material. To recap, *key-words* or *concepts* are what may be called 'buzzwords' – frequently used and seemingly meaningful words or phrases the meaning of which nonetheless may be difficult to exactly pin down and define; *hierarchies* are explicit or implicit relations between things, often implying a 'better'–'lesser' or 'either-or' relation; *categories* are things sorted and classified, labelled and separated, which may imply opposites.

7.1.1 Choice

A keyword in the representation of the problem as lack of sense is *choice*. For the transport system to function properly and sustainably, more people must *choose* not to use the car but other modes of transport (e.g. Walkable City, p. 20; Mobility Strategy, p. 5). Choice implies responsibility, for both the action and the effects of the choice: "Your travel choice will have consequences, not just for you, but for the whole of society" (Mobility Strategy, p. 6). 'Freedom of choice' is presented as desirable in policy – the free school choice (which may let parents choose schools far from their homes) is so important that it becomes a transport 'problem' or even a matter of rear-ranging the city, rather than one of the choice itself; the limitations on the freedom to choose mode of transport, as expected in the *Mobility Strategy*, is described as a drawback acceptable only in light of the benefits (Mobility Strategy, p. 39); and freedom of choice in the transport system will "provide all Stockholmers with excellent accessibility to all of the city's opportunities" (Mobility Strategy, p. 23).

The focus on individual choices and responsibility is perhaps best illus-trated by the blurb on the back of the *Mobility Strategy*: "You're not stuck in traffic; you're part of the traffic" (p. 70). The text goes on to say that, "This is what this strategy is all about. How individual road users should use the city's streets and roads, the vehicles they travel in and the parking areas where the vehicles are kept, to ensure the system is as efficient as possible" (Mobility Strategy, p. 6). The message of the *Mobility Strategy* is that as population growth and regional expansion will result in a significant increase in travels in the city as a whole, individuals should travel less and differently than they otherwise would have to ensure that the 'transport supply' remains func-tional and sufficient for all. In one sense, a communal problem becomes the responsibility of the individual. However, this responsibility is to be encouraged by fairly firm measures from the city and made easy by for example public transport.

Policies devote quite a large number of measures to influence citizen's behaviour, be it through information, various trial campaigns, or simple fiscal punishment. The 'problems' of urban transport are represented to arise because the individual transport user chooses the wrong transport mode, the wrong kind of car, the wrong type of fuel – or the wrong time or route to travel altogether. The conflict between the 'common good' and the interests of individuals is recognized in several instances (e.g. Roadmap, p. 39). Measures represent this conflict as being on the one hand a fair response to a situation partially caused by individuals themselves (through for example charges and information to grow acceptance among travellers), but on the other as a condition which should be limited (e.g. through lower congestion charges than suggested by the associations for taxi- and bus companies, Forssén and Juth 2013; through reluctance to implement the 'car-free inner city' proposed by e.g. Young Feminists, Nathanson Thulin 2018; and through continued road investments).

The air cleaner

A 2016 campaign from SL and bus company Keolis, *Fördel buss* (Advantage Bus), uses economic, environmental, and time arguments for choosing bus over car (SL 2016). The ads speak to the individual's economic self-interest, but especially to the individual's sense of responsibility for society and the environment. The campaign constructs bus users as extra considerate to the needs of society and the environment, and car users (a target of policy) as ill-informed people who will switch over to the bus when made aware of the benefits to society and the environment. The placement of a series of posters on buses – compared to ads visible primarily by drivers – represents a desire to encourage public transport users to keep not choosing the car, perhaps by bolstering their sense of morality. Public transport users have, after all, already chosen the bus for whatever reason. These ads, when visible to public transport users only, represents a problem of disloyal public transport users and/or of public transport users unaware of their contributions to societal and environmental benefits; overall, a 'problem' of a lack of a wide public agreement that public transport is better is represented.

The individual's responsibility for the health of the environment and reduction of climate gas emissions constructs the environment/planet as something which must be protected, and which can be protected primarily through the choices of the individual. But the environmental benefits are also linked closely to social benefits, such as clean air, healthy kids, and improved mobility, as well as saving money. This constructs environmental sustainability as wholly compatible with social and economic benefits, and public transport as one unproblematic solution to several problems.

Figure 6.1: The video screen of a bus. It reads "Welcome aboard the air cleaner" and "1 bus = 92 cars". Sender: SL and Keolis. Picture by author, n.d.

Figure 6.2: A more recent campaign gives thanks to "involuntary environmental activists". Campaign by SL and Ehrenstråhle, 2019. Picture by author, 2019-05-22.

7.1.2 'Necessary' and 'unnecessary' traffic

The *Mobility Strategy* describes the car's advantages as "lost in the big city traffic", stating that "[w]hile in many contexts, the car has a crucial function, efficient car travel in a major city requires people to make the majority of journeys by other modes of transport" (Mobility Strategy, p. 6). Reducing car use is described as a necessity to make car use work efficiently, and "not working to reduce car traffic would be an anti-car strategy" (Mobility Strategy, p. 6). The *Walkable City* similarly asserts the "natural and irreplaceable" role of the car, and states that "unnecessary" journeys can be prevented through the location of destinations (presumably but not explicitly stated to be done by ensuring access by public transport; Walkable City, p. 20). According to the *Mobility Strategy* (p. 37), parking problems limit the car's efficiency. The *Mobility Strategy* sets two goals here: freeing up space for moving traffic by removing 'unnecessary' moving or parked cars, and making parking easier so that 'necessary' car users have an easier time to 'arrive' and residents can leave their cars at home. This may seem an oxymoron (and there is some tension in policy between seeking to limit car use on the one hand and seeking to facilitate car use on the other hand), but 'necessary' is here the key word – space needed for moving traffic and parking will be freed up by removing 'unnecessary' cars. But what is meant by 'unnecessary' traffic? While constructing the dense city, very clearly a task of the municipality or even the state, is held as a crucial way to remove the need to travel, the measures proposed in policy frequently rely on altering the choices made by individual transport users through information or pricing.

The reliance on 'user pays' schemes in Stockholm policy show that the 'necessary' vehicle is the one whose owner will pay for its use, while the 'unnecessary' vehicle is the one whose owner won't or can't pay. Strictly speaking, this implies that the wealthy user is less likely to be 'unnecessary'. But the 'user pays' schemes also show which kind of transport use is particularly 'necessary' and so exempt from the congestion tax or allowed to pay lower fares for parking. Table 7.2 shows which vehicles are covered by or exempt from the congestion tax; those not charged can be read as particularly 'necessary'. These vehicles are emergency vehicles, public transport vehicles, buses over 14 tons regardless of ownership, military vehicles, diplomat vehicles, and motorcycles. While it is no surprise that emergency vehicles and public transport are exempt from the congestion tax, it may surprise the reader that services for the sick and accessibility users[18] are taxed. Those with an accessibility parking permit may apply to the Swedish Tax Agency to exempt one vehicle from the congestion tax. The congestion tax applies to vehicles, which are either charged or not charged, and so taxis (which may serve any traveller) cannot be exempt from the tax for journeys in the service of the sick or accessibility users. Accessibility permit holders in possession of their own car can make their journeys 'necessary' by application, but they are not automatically considered so. The parking strategy further underlines the 'non-necessity' of residents with accessibility permits: accessibility parking spaces are also charged under the new parking strategy, where before they were free of charge. The proposal for the new parking plan states that this is due to new technical solutions which don't require access to the parking meter (Stockholms stad 2016b, p. 11). Permit holders may apply with the municipality for a reduced charge (paying 500 SEK per year) which applies to all parking spaces, regardless of designation, giving the accessibility permit holder a wider choice of parking (where before, the accessibility permit was only applicable to accessibility parking slots). As with the congestion tax, accessibility permit holders can apply to have their car use designated as more 'necessary' than other car users', but it is not automatically so.

Table 7.2: Vehicles charged or not charged under the congestion tax.

Congestion tax	
Charged	*Not charged*
- Private cars, including 'green' cars and cars with accessibility permits (the latter can apply to be exempt) - Taxis, including services for the sick and accessibility users (*sjukresor* and *färdtjänsten*) - Private busses under 14 tons	- Emergency vehicles - Public transport - Busses over 14 tons regardless of ownership - Military vehicles - Diplomat vehicles - Motorcycles

The inclusion of 'green' vehicles in the congestion tax (as of 2006, when the tax was made permanent) underlines its function as a space-saving rather than

---

[18] An accessibility user in this example is a person who uses *färdtjänst*, a mobility service for those who, due to disability, cannot drive themselves or use public transport. These services are carried out by taxi companies contracted by the county council. An accessibility permit holder has a parking permit allowing them to park in parking spaces designated for the disabled (e.g. near the entrance of a building).

air-cleaning measure, as does the exemption of motorcycles. Pedestrian or cycle traffic is by this definition never 'unnecessary', which aligns with the idea of bicycles as space-saving vehicles and pedestrians as highly space-efficient non-motorized travellers (more on this in Chapter 8). While motorcycles are exempt from the congestion tax, the new parking strategy has removed free parking for motorcycles (as with accessibility parking, due to new technology; Stockholms stad 2016b, p. 11). The cost for motorcycles is somewhat reduced, to reflect that several motorcycles can use one parking space designed for cars (a motorcycle is charged half of what a car is, while motorcyclists have argued that they only take up one-fifth of the parking space and reported the Traffic Office and Board in Stockholm; Blomberg 2016). This represents motorcycles as 'necessary' when mobile, but less so when parked; Chapter 8 will expand on the representation of transport work as insufficient, while Chapter 9 will expand on the representation of urban space as limited and precious. The pricing system for motorcycles neatly demonstrates these two problem representations: a moving motorcycle takes up less street space than a car and can so be considered 'space-saving', but a parked motorcycle takes up valuable street space, albeit less so than a parked car, and can be considered 'space-craving'. The focus of pricing strategies is in part to ensure the mobility of *moving* transport, by enforcing a limit on the demand for street space from moving but in particular from parked vehicles. This is made clear by the zoning of the parking costs, with the highest costs in the inner city and gradually lower costs in the surrounding areas. That parking charges were introduced in areas previously free of charge reflects the aim of extending the urban core, and perhaps also the changing (that is, intensifying) traffic situation in Stockholm. In the very centre of the city, there is no residential street parking. This also ties into the value of urban space, see Chapter 9. The concentration of services and workplaces to the city centre makes it possible to charge more than in suburbs.

Public transport use is never explicitly referred to as either necessary or unnecessary. The exclusion of public transport from the congestion tax implies the necessity of the public transport system as a whole, or simply that it would be strange for the government to tax public services – although, as the case with accessibility mobility services and the congestion tax shows, it's not unthinkable. The omission of lower public transport fares as an incentive for choosing public transport over car together with the continued raise of fares, as well as the focus on 'efficient' ticketing, implies that if you as an individual cannot buy a ticket your personal journey is unnecessary. In the case of public transport, the space for which a person is charged is not on the streets, but on the vehicles.

Another way of sorting 'necessary' from 'unnecessary' transport is by looking at how the promoted strategy of the dense city is described as a way of 'building away' the need for transport. To create the dense city, transport, housing, and services are to be co-planned (Walkable City, Mobility strategy, Roadmap, Vision 2030, and 2040). This is to be done by constructing housing in areas with good public transport services, extending public transport along routes where housing is to be constructed (as with the new rail extensions), and assuring access to services with supplement from internet shopping. The *Roadmap* (p. 40) presents the free school choice as a cause of car journeys which may be difficult to replace by public transport, but argues that these journeys may be reduced in the dense city. This assumes that parents will choose the daycares and schools closest to their homes. The journeys to be 'built away' with the denser city are thus social and service-related. The work commutes, however, are to remain (except for the smaller group of people who are to be encouraged to work from home or local job cafés, or some of those who work in the services made more locally available). Commutes, then, are constructed as 'necessary' transport, and school runs may be 'necessary' (note that the freedom to choose a school far away is not presented as a 'problem'; rather the long school journeys are presented as a matter of available schools); journeys for acquisition of goods and services are 'unnecessary' (although then-mayor for the environment Per Ankersjö (2013) has stated that the Stockholm Bypass is necessary for people to "bring home furniture they buy on [virtual market site] Blocket").[19]

The division of journeys into necessary and unnecessary suggests a view of journeys as creators of value – they must be of use, of necessity, to be considered valid. It is the destination, the 'arrival', or the service sought which determines the value. The motorized journey made for the journey's sake – *nöjesåkning* – is not recognised in policy as valid (or, indeed, as existing), in either car use or public transport. Pedestrian or cycle traffic is argued to have recreational or health values in addition to mobility, but new cycle ways are centred on public transport nodes suggesting that they are to connect cyclists to commutes. The strong emotional ties to car use, where the car becomes a

---

[19] That internet shopping contributes to greenhouse gas emissions, particularly international purchases which offer quick delivery by airplane, further strengthens the impression that policy is not designed for reducing emissions so much as reducing local congestion. Additionally, not all purchases made online reduce the need to travel, particularly in the inner city where many have shops and grocery stores within walking distance but may choose home delivery for the convenience.

home away from home or a 'purse' (e.g. Salzer in UT 2010), are omitted from policy texts. Transport becomes in this sense a technical issue, subject only to rules of rationale and efficiency. Necessary transport is constructed as a means to an end, and this end is socially productive: work, school, and to a smaller degree the acquisition of goods and services. Further, the continued emphasis on pricing of both car use and public transport constructs transport and street space as a commercial good. If the value of transport was only determined by what individual travellers use it for, the demand for 'necessity' – an essentially moralistic stance on transport use – might be expected to lead to stronger limitations of transport use. But transport is held to create values for society as a whole, by carrying workers to sites of employment. These strong ties between transport, work, and economic growth will be further discussed in Chapters 8 and 9.

7.2 An individual understanding of the problem

The representation of the problem as one of wrong choices by individuals is supported by conceptual premises of individual choice and necessary versus unnecessary transport: that transport 'problems' are created by individual transport users causing 'unnecessary' traffic. I showed that 'necessity' is largely defined by willingness or ability to pay and underpinned by an expectation of value and benefit to society, in particular through wage labour (represented by commutes). Soneryd and Uggla (2015) have pointed out how an individualization of responsibility is a defining feature of contemporary politics, especially in environmental issues. An important feature of Stockholm policy for transport is the placement of significant responsibility for both congestion and emissions on individual transport users, using on the one hand information and on the other hand market measures (that is, pricing). While policy makers assume great responsibility for ensuring the means held crucial for future urban and economic growth – extending the commuter system and ensuring the construction of homes for future residents-workers – the environmental targets are made dependent on individual choices. These choices are more often between types of technology: biofuels over petroleum, electric cars over fossil fuel vehicles, public transport over cars... This focus on changing *how* people move avoids questioning the commuter system as such, especially an expansion of the transport system, and de-problematizes both public transport and the linking of commutes to economic growth, as well as the primacy given to economic growth. Of the "priorities" called for in the *Mobility Strategy* (p. 4), 'economic growth or the environment' is not one of the choices to be made. While the car has, at least to some degree, been taken off the pedestal, public transport has entered the spotlight as the solution to nearly all of the city's problems: space; emissions; and growth.

7.2.1 Discursive elements

The representation of the 'problem' as one of too little sense among transport users has been shown to be centred in a discourse of individual responsibility and choice. This discourse precludes attention to those who may – despite information or even economic incentives – be unable to make the 'right' choice: those who cannot afford an electric car yet whose lives require them to commute routes that are not covered by public transport (or who, for health reasons, cannot use public transport), for example. The focus on removing 'unnecessary' transport negates attention to the details of those journeys: who makes them, and why? Hinging 'necessity' on the ability or willingness to pay within a discourse of choice closes off questions about socioeconomic status – or class – and a discussion about for whom the city is to be open and accessible. Finally, the discourse of individual responsibility masks the fact that individuals may have very little option *but* to travel in search of work, education, or other opportunities and satisfactions. Individualization of responsibility simplifies the issue (cf. Soneryd and Uggla 2011) and limits the possible actions: rather than for example social change, the solutions focus on technological change and habits which individuals may be held responsible for. This makes it hard to discuss systemic causes of transport choices and patterns: an individual cannot reasonably be held responsible for urbanization trends or the decline of rural areas, concentration of workplaces and services, housing costs, or the increasing use of short-term employment (for example).

7.2.2 The subject

The representation of the 'problem' as emissions caused by people choosing the 'wrong' technologies for transport out of insufficient or faulty information or some form of carelessness, rests highly on the understanding of people as narrowly rational beings, for whom information and financial incentives may serve as tipping factors, and environmental health as a matter in the hands of individuals. It also shows the state, or in this case municipal government, as a facilitator of good choices: a provider of information, and of incentives. The state, however, is not ultimately responsible for making those choices: that is up to the individual. The transport system itself, as has been shown, serves especially to promote commutes. It is then up to the individual to use that system wisely, or pay. As was noted in Chapter 6, the focus on technology reinforces sustainability as an effort performed through consumption: one is to become sustainable through consuming the right transport services or vehicles (see for example bonuses for 'green' cars). The individualization of responsibility in transport policy thus constitutes the subject as a consumer; as shown in Section 6.2.2 either a moral consumer of green vehicles or services, or an immoral consumer of fossil fuel energy.

Policy then constructs especially car users as wilfully 'bad' or selfish. The focus on financial incentives helps to form a view of the urban driver as a rich, selfish person to whom congestion taxes and parking charges do not matter; while many may think of themselves as 'the little person' paying for other people's mistakes (most notable in letters from readers in local papers and on online forums). The individualization of responsibility means that the individual, through her choices in transport, is responsible for the well-being of the entire planet.

The material shows a tendency towards shame as a policy tool – consider for example the strong focus on information as a means to change behaveours. The ads (shown in section 7.1.1) that highlight the benefits of people taking the bus by necessity (and explicitly) point to the car as a less smart and less environmentally friendly choice. Slogans such as "you are a part of traffic!" (Mobility Strategy), the inherent question to car users whether their journey is necessary, and the mayor of transport's assertions that cars should be removed from the city (e.g. Frenker 2018a) also contribute to depicting the urban driver (especially when visiting) as making fewer moral choices (the same is not true for car users outside the city). This relates strongly to the individualization of responsibility, which by placing the burden of doing the 'right thing' on the individual bridges moralization (the idea that someone is a 'bad' person for showing a certain behaviour) and rationality (the idea that a person will make choices based on self-interest). The combination of individualization of responsibility, through costs and information campaigns, and the pressure of the commuter paradigm could then incite people to feel shame for their own behaviour and/or blame for their fellow citizens.

However, letters from readers and interviews with car users in local papers suggest that the measures instead incite car users to feel victimized. Car users complain about being 'punished', "fleeced" (Swedish: *pungslagen*, literally 'hit in the wallet'), or 'hunted' for owning a car (e.g. Dahlin 2015; Henrik 2016; Trött på MP 2017; Gabrielsson 2018) and argue that "one parking space per home should be the rule" (Ydstedt 2017). The car is described by these readers as a necessity for their lives (e.g. Roosmark 2016), and the parking charges and fines as unfair and disproportionate to their effects on traffic (e.g. Berglund 2016; Gabrielsson 2018). References by policy makers to improved mobility is called "qualified snow mush" (Swedish *snömos*; Berglund 2016). Letters from readers and interviews with car users then show clearly that rather than ashamed, car users in the city feel angry, abused, and helpless as their everyday lives depend on commutes which they are 'punished' for. Letters from readers also call attention to a conflict created by policy between car users and motorcycle users (e.g. Gabrielsson 2018; Motorcyklist på söder 2018). Residential parking for motorcycles applies only to regular parking spaces; motorcyclists may not use the spaces for motorcycles if they have residential parking, as these are for visitors (Stockholms stad 2018d). This creates tension between car users and motorcyclists as they compete for the same parking spaces, causing some car users to leave "angry notes" on motorcycles using car spaces (Motorcyklist på söder 2018), while some motorcyclists may feel entitled to using half a car space instead of one-fifth, as they pay half of what a car user does (Gabrielsson 2018). Residential parking is described as a "lottery" (Trött på MP 2017) as free space is not a given. This also creates tension between car users, competing for the same spaces. Most clearly, however, the letters from readers reveal a frustration with politicians – most notably with the Mayor for Transport – who only represent "plush trolls" (Swedish *plyschtroll*), and "most of all want to see a city where everyone cycles and there are no cars, where the air is cleaner than the wilderness of Sarek and where lions, dodos, polar bears, and orcas live in harmony next to humans, in the middle of the inner city" (Gabrielsson 2018), reinforcing the reading of a perceived victimization of car users.

At the same time, one reader wishes to coin the term "car shame" (Rudbeck 2019; similar to the recent term "flight shame" for travelling via air plane), and other readers encourage car users to sell their cars and rent one when they need it (Sommarskog 2016), or move closer to their work (Önneby 2015), and urge city planners to remove parking spaces and make room for more public transport (Wikesjö 2015). Overall, though, the majority of opinion pieces promoting less car use come from political groups and researchers (e.g. Fendert and Andersson 2013; Tovatt and Askeljung 2013; Ståhle 2016; Friman 2017). This might further reinforce the sense among car users that green politicians are 'out to get them' and strengthen their affect. It also suggests that the affect experienced by car users is – in recent years –

stronger (in the sense that the urge to write letters to papers is stronger) than the affect of car critics.

7.2.3 Lived effects

The representation of the problem as one of wrong choices made, with the discursive effect which draws attention away from the structures which may create a *lack* of choice (whether perceived or real), coupled with the sub-jectification effect of the conscious vs. selfish consumer, places a great deal of pressure on the individual to make 'good' choices. As noted above, the attempts to steer people's choices incites frustration and anger in residents.

The representation of the problem as one of too little sense, and the measures which form it, primarily affect the cost of car use and car owner-ship in the city. The congestion tax has been found to reduce traffic in the city, but the relationship may not be linear. Statistical data from the Trans-port Agency shows that registered passages across the congestion tax borders increased in 2017 (Transport Agency 2018b) by 3,300 cars per day (Lund-berg 2018). Reasons cited are the road extensions around Stockholm, which make taking the car easier, and the expanding economy which helps people afford the higher charges (Lundberg 2018). Private conversations with car users further suggest that the new tax on Essingeleden removed the incentive to avoid the inner city. Between 2017 and 2018, passages per taxed day decreased by 3,500 per day, and up until June 2019 passages had further decreased by nearly 2,000 cars daily (Transport Agency 2018b; 2019). The Stockholm Environment Barometer also reports fewer passages across city sections, but an increase in road transport work since 2012 (Stockholms stad 2019c). The introduction of parking charges in areas where parking was free has had unclear effects; a survey made by a parking company found that around 40% found it easier to find a space, while almost 10% found it harder, and the majority found no difference (Brandt 2017). Local news report that in some areas parking access has increased (Fagerström 2017a; 2017b; 2017c). If a person has access to free parking at work, they may be en-couraged to take the car to work instead of leaving it at home, as leaving it at home would cost them more in parking charges than driving it to work – or as one letter from reader puts it, it's "expensive to go/walk [Swedish *gå* can mean both] to work with residential parking" (Johansson 2015).

In the long run, policy is explicitly aimed at making people in the city get rid of their cars. This would of course have impacts on their daily lives – for example, it might be harder for them to get around their daily activities, visiting friends or family, or doing weekly shopping – but also on the local environment as a whole. Fewer cars on the streets would likely mean, as policy argues, easier traffic flows and more available parking slots; it might also mean fewer local and greenhouse gas emissions (depending, to some degree, on how often those residential cars were used), and less noise. In the winter, fewer cars parked might mean that it would be easier to clean snow off streets and sidewalks. For visitors to the city finding parking might be easier if fewer residents had cars parked on the streets. This might, on the other hand, also contribute to higher car use among people who can pay for it; easier access to parking and reduced traffic flows may make car use more attractive to those who can pay for this improved mobility. Meanwhile, the lack of attention to patterns and structures as well as individual situations (such as health) which create 'need' for transport could risk create adverse situations for e.g. accessibility users. Measuring 'necessity' by willingness or ability to pay may skew results in disfavour of those who use the car as an accessibility aid.

8
The problem as too little transport work

To answer my research question of *what kind of 'tool' is produced by policy for transport in Stockholm municipality* I continue my analysis of what transport *does*. In this chapter I discuss in more depth the representation of the problem as *too little transport work*. As in previous chapters, I address the questions from the WPR framework: What conceptual premises underlie this representation and What effects (discursive, subjectification, and lived) follow from this representation of the problem?

While for example the *Mobility Strategy* (p. 3) argues for a reduction in transport need to meet the city's sustainability needs, supported by the *Walkable City*, this explicit presentation is contradicted by the measures proposed. Rather, as shown in Chapter 5, policy represents a need for more transport work. The problem representation of too little transport work draws on a recognition or assumption of increasing transport demand, partially as a result of population growth and partially as the result of measures taken. That is, there is an explicit representation of the problem as increasing transport demand and work, which leads to measures for increasing transport capacity – that is, transport *work* – which represent the problem as too little transport work done at present. The same recognition of increasing transport demand could have led to a representation of the problem as too high transport demand, through measures for reducing demand, or at least measures for reducing demand for car transport. However, while road extensions are recognized to contribute to higher car use and stagnant or decreasing shares of public transport use (e.g. *Action Plan 2012–2015* p. 17), policy overall represents this as a problem of 'wrong' technology causing emissions rather than one of too high demand for car transport. Hence, my reading of the problem represented as one of *too little transport work*, whether it is a genuinely desired outcome or a response to prognoses.

Table 8.1: 'Problem' representations related to insufficient transport work.

'Problem' category	Problems represented within this category	Measures
Too little transport work	Too low use of public transport	Rail extensions More intense use of public transport system Information campaigns to increase public transport use
	Too low use of cycling	Extensions of bicycle paths Bicycle lanes on streets Information campaigns to increase cycling
	Too low use of car outside the city	Stockholm Bypass, other road extensions
	Insufficient funding for new infrastructure	Congestion tax (used for infrastructure investments and extended to cover more investments)

8.1 Conceptual premises

In this section I discuss the conceptual premises, drawing on identified keywords or concepts, binaries, and categories from the material. To recap, *keywords* or *concepts* are what may be called 'buzzwords' – frequently used and seemingly meaningful words or phrases the meaning of which nonetheless may be difficult to exactly pin down and define; *hierarchies* are explicit or implicit relations between things, often implying a 'better'-'lesser' or 'either-or' relation; *categories* are things sorted and classified, labelled and separated, which may imply opposites.

8.1.1 Capacity

The *Mobility Strategy* (p. 23) states that the capacity per hour on the streets and roads of the transport system (during rush hour) should increase more than the percental population growth until 2030. The main scenario of the *Roadmap* (p. 40) argues for a 90% capacity increase in public transport to meet future demand while addressing CO_2 emissions and preventing congestion. The focus on rush hour capacity reflects the fact that this is when most people use transport at the same time, but also suggests that the local government is more invested in ensuring commutes than other types of transport use. The capacity to be measured is then primarily the number of commuters who can be moved within a limited amount of time and space.

'Well-functioning' transport system

That a transport system should be 'well-functioning' may seem like a given. However, it is interesting to consider what is *meant* by 'well-functioning'. *Walkable City* (p. 20) stresses the importance of a "well-functioning transport system with minimal climate impact" (see also Vision 2030, p. 15). Similarly, *Vision 2040* (p. 13) cites a need for a "well-functioning infrastructure ... and though-out urban planning which makes it easy and natural to live environmentally friendly". This is held as the condition for the region as a cohesive labour-, housing-, and educational market "giving people unique opportunities to use the qualities of the whole region" and positioning Stockholm as the "natural centre" of the region (Vision 2030, p. 10). Transport, especially new cross-connections, is also held to remove barriers between the different parts of the city and enable people to "move quickly and easily throughout the whole region" (Vision 2030, p. 15; see also Walkable City, p. 17). In *Vision 2040* (p. 21), "Businesses are supported by a well-functioning transport system". Transport is held as a remedy to geographical or social exclusion, as well as a key to opportunities for both business and individuals. But inherent in both of these aspects of 'good function' is the reliance on more transport work to take place; otherwise the opportunities and integrating interpersonal meetings would remain the same as today. A 'well-functioning' transport system is then one which facilitates and promotes more transport work. It follows that a less 'well-functioning' transport system is one which does not include new cross-connections or bypasses (e.g. Vision 2030, p. 15), does not promote intra-regional travel, and does not enable more transport work. The *Mobility Strategy* (p. 49) also states that, "Efficient traffic flows and a vibrant urban environment demand growth in vehicular traffic [in the Swedish version, it says 'cars'] to be suppressed in crowded urban environments to enable a better balance between supply and demand". This implies that cars are not part of a 'well-functioning' urban environment – but the specification of "in crowded urban environments" shows that the transport system overall might tolerate cars.

While the *Mobility Strategy* (p. 5) states that "traffic is people and goods – not vehicles", the focus on transport work as an indicator for opportunity and development remains.

This problem representation is continued in the recent City Plan from 2018, which cites a need for "well-functioning services" and "well-functioning and resilient urban structure and technical systems" (in light of coming climate change; City Plan 2018, p. 6), and "well-functioning connections" as well as "high mobility" in the transport system (2018, p. 80). Here, too, 'well-functioning' is linked to the quantity of transport work.

8.1.2 'Framkomlighet' through mobility or accessibility

Policy, in particular the *Mobility Strategy*, presents a difference between mobility and accessibility as ways of achieving what in Swedish is dubbed *framkomlighet*. This is strongly linked to expressed aims to reduce car use and construct the dense walkable city, for environmental sustainability as well as space efficiency. However, this presented binary of mobility and accessibility, which texts hierarchize with accessibility on top, is in practice more of a sliding scale which sometimes promotes accessibility and sometimes mobility.

'Komma fram' means 'to move forward through a space' but also 'to arrive'. 'Framkomlighet' in daily speech is often used to mean the ability to move forward, or the quality of a space (such as a road) which allows one to do so. In the material it's used to mean 'the ability or quality of a space which allows one to arrive'. The *Mobility Strategy* (p. 5 Swedish version, my translation) states that "travelling is about arriving ['komma fram'], not moving forward ['ta sig fram']" (in English, this reads, "Travelling is about reaching the destination, not the journey itself"; Mobility Strategy, p. 5 English version). It goes on, "Flows and mobility are not goals in themselves. The key element is accessibility, to easily reach one's destination" (Mobility Strategy, p. 5).[20] In this part of the material 'framkomlighet' is linked strongly to 'accessibility'.

---

[20] By comparison, The EU White Paper on Transport (European Commission 2011, p. 6) states that "curbing mobility is not an option", suggesting value in the movement itself, rather than in reaching whatever is at the end of the journey.

The understanding of accessibility in Stockholm policy is strongly focused on *time* needed to reach opportunities.[21] 'Accessibility' in the material is limited to physical access to places and services, while other barriers to access such as costs are largely excluded from policy (except where higher costs of car use is held to improve accessibility for remaining cars). *Walkable City* cites accessibility ('tillgänglighet') as the quality which must improve in the transport system, but in a way that suggests it is concerned with accessibility through mobility. For example, it states that, "concentrating services in the nodes is more advantageous than continuing development towards more external trade. It assumes that *accessibility from adjoining areas is high* and proposed improvements to public transport are thereby significant" (2010, p. 42; emphasis added). In another section, *Walkable* City states that "[a]ccessibility to and from the inner city is excellent from the suburbs and is one of the reasons why Stockholm has such a high proportion of public transport users" (Walkable City, p. 34). In this context, 'accessibility' comes to mean 'potential to travel to'; it is not a case of getting services and opportunities to people where they live. In further support of this, the Stockholm Bypass highway is held to provide for example western Vällingby suburb with "much better regional accessibility" (Walkable City, p. 66). The proposals for enabling teleworking, such as job cafés, address accessibility issues as getting opportunities to people, but the majority of actual proposals deal instead in getting people to opportunities and reducing congestion for better *framkomlighet*. Note that *Walkable City* (e.g. p. 44) does not address access to services or other opportunities for the people who use them (such as local shops) but rather the (public transport) accessibility to places where opportunities are centred. Similarly, the *Mobility Strategy* (p. 23) states that capacity in the transport system should increase because "[i]ncreased flows and freedom of choice regarding the transport system provide all Stockholmers with excellent accessibility to all of the city's opportunities."

This model for accessibility is in practice centred on the ability to move. The "improved regional accessibility" provided by the Bypass will also encumber pedestrian and cycle accessibility where the Bypass joins the existing roadnet, and accessibility by bus will not be quite as good as that by car (due to the lack of dedicated bus lanes in the tunnels, but also to the fact that busses must exit the tunnels every time they make a stop for passengers). There is also the question of *what* the Bypass provides access to, when it was

—

[21] One example is a report from the office of City Planning which traces the number of workplaces one can reach within 30, 45, and 60 minutes from each of the stops of the Stockholm rail system (Stadsbyggnadskontoret 2004).

chosen for its ostensible capacity to connect places difficult to provide with high-frequency public transport (RA 2005, p. 216) and SL made the assessment that there was no significant demand for rail transport along the route (Trivector 2009).

8.1.3 A 'sustainable increase' in transport

Stockholm transport policy works to promote an increase in transport work, while encouraging a shift in technology – this is what the *Mobility Strategy* (p. 48) dubs a "sustainable increase in transport". Measures connected to this are the extensions of public transport, cycling, and walking, but also roads in certain locations. There are two parts to the concept of a "sustainable increase in transport: 'sustainable' and 'increase'. As was shown in section 5.1, 'sustainability' is closely linked to energy and space efficiency and a reduction of CO_2 emissions, while the previous section showed a focus on an increase of transport work through higher capacity in the transport system. While the exact phrase is not used extensively, it is echoed throughout policy documents. *Walkable City*, for example, states that, "One of the single greatest challenges for the region and for the City Plan is to increase access to the transport system while at the same time minimising the environmental impact of the transport sector" (Walkable City, p. 10).

Transport work, in the form of commutes, is held to be necessary, even crucial, for the function of society, for creating economic growth (e.g. Tamsons et al. 2016) which in turn is a highly-held aim in nearly all policies and laws and presumed a requirement for sustainability (such as the Planning and Building Act [Swedish: *Plan- och bygglagen, PBL]*; SFS 2010:900, chapter 2:3, and the National Strategy for Sustainable Development; 2001/ 02:172, p. 58). The necessity for an extended transport system is motivated with expectations for the future, as in the circular reasoning in *Walkable City*: "There are strong indications that the labour market region will continue to expand in the future, at least if the planned improvements to the transport infrastructure are realised" (Walkable City, p. 8), and "As the labour market grows, commuting will take place within an increasingly large area" (p. 16). *Mobility Strategy* differentiates between inner-city and regional transport, but is on a similar track:

> Stockholm is growing. Forecasts indicate that the City of Stockholm will have 25 per cent more inhabitants by 2030. The City's Vision 2030 describes what it will be like to live in, work in and visit Stockholm. Exactly how the city will grow is described in the City Plan, the Walkable City: the density of existing

housing developments is to increase and 100,000 new homes are to be built thus enabling more people to live and work in the same area.

Roads, the metro and rail lines must be extended to support this regional development, however, the demand for transportation within the city's boundaries will, in all probability, be greater than the physical capacity of the transport system (Mobility Strategy, p. 3).

Measures addressing transport work are represented in contradictory ways. While some policies state that only reducing the harmful emissions from vehicles is insufficient (primarily because these still take up space; e.g. Road-map, p. 37), and that reductions in transport work are necessary, most – even the same policies – also contain proposals for extensions of motorized trans-port work (see e.g. Walkable City, p. 74 for a list of proposed roads). In *Walkable City*, road transport is noted to have negative effects:

> The impact of transport on the climate and environment is well known. The transport sector is responsible for around half the county's carbon emissions. A host of measures are required in this sector if the target of becoming a fossil fuel free Stockholm by 2050 is to be achieved. There is great hope that technical advances may result in emission-free and carbon-neutral fuels in the future. However, an increase in road traffic also brings other undesirable effects such as congestion, noise and physical barriers (Walkable City, p. 22).

At the same time, "The city is also prioritising the Stockholm Bypass (Förbi-fart Stockholm)" (Walkable City, p. 43). *Mobility Strategy* notes that the Bypass is unlikely to have significant impact on urban congestion (Mobility Strategy, p. 11) and that road traffic has several negative aspects:

> Road traffic can comprise a danger in itself but is also a source of air pollution and noise, which are damaging to people's health. How we choose to trans-port ourselves also impacts our health. Our access to a variety of travel alternatives impacts our social lives. Transport infrastructure is expensive to build and the multitude of tunnels and bridges in Stockholm require signi-ficant resources to operate and maintain.

> However, the greatest challenge is the contribution made by traffic to global climate change and the significant efforts that will be required to achieve the ambitious target of a fossil-fuel free city by 2050 (Mobility Strategy, p. 6)

But *Mobility Strategy* refers to reducing car use as a way of making car use easier (p. 5) and goes on to say,

The Stockholm Bypass will divert regional traffic that does not need to pass through central Stockholm, and enable the Essingeleden motorway to play a more local pressure-relieving role. Through-traffic will no longer pass through inner-city streets, leaving space for a higher degree of local travel by public transport (Mobility Strategy, p. 48).

Mobility Strategy, and the material overall, is formed around the idea of decoupling – in this case, decoupling accessibility, regional growth, and transport increase from harmful environmental effects: "One of the greatest challenges for a growing city is increasing accessibility while minimizing the vehicular traffic's environmental impact" (Mobility Strategy, p. 45). Limiting traffic growth is recognized as a "major challenge", which must be met with the help of "alternative modes of transport" (Mobility Strategy, p. 65) – that is, a *shift* (to speak with Banister) will allow for the growth already assumed and not demand a too-difficult *avoidance* of transport use. It does, then, seem that 'traffic' is often used in place of 'inner-city car traffic' – otherwise the demand to limit traffic growth *and* increase capacity would hardly make sense. Public transport becomes de-problematized in this context: it is so efficient that the municipal government can take – or promote – a continued growth in transport (and a regional expansion encouraging this further) as a given.

As stated, it is also clear that cars are not to be removed entirely – only from the inner city. As I have shown, bypasses around the city (most notable the Stockholm Bypass, as the Eastern link has been put on hold) funded largely by the congestion tax are to facilitate 'regional cohesion' and shift car traffic away from the inner city. While the congestion tax is argued to reduce car use, congestion, and emissions *in the city*, it funds increased car use *outside* the city – thus asserting the car as a desired mode of transport. That the inquiry for the Stockholm Bypass showed that the highway would increase car use and decrease public transport use is not raised as in contradiction to the stated aims of policy, confirming the focus on reducing only inner-city car use.

In a somewhat puzzling paragraph, *Mobility Strategy* states that, "A growing city with a healthy economy acquires the exact amount of traffic in peak hours for which the road capacity has been created. Less vehicular traffic requires other measures, such as congestion tax or other user fees. To ensure continued growth in the region, there must be alternatives" (Mobility Strategy, p. 30). It might seem that this is an argument for limiting car use rather than building new roads, and promoting "alternatives" instead. While this paragraph – and *Mobility Strategy* as a whole – states that increasing capacity (i.e. constructing more or bigger roads) cannot solve the accessibility issues caused by congestion, it does not argue against building new roads to meet demand. Instead, there is a sharp delineation between the city and places outside of the city. For further example of this, see *Mobility Strategy* on the objective of limiting through-traffic by 2030 to present levels at 5%: "The major investments in ring roads creates scope for a sustainable increase in travel and an attractive urban environment" (Mobility Strategy, p. 48). That is, *Mobility Strategy* suggests that shifting car use outside the city makes both car use and the city more sustainable. That ring roads will increase car use is recognized by *Mobility Strategy* as troublesome (p. 30), but an increase in car use – recognized elsewhere as harmful and against policy – seems acceptable if it takes place outside city borders. This is particularly interesting when one notes that the Strategy explicitly "indicates the need to limit traffic growth to achieve a transport system that is environmentally, economically and socially robust and sustainable" (Mobility Strategy, p. 65).

8.1.4 The growth engine of Sweden

Stockholm is frequently described as the "growth engine of Sweden". *Walkable City* states that, "Central Stockholm enjoys a unique position in the Stockholm-Mälaren region and operates in many respects as an engine for the entire county's growth" (Walkable City, p. 36). The budgets also refer to Stockholm as a growth engine. The *Vision 2030* states,

> The Stockholm–Mälar region is of great importance for the whole of Sweden's economic growth. This requires that national policies have an urban perspective and consider the region's specific circumstances, with high costs for housing, premises and salaries, long travel times, complex decision-making processes and the risk of segregation. The municipal equalisation scheme must be modified, and the allocation of state funds for infrastructure must increase (Vision 2030, p. 16).

This is often couched in a sense of urgency – certain aims or measures must be safeguarded in order to ensure the well-being of not just the city, but of the whole nation. The *Roadmap* is for example prefaced by then-mayor of transport Per Ankersjö stating that, "As the capital of Sweden and the nation's engine for growth, Stockholm has an opportunity to take the lead in this work by demonstrating that it is possible to phase out fossil fuels and reduce emission levels while still sustaining growth and meeting the challenge of a rise in population" (Roadmap, p. 3). That is: despite doing the hard and crucial work of running the vehicle of economic growth for a country of almost ten million people while making room for more residents in the front seat, Stockholm can *still* phase out fossil fuels – this should be a sign that others can do it, too.

But the sense of urgency also brings with it calls for special attention to the needs of Stockholm. The equalization scheme – the give and take of tax money between municipalities in place to ensure equal provision of social services – should be modified, the state should put more money into Stockholm's infrastructure (e.g. Vision 2030). Transport is given a key role in Stockholm's role as the nation's 'engine' – the 'growth engine' is to be driven by more or less literal engines, taking people to work across the whole region. For example, traffic county council Kristoffer Tamsons and other councils wrote that failing to invest in public transport in the Stockholm region would be a "brake" on the labour- and housing market in the region and the (economic) growth of the whole country (Tamsons et al. 2016).

The idea of Stockholm as the 'growth engine' also carries a strong focus on the status of the city as 'attractive' (for residents, companies, and visitors). Sustainability, greenness, clean air and water, as well as good public transport, are described as features which attract new residents and tourists, as well as businesses. The concern with maintaining Stockholm's attracttiveness (in comparison with other cities), particularly for business, is evident throughout all texts. *Walkable City* even states that "the most important issue" is,

> to meet the need of the business world for skilled labour and improved communications. Another priority task is to promote and develop Stockholm as a good city with a high quality of life, so that the workers of the future will want to live and work here. In an increasingly internationalised world, a people-friendly urban environment, a rich variety of housing and workplaces, well-developed services and a broad range of culture and entertainment are becoming ever more important in gaining a competitive advantage. Through this, the attractive metropolis of Stockholm could become an even stronger brand (The Walkable City, p 9).

The traits of urban entrepreneurialism – in which city government works to attract business and residents and implement measures which are assumed to stimulate economic growth, rather than administer welfare (Harvey 1989b) – are evident in much of the Stockholm material. The reference to the city's 'brand' is also present in the budgets: "the brand Stockholm – the Capital of Scandinavia" (e.g. Budget 2017, p. 300) or "the environment is a large part of the city's brand, and thus environmental policy is ambitious" (Budget 2012, p. 1), as well as "the City Archives should therefor highlight the history of the city and its operations in work with the brand Stockholm" (Budget 2015, p. 142), or references to spreading the city's "cycling brand" (Budget 2014, p. 7). The city is described as if it were a business aiming to sell products.

8.2 A 'technical' understanding of the problem rooted in narrative

The representation of the problem as too little transport work is situated in a conceptual context of seemingly rational-technical premises, which on a second look become harder to pin down. What is for example meant by a 'sustainable increase' in transport? What does *framkomlighet* mean? While a focus on capacity in the transport system may be a technical – even mathematical – focus, what about the assumption that more people should travel longer distances for work?

The understanding of transport as a vehicle for development is old. For example, Oldenziel and van der Vleuten (2017) show how transport was believed to hold the answer to all of society's ills during the 'Age of Promise' (ca 1815–1914) through the capacity of rail to connect and expand society, literally driving civilization forward. However, even at the beginning of the Age of Promise, the focus was on the urban middle-class. Demolitions and new constructions in 19th century Paris pushed the working-class poor out of the city, much like the 'sanitation' of Stockholm City did in the mid-20th century. Transport ensured that the working classes were still available to the labour market (Oldenziel and van der Vleuten, 2017). While the linking of transport to prosperity can be traced back to the first trade routes, and the rail lines of the 19th century extended both cities and the labour market, it was the advent of the car that truly enabled the contemporary commuter lifestyle and the connection between daily personal transport and economic growth: "The car creates distance only it can overcome" (Lutz and Hernandez 2010). While the Stockholm metro of the 1950s provided the city with a non-car-based means of growing, and its residents one of traversing long distances, Börjesson et al. (2014) argue that it may also have created a stronger dependence on cars than would otherwise have been the case through the following spread of the urban structure into a widespread pattern.

This seemingly rational framing – that we need more transport to create jobs, provide homes, promote development and growth – has deeply emotional elements. There is a utopian side, which presents a bright future if these extensions (and maybe some more in the future) are built, a future without (or with less) congestion but with more opportunities, easier lives, more time for 'what matters', welfare and prosperity. This will be achieved through 'sustainable growth': so hard to define yet paramount for the future. There is also a dystopian side, which warns that if we do not build them, not only Stockholm but the whole country will suffer; we will be stuck in traffic, we won't get good jobs, emission will increase, we will have to spend more time in traffic and less time on 'what matters', economic growth will stagnate leading to a decrease in welfare and prosperity. We will 'stop' – see for example the motto, "without the Bypass Stockholm will stop" (Stockholm Chamber of Commerce 2010). As implied by the phrase 'sustainable growth' (and by e.g. the National Strategy for Sustainable Development), sustainability without growth is not sustainable at all. While the connection of extended transport, more opportunities for work, and economic development has historic precedence, it is interesting that in a region such as Stockholm – with an extended transport system and a strong economy – continued extensions are framed as 'do or die' projects.

There is a representation of absolute certainty of the compatibility of economic growth and environmental sustainability, and in the capacity of 'climate smart' solutions, which eliminates 'tough choices' between a cohesive labour market and climate targets. Within this narrative of sustainable growth, even the Stockholm Bypass can be depicted as 'climate smart'.

8.2.1 Discursive elements

As has been shown, the representation of the 'problem' as one of too little transport work takes place within a discourse of technological development and economic growth. Within this discourse, transport 'problems' should be addressed by extending the supply. Even though this is explicitly contested in for example the *Mobility Strategy* and *Roadmap*, the measures proposed show a pattern of extensions as the key 'solution'. Against the large-scale projects for metro extensions and the Stockholm Bypass, the proposals for local job cafés (thus far without any significant implementation) and improved internet access (a measure further related to the discourse of technological development) are quite small. The optimism and hope invested in technology (in particular the metro) and growth distract from the question of whether the metro extensions were the best option, along the best routes.

The extensions have been criticized especially due to decisions taken before traffic- and cost-benefit analyses were made (e.g. Delling and Hennel 2013; Gustafsson 2014). Extensions become such a given, deproblematized through optimism of 'high-capacity' technology, that the increasing demand for electricity to power the new metro lines (for example) is not addressed.

8.2.2 The subject

The focus on commutes in policy – improving capacity during rush hour, the vital task of extending the labour market through the transport system, attempting to discourage 'unnecessary transport' – sets the subject as a worker. As Chapter 7 showed, necessary journeys are those which create value, primarily through wage labour. People are also often described as "labour" – see for example *The Walkable City* (p. 10) on the number of people outside the labour market: "All the indications are that it will be imperative to make better use of this reserve of labour in order to secure long-term growth". The very first section of *Vision 2030* reads, "The Stockholm-Mälar region needs labour. Here you can find an occupation that matches your interests, education, background and experience" (Vision 2030, p. 6). This is later followed up in a description of Stockholm as "the centre of a strong, growing region":

> Investments in education, from the first years of school to research at a high academic level, have provided the region with a skilled labour force that few others can match. This is one of the reasons that so many businesses choose to establish operations here (Vision 2030, p. 10).

The *Walkable City* (p. 8) states that, "There are strong indications that the labour market region will continue to expand in the future, at least if the planned improvements to the transport infrastructure are realised" and "The most important issue is to meet the need of the business world for skilled labour and improved communications" (Walkable City, p. 9). The transport system is then to extend to provide businesses with (highly-skilled) labour, to secure future economic or urban growth:

> Efficient transportation makes Stockholm the hub that links the entire Mälar region together. All the prerequisites for the business community are here. Many companies, particularly international ones, choose to locate their headquarters and research and development operations here. This applies especially to companies in the IT, life science, environmental technology, financial and other knowledge-intensive industries (Vision 2030, p. 10).

The problem representation of too little transport work then rests on a construction of the subject as a worker, to be made available for employers around the region and make the most out of her education. This also limits the attention to the subject as a citizen, a political subject, a partner or parent in a family, or simply the curious, playing *homo ludens* – if every journey should create benefit, what about the journey taken just to see something new?

8.2.3 Lived effects

The focus on extending the capacity of the transport system can be assumed to have several effects on people's lives.

First, there are the quite physical effects of the new transport routes, both rail and road: new incursions into landscapes, new stations and junctions, and various supporting constructions (such as air vent towers from the Bypass tunnels or entrances to underground metro stations). Traffic junctions between the Bypass and other roads will on the one hand provide access for car users, and some bus users, but will also form barriers for pedestrians and cyclists. The placement of traffic junctions near the natural reserve and cultural heritage at Lovö will affect both of those, and the Bypass has been identified as a potential "infrastructure threat" to the world heritage Drottningholm castle area (Månsson 2016; Unesco 2016). The crossing of the Bypass over the E18 highway near Hjulsta and Akalla northwest of the city will take up formerly natural landscape and recreational areas and lead the new highway on ground level just a few hundred meters from residential areas (e.g. Mahovic 2015). The metro lines will, at least as at the time of writing (2019) run in tunnels, and will so likely impact mostly through some noise and the stations aboveground. The light rail lines are all above grounds and so noticeable for all nearby; the light rail line *tvärbanan* has been met by complaints of noisy trains from residents along the tracks. Of course, all projects will have wider impact areas during construction.

Figure 8.1: Construction of the Stockholm Bypass tunnel entry at Lovö, Ekerö municipality. The area was previously woodland and crop fields. Picture by author, 2019-09-18.

The new routes also create new travel patterns: there will likely be more public transport use in, to, and near the city, and more car use between north and south of the city; the cross-connections of the light rail lines mean that people to a lesser degree will go by the inner-city stations; the busses and local rail from Nacka may get fewer passengers as the metro opens. The Stockholm Bypass makes it easier for many to commute between the north and south parts of the region. As noted by e.g Caro (1975), Duranton and Turner (2011), and Shove and Trentmann (2018), new roads lead to higher car use, and faster transport or increasing flexibility creates new norms for distances travelled and number of tasks performed during a day. Together with the construction of the subject as labour, and of traveling for work as more necessary than other journeys, commutes can be expected to stretch out in time and space. These new commuter patterns bring side effects. For example, Mattisson et al. have shown that long commutes impact both mental and physical health, relationships, and political participation negatively (Mattisson et al 2017; Hansdotter 2017; Backman 2017). While longer commutes are associated with higher wages (Sandow, in Backman 2017), there is then also cause for concern about the social sustainability of policy-making for more and longer commutes. Among heterosexual couples with children, it is also often men who commute longer for higher wages, while women work part-time for lower wages in order to take care of children before and after school (Scholten, in Backman 2017), which implies that commuting may also reinforce gender roles, to the detriment of women (short- and long-term, as lower wages also means lower pensions in the future); in this way, commutes may exacerbate stress also for the non-commuting partner. But also women who do long-distance commutes tend to experience higher levels of stress than men (Backman 2017) and stress is rising as a public health issue, especially among young women (e.g. Swedish Social Insurance Agency 2016; Public Health Agency of Sweden 2019).

Lastly, the heavy investments in infrastructure in Stockholm naturally excludes investments in other parts of the country, just as the investments in the Stockholm Bypass necessitated premature introductions of the congestion tax to Essingeleden to provide funding for public transport investments, as the public treasury is not unlimited. If it is a recognized fact that it is more cost-effective to build for 'sustainable increase of transport' in cities that rural areas (e.g. Börjesson, in Dietl 2018), one might ask when it will be worth spending money to promote sustainable transport practices outside urban areas?

9

The problem as too little urban space

To answer my research question of *what kind of 'tool' is produced by policy for transport in Stockholm municipality* I continue my analysis of what transport *does*. In this chapter I discuss in more depth the representation of the problem as *too little urban space*. As in previous chapters, I address the questions from the WPR framework: What conceptual premises underlie this representation and What effects (discursive, subjectification, and lived) follow from this representation of the problem?

The Walkable City shows the public transport system as the answer to many needs. Not only does it allow people to go about the business of their days, it is also "a key component of sustainable growth" (The Walkable City, p. 22); a key to social cohesion (in "poorly integrated" areas a "strategy to physically link together" the city "would increase the opportunities of local people to meet and travel to work, education and leisure activities in a sustainable way", p. 43); improved air quality (through promoting a traffic system "that reduces the need to travel by car", to complement the key measures of "exhaust gas cleansing and reduced use of studded tires", p. 30).

First and foremost, public transport is necessary to ensure the mobility of the city's residents *given the available space*. This last is very important: throughout the city plan, there is a great deal of attention on the dire need for urban growth, for expansion, for more homes to live in and businesses to work in, and so, when the worker-residents of the city are to go about their day, the hunt is on for the transport mode with the *highest capacity*.

In the material I have found that 'problem' representation of insufficient urban space is supported by a discourse of an 'urban crisis' visible in calls for homes to the "new Gothenburg" taking up residence in Stockholm between present day and 2030, in the division of transport into 'space-craving' and 'space-saving', and in the stress on promoting Stockholm as the 'growth engine' of Sweden. Within this discourse, and in light of measures to increase transport work, the 'walkable city' is easily read as a means to make room for more people first, and a means of reducing emissions or preserve green areas second.

Table 9.1: 'Problem' representations related to insufficient urban space.

Problem category	Problems represented within this category	Measures
Too little space	Insufficient space for transport on land	Extensions of transport Public transport on water
	Too few homes (and recalcitrant municipalities)	Demanding homes for metro extensions
	Cars get in the way of public transport and cyclists	Turning car parking or car lanes into public transport or bicycle lanes Signal priority to public transport and bicycles

9.1 Conceptual premises

In this section I discuss the conceptual premises, drawing on identified keywords or concepts, binaries, and categories from the material. To recap, *keywords* or *concepts* are what may be called 'buzzwords' – frequently used and seemingly meaningful words or phrases the meaning of which nonetheless may be difficult to exactly pin down and define; *hierarchies* are explicit or implicit relations between things, often implying a 'better'–'lesser' or 'either–or' relation; *categories* are things sorted and classified, labelled and separated, which may imply opposites.

Throughout the *Mobility Strategy* is mention of modes of transport which are 'high-capacity' and 'efficient in use of space' – in the strategy, this means public transport, cycling, and walking. It is clear that the main resource to mind and manage is urban space; air quality and green spaces, for example, are treated quite marginally, even as traffic's contribution to global climate change is cited as "the greatest challenge" (Mobility Strategy, p. 6). Under the headline "Sustainable accessibility" the *Mobility Strategy* notes that, "This strategy has its primary focus on promoting efficient use of a shared and limited resource: street space. How we use and plan this resource plays a decisive role in the city's ability to reach its targets for sustainable social, economic and environmental development" (Mobility Strategy, p. 6). As the quote suggest, efficiency is assumed to yield sustainability, neatly aligning environmental goals with those of the municipal government and opening up for the intensification of traffic that is both predicted and prescribed. Reinforcing this, the *Walkable City* states that sustainability is to be achieved by focusing urban development on "places where growth can be concentrated so that development will be long-term sustainable from an economic, social and environmental perspective (Walkable City, p. 6). The *Walkable City* states that:

> A dense city core in the central parts of the region also encourages sustainable development in many respects, particularly due to the excellent opportunities created for sustainable transport. The city should therefore continue its planning to strengthen central Stockholm (Walkable City, p. 36).

and later:

> Existing land resources are exploited efficiently and high accessibility to public transport is preserved. From a social perspective, too, there are gains to be made from seeing the inner city expand beyond its historic boundaries, the old tollgates (Walkable City, p. 38).

A key aspect of 'sustainable transport', as touched upon in Chapters 6 and 7, is then the efficient use of urban space.

9.1.1 The 'walkable city'

Often used synonymous to 'dense', the 'walkable city' is held up as a solution to many of the city's problems: the lack of homes (see below), preservation of green areas, CO_2 emissions, and the need for an 'attractive city' (see below). This model for urban development is based on in-fill urban growth, mixed-use neighbourhood block structure, and ensuring homes and public transport (as well as cycle lanes) are planned jointly. For urban transport, the ideal of the walkable city is that local journeys should be made by bicycle or on foot, while longer-distance journeys should be done by public transport. The *Walkable City* (p. 22) states that,

> The environmental impact of transport is clear in cities, but they also have the best potential for sustainable travel compared with the situation in rural areas. A dense and concentrated city encourages walking and cycling, and promotes the need for reliable public transport. It is also possible to use the infrastructure more efficiently, because it can perform different tasks at different times of the day.

What exactly this means for urban structure is not immediately clear, however. The organization Yimby suggested that "the Walkable City is stone dead" when the plans for Årsta fields were revealed (Thörnqvist 2016), since the schematics for local roads would not allow the Årsta area to connect

Gullmarsplan and Liljeholmen as planned. The high-profile Stockholm Royal Seaport (Swedish: Norra Djurgårdsstaden) has been marketed as a sustainable quarter but is allegedly "difficult" to cycle (Nyman 2016), and most new residential areas lack adjacent playgrounds for preschools, forcing longer journeys for preschools (Ritzén and Mahmoud 2018).

At the same time, the free choice paradigm operating in for example schools and health care means that even if there are services within walking distance, there are no guarantees that these will be the first choice of nearby residents (or that they will accept the resident seeking their services, as private providers are or perceive themselves to be freer to pick and choose between 'customers', as for example charter schools have done; Fegan et al. 2013). Within the free choice paradigm assuring citizens influence over where they access services, few promises are made to ensure equal quality of services regardless of location, even under the walkable city label.

The walkable city is then a seemingly well-defined concept which becomes tenuous when one considers practice. If the dense, walkable city does not necessarily guarantee walkability between residential areas (as in Årsta fields), access to services such as play areas, or convenient cycle routes, and if the free choice paradigm remains in place in the stead of equal-quality services, what *is* necessary for the walkable city? Policy and practice suggests that the central feature of the walkable city is density of housing and access to public transport. Neither of these features precludes travel nor makes it unnecessary, and recent studies suggest the connection between density and reduced traffic is not as strong as policy text would have it (an American study found that a high increase in density yielded only a small decrease in car use; Duranton and Turner 2018. See also Holman et al. 2015). The walkable city ideal in practice then relates to population density and access to longer-distance transport; supporting the problem representations of too little transport work as well as too little urban space.

> The vision of a world-class Stockholm is all about creating a vibrant and growing city that mixes different functions. The model often used is the intensive urban environment of the inner city, with its diverse range of housing, workplaces and services that attract many Stockholmers and visitors (Walkable City, p. 34).

It is not discussed, in the *Roadmap* or in other texts, what other environmental effects a denser city structure will have, or whether this plan is socially sustainable. In the *Roadmap*, justice is not discussed in the local context – social sustainability is only mentioned in relation to clean development mechanism projects and involving locals in host nations (Roadmap, p. 52). In the *Walkable City* (pp. 10, 18), social sustainability is constructed as a lack of cohesion caused largely by unemployment, which should be addressed by removing physical barriers and increasing, through transport, access to work. The dense city is here envisaged to break through barriers, such as green areas, and provide meeting spaces (Walkable City, p. 45).

9.1.2 Urban nodes

The representation of the problem as one of too little urban space also rests on an extension of urban space, into "urban nodes". The walkable city should not fit the whole "new Gothenburg" into the city centre; rather,

> Sustainable growth and development towards a world-class Stockholm demand a better balance between the different parts of the city than is currently the case. The city therefore needs to support the development of a polycentric structure with dense and high-amenity nodes in the outer city (Walkable City, p. 39)

These 'nodes' should share the inner city's urban qualities, such as density and mixed functions, and be connected to the city and other nodes by high-capacity transport. They should ease the burden on the inner city by taking some of its hopeful residents, and contribute to the growing labour- and housing market.

> The idea behind a more polycentric structure is to exploit growth potential across the county in a sustainable and effective way (p. 9).

The urban nodes show that it isn't just that there is too little space in the inner city, but also that there is too little city in the region. They tie into the 'smart city' concept, where the urban is recognized as more sustainable and so preferable as a structure for the built environment. With the help of the urban nodes, more people can live in dense urban areas with efficient transport, and more people can be a part of the extended, cohesive labour market of the Stockholm-Mälar region. The nodes should, however, not challenge Stockholm's role as the main character in the region: the *Walkable City* makes it clear that development should continue to strengthen the inner city as a site of employment, services, and culture (Walkable City, p. 36).

9.1.3 'Lack of homes' (Swedish: 'bostadsbrist')

Public transport extensions, especially the new metro lines, are associated with housing considered vital for the development of not just Stockholm but all of Sweden (e.g. Tamsons et al. 2016). As stated in Chapter 6, the demands for municipalities to construct a large number of homes in exchange for extended public transport infrastructure ties transport inextricably to an anticipated and promoted population growth in the urban region. The extensions of transport capacity are couched in a narrative of a large future population putting pressure on the urban system. The *Roadmap* (p. 16) states that, "The capacity of public transport must be expanded so that, as a minimum, it can cope with the 350,000 new journeys that will be created by the population increase". The *Mobility Strategy* (p. 10), meanwhile claims that, "Population growth in the city and the region is of such an extent that even these major investments in new roads and rail lines will be insufficient and significant capacity deficiencies will continue to exist in parts of the transport system even after these expansions". In this context, the urban space is not necessarily to be 'freed' from congestion for the enjoyment and convenience of the present-day population (just like it may not necessarily be the present-day population who should shift their transport mode; Mobility Strategy, p. 26), but to make room for more residents and more travellers in the future.

This 'crisis' may well be the reason for the shift from the concern of the 1999 City Plan (*Översiktsplan 1999*) for comprehensive green areas, to the concern of the *Walkable City* for comprehensive urban areas. The green areas were even pointed out as a source of unsafety by Kristina Alvendal of the Moderate Party, who said,

> When you talk about biological diversity you often get down to beetle level. We have set the aim to be one million people in Stockholm, that has to matter too. If it's about keeping unsafe forest areas with rotten trees near where people live, then there is a higher aim than biological diversity and that is the safety of Stockholmers (Kallin 2008).

Similar thoughts were expressed by Jessica Sjönell, local representative for the Liberal Party in Skarpnäck south of Stockholm, who argued that the forest of Bagarmossen south of Stockholm was unsafe and should be turned into a residential area connecting suburbs Bagarmossen and Skarpnäck (Jonsson 2016b).

The city must continue to grow; this is strongly asserted in *Walkable City*. Growth is necessary not only for the city itself, but for the region and the entire nation as well: Stockholm's needs are Sweden's needs. *Walkable City* assumes the absolute necessity of a growing urban population, and economy:

"population growth in Stockholm is a basic condition for a positive economic development and increased welfare" (Walkable City, p. 6). This goes for the urban structure itself, too: "A high rate of home building is crucial for sustainable growth in Stockholm" (Walkable City, p. 24). That this growth may expand into green areas (see Walkable City, p. 45), and was found by Ban and Furberg (KTH 2019) to have increased built environment by 15% at the expense of green areas, implies that 'sustainable growth' does not require preservation of green areas in or near the city.

INSÄNDARE: Skövla skogen i Söderort och bygg stad

Bostadsbristen kräver att Stockholm bygger fler bostäder – även i Söderorts skogar, skriver signaturen Skövlarsyntharen.

Debatt

Publicerad 11:55, 18 sep 2017

Det här är en debattartikel/insändare på StockholmDirekt. De åsikter och synpunkter som framförs är författarens. Vill du skriva en debattartikel – klicka här!

"Det är ett jäkla gnällande om träd i Söderort. Man skulle kunna tro att våra gator och hus är fyllda av ett gäng skogsmullar istället för äkta Stockholmare! Senast i raden av bostadsbyggen som det ojas om är så klart slyskogen som nu fått det tjusiga men påhittade namnet "Östra Kärrtorpsskogen". Ett litet stycke sankmark som plötsligt upphöjs till "Ekologiskt särskilt betydelsefullt" och "spridningsväg för flera artgrupper".

LÄS ÄVEN:
Beskedet: Så mycket vill staden spara av Årstaskogen

Den artgrupp som främst behöver spridas i stan är så klart vi människor. Våra barn står snart på gatan, utan bostad. Det är så svårt att hitta ett hem i stan att våra unga tvingas flytta utomlands, eller ännu värre: till Göteborg.

Figure 9.1: A blunt example of an opinion letter proposing less woodland and more housing, lest Stockholm children be "forced to move abroad or worse: to Gothenburg".

Skövlarsyntharen 2017.
The signature, Skövlarsyntharen, has also made a song called Bygg stad, *about "asphalting the forest" to build houses (Jonsson 2016a).*

9.1.4 Space-craving and space-saving modes of transport

As was shown in Chapter 6, policy for Stockholm transport is occupied with promoting *efficiency* – efficiency of space, of energy, of time, and of vehicles, all addressed through 'high-capacity' vehicles such as buses or metro cars and a removal of congestion – and implicitly with eliminating *inefficiency*. This can be seen particularly clearly through the sorting of vehicles into 'space-craving' and 'space-saving'. For example, *Walkable City* (p. 22) states that, "Public transport is by far the most efficient way of moving people around, with just one metro line transporting as many people per unit of time as 16–18 lanes on a road".

Figure 9.2 shows an image from the *Mobility Strategy* (p. 7), depicting the relative use of different vehicles in Stockholm. The most interesting thing about the image is that it separates person transport into 'public transport' and 'individual', and further individual transport into 'space-saving' versus 'space-craving'. The schema shows that 'space-craving' transport using personal cars is undesirable: they "could be saved or performed in another manner". While taxis are considered "both shared and individual trans-portation", and space-craving to the extent that they are individual (and ul-timately deemed 'non-necessary' through the congestion tax), public transport and goods transport are marked "vital for the city's function" and not sorted by their craving or saving of space. Only private transport of people is seen as capable of being space-craving.

It must be noted that the Swedish version uses the words *ytsnål* ('space thrifty') and *ytkrävande* ('space demanding'). Especially the use of *ytsnål* better relates a view of vehicles as more or less *demanding* of space – rather than suggesting that some vehicles could, somehow, *save* space, when all vehicles must by laws of physics use some urban space (at least, until tele-portation).[22]

---

[22] I am obliged here to the students at *Miljökonsekvensbeskrivning* spring semester 2019 (April 26, 2019), who made the note of the difference between the Swedish version I showed them and the English version I have used in my dissertation. You saved me from making an erroneous and un-necessary observation!

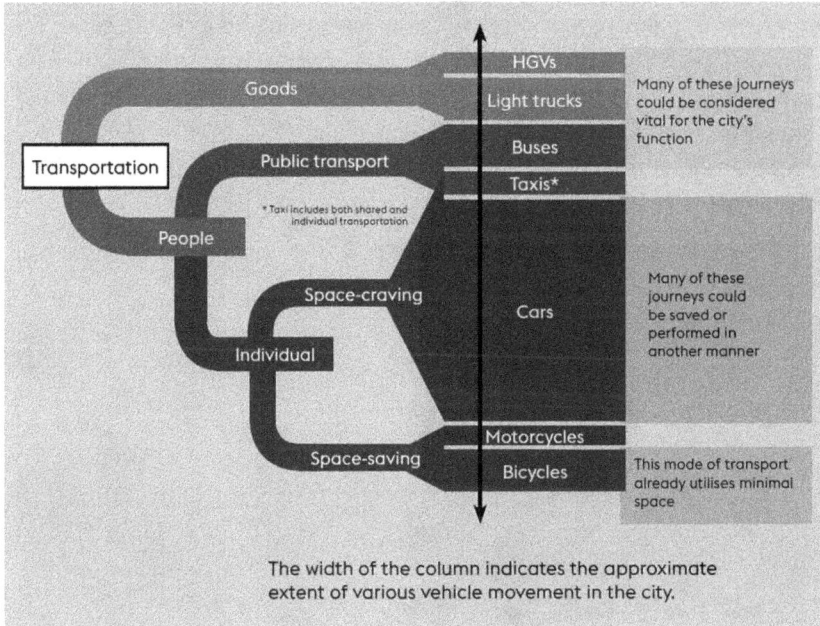

Figure 9.2: A schematic of transport modes' relative use of urban space (Mobility Strategy, p. 7).

Bicycles are explicitly represented as a space-efficient, 'space-saving' means of transport. The bicycle plan includes new bicycle routes, space taken from cars and given to cyclists – "The needs of the cyclist when moving will need to be prioritised over the needs of stationary cars, in other words, parking places will need to be removed to create space for cycle lanes and cycle paths." (Mobility Strategy, p. 60) – and promotion of more bicycle parking spaces. Cycling is to be encouraged because it frees up space on public transport (Mobility Strategy, p. 23), and also "utilizes minimal space" (Mobility Strategy, p. 7) to get people places. Where before cycling was seen as something which took space needed by cars, put cyclists at risk, and was unnecessary because it was mostly used for leisure (cf. Emanuel 2010, p. 2), it is now described as something which saves valuable city space and should be promoted over the car.

This division into space-craving and space-saving is reflected in many measures for the inner city of Stockholm. However, as I have shown, the designation of private cars as space-craving does not mean that all cars are marked as undesirable. Taken together, it can be said that some cars (as Section 7.1.2 showed, primarily those whose users cannot or will not pay for urban street space) are more space-craving than others. As the *Mobility*

179

Strategy (p. 5) refers to reducing car use as a way of making car use easier for 'necessary' car traffic, it can be inferred that congestion is to be blamed on people who perform 'unnecessary' (unpaid for) car journeys. The view of congestion as a 'problem' of insufficient supply has been replaced by a representation which instead puts the blame on individual drivers making bad choices.

Figure 9.3: A model of a metro train versus the number of cars necessary to carry the same number of passengers. Picture by author, 2017-09-08. Picture taken at the Stockholm Transport Museum (now closed for relocation).

9.2 A narrative of space

The representation of the problem as too little urban space rests highly on narrative rather than technical rationale, although the 'walkable city' is depicted as a 'smart city' solution (i.e. technical and depoliticized) and the housing crisis is often accompanied by numbers of people waiting for a home. This representation is strongly informed by understandings of urban development which are emotional in character – see for example the con-struction of the urban housing crisis, often accompanied by questions about 'where our children will live' or accusations of selfishness towards those who want to move to Stockholm. The walkable city is here the utopian vision, where everybody in and near Stockholm (thanks to the nodes) can walk to work, schools, and shops, and use public transport when they must go further. The dystopian vision is clear in the construction of the housing crisis, which is said to not only affect the people without a permanent home, but the economic growth of the whole country. The promise is that what is good for Stockholm is good for Sweden – and implicitly, the warning is that what is bad for Stockholm will be bad for Sweden. What is good for Stockholm, in this case, is building a lot of homes. Again, the idea of 'sustainable growth' covers over any conflict between building more homes and more city, on the one hand, and ensuring environmental and public health, on the other.

9.2.1 Discursive elements

The discourse of rapid urban growth – "a full bus every day" (Tottmar 2018) – portrays a kind of crisis mode of an ever-increasing population putting constant pressure on the urban fabric. This discursive frame makes it difficult to ask to preserve green areas or other 'unused' spaces without implicitly suggesting that new residents should not have homes to live in.

The 'problem' themes of too little transport work and too little urban space are both rooted in a discourse of determinism: the urban population is assumed to grow, and with it the need for homes and the number and distance of commutes. While this is simultaneously an aim, it is also a variant of the old 'predict and provide' model. The growing city is never represented or discussed as a dependent variable, effected by policies made by the national or local governments, only as a given. The discourse of determinism constructs the government – municipal, regional, or national – as powerless in the face of a development which functions as a natural law. The city is in this narrative not unlike a magnet, inexorably drawing subjects to it: only the inherent *pull* factors (the city's attractions or opportunity for work) drawing people to the city are acknowledged, while the *push* factors that might incite people to move from smaller towns and rural areas go unaddressed. Could anything be done to make non-urban life easier, better, and more feasible? Is this desirable? The material shows no signs that this is even a question. Instead, the representation is that it is up to the municipal government to predict and provide what is needed to adapt the city to the 'bus loads' of new residents coming in.

The debate concerning the housing crisis leaves out the fact that a rapidly growing population is an explicit target of the city (see e.g. Walkable City, p.

181

8; Vision 2030; City Plan 2018, p. 6). This explicit goal puts the representation of a helpless local government to question. My reading suggests that the 'predict and provide' model represented is rather a case of 'prescribe and provide': population growth is expected, and because it is desirable it is further enabled and encouraged through policy measures. The representation of a 'crisis' allows these measures to conflict with other aims, obscuring the political choice made to promote this development. The "full bus" analogy is also misleading, representing the population growth as due to influx from other parts of Sweden and a transfer of the population from rural areas to urban. Statistically, the population growth in Stockholm is primarily from newborns and immigration from abroad (SCB 2015; Stockholms läns landsting [SLL] 2018). Similarly, principles which are acknowledged to create transport, such as the free school choice (Roadmap, p. 40), are not questioned; the dense city is expected to reduce the transport demand by ensuring schools nearby. The many factors behind families' choice in schools (and other services) and the effects are in this way put aside, to be solved by a future dense city structure.

Parallel to the 'crisis mode' or urban growth is a discourse of urban excellency. The same way that the term 'climate smart city' links 'climate smart' to the urban, the 'walkable city' represents the inner-city as the ideal structure for human habitats. The continuous efforts to promote further urbanization of both the inner city and surrounding areas, through new homes and continued focus on the inner city of Stockholm as a site of culture and opportunity (e.g. Walkable City 2010), indicate a view that not only do more people want to live in the city, but they *should* want to – for sustainability's sake, and because the city is simply a better place to be.

The discursive frame of modernity which articulates 'sustainability' with 'growth' precludes critique against the perceived demand for continuous economic growth, as the silence surrounding the negative effects of economic growth and the attribution to economic growth of all social benefits makes it difficult to address those costs. This in turn makes it hard to question the priorities and calculations of policies and plans, for example the weights attributed to social gains (in travel times) and social costs (e.g. CO_2 emissions) of the Stockholm Bypass, and the starting assumption that commutes create benefit and should be promoted.

9.2.2 The subject

The problem representation of too little urban space assumes a willingly urban subject. The pressure of a growing population is taken as a sign of the city's excellence (ref), rather than of the difficulties of living rurally. The hinders to development brought on by appeals (i.e. 'Nimbyism') are frequently debated, and the shrinking space for playing children has been brought up in media (see the 2018 article series in DN on the reduction of green space; Ritzén 2018). The subject in transport is, through the division of modes into space-craving versus space-saving, at risk of being a space-craving egotist, who not only causes congestion but in doing so also hinders growth in the city and the country. The public transport user and the driver outside the city, meanwhile, become crucial pieces in the urban growth machine; parts of the labour force ensuring Stockholm's attraction to business and role as the growth engine of Sweden. The urban subject is depicted as highly educated and attractive on the labour market (e.g. *Vision 2030*). Those who do not meet these criteria, who do not have the same conditions of life, are described as a "labour reserve" which must be tapped into to safeguard future growth (Walkable City, p. 10). This (as with the representation of the problem as too little transport) constructs the subject as labour, and as a responsible or irresponsible consumer of transport.

The city itself is portrayed as more important for achieving sustainability targets than other parts of the country, and the implication is that if more people live in cities sustainable transport for all will be possible. Negative effects of such a scenario are not discussed.

9.2.3 Lived effects

The dense, walkable city aims to push together activities such as living, work, accessing services, and social activities. This is held to create conditions for sustainable transport and the kind of urban structure promoted as 'attractive'. However, whether this is the type of city residents want is uncertain. For example, in the southern district of Stockholm, Södermalm, there are frequent complaints from residents over noise from preschool children playing, church bells, and beer gardens (Jonsson 2018; Joelsson 2018; Thuresson Kämpe 2019). In a dense, mixed-function city, these types of noises can only be expected to increase. It is possible that new residential areas, often planned without adjoining play areas, will avoid at least this disturbance, but on the whole more people in a smaller area will mean more noises.

In Stockholm, as in many places, closeness to public transport raises the value of housing, especially when it comes to the metro. The new metro stations can be expected to increase value of housing near the extensions by as much as 1,300 SEK per square meter within a decade or so, according to realtors (e.g. Sköld 2013; Offentliga affärer 2013). Hemnet (2016) shows that commuter times are linked to housing values: the longer the commute from the city centre, the lower the value of a *bostadsrätt* (co-op housing) near that station. This suggests that while residents of Nacka, Hagastaden and Barkarby may see their homes worth more on the market, residents of Hagsätra – where the metro line will change designation colour from green to blue, adding about ten minutes to a commute to Södermalm – might see less benefit, unless the new nearness to Kungsträdgården and Nacka acts as counterweight.

While the new metro lines will allow some to make a bigger profit off their homes, this will also mean a greater barrier for others, with less money, to live near the city. The new metro can be assumed to bring further gentrification of many areas (a trait of the 'walkable city' and the urban nodes spreading the qualities of the inner-city), possibly making the city more inaccessible to many, rather than less. Thus, it is clear that the new metro extensions will have winners and losers: winners include those owning homes (especially apartments) near the planned extensions; losers include those who can no longer afford to live in or move to these areas (especially if market-regulated rent becomes a reality).

The urban imperative

Pragmatically, spending state funding on expanding urban areas means less funding for the non-urban. While this may be a rational and cost-efficient priority – see for example Börjesson (Dietl 2018) on the urban areas being able to provide more green transport (e.g. a shift from car use to public transport) per monetary unit due to population density – it does also mean that non-urban areas will fall behind on infrastructure investments, with the risk of 'green' transport choices becoming comparatively more difficult outside of cities.

The stress on the 'green' city and the value of urban space, and the encouragement for further car use outside of the city, coupled with the high costs of living within city limits (and the greater tendency of high-income residents to complain and appeal controversial projects, compared to low-income residents), further risks cementing the environmental injustices noted by e.g. Bradley et al. (2008). Strong measures are taken to reduce emissions within city limits while a highway for 200,000 cars is placed quite near lower-income residential areas of Hjulsta and Akalla. While the air quality in the inner city is lower than areas further out, due to the closely-placed houses preventing circulation, this does not negate the higher emission rates placed on densely populated and socio-economically vulnerable areas. If the pattern for the 'sustainable' city is to shift heavy traffic outside city limits, while housing costs within the 'green' city continue to rise, this will have implications for socio-economical justice.

One very important effect of the problem representation of too little urban space is the calls for reducing the possibility to appeal new construction (e.g. Rosenholm 2013). The right to appeal (for a limited selection) is a relatively new feature of citizen rights. Until 1960, citizens could partake of information about projects but had no say; after the hard protests of the 1970s against the construction of a metro entrance in a popular park – *Almstriden*, the Elm Battle – it became clear that clearer channels for citizen participation were necessary and it took until 1987 for the new Planning and Building Act to finally formalize how it should be done (see Zetterlund 2015 for a summary of the history of the right to appeal). A common reason for appeal is a desire to preserve green areas and playing areas, or to prevent a drastic change in 'identity' of an area, such as constructing high-rise buildings in an area of separate housing. Municipal government proposes to limit a citizen right, given after several decades of large-scale upheaval over which citizens had no say, in order to make construction of homes quicker and easier. In effect, residents are to have less say over their environment and their city. That it is typically high-income neighbourhoods who use the right (Falkirk 2017) does not necessarily mean that they complain too much; perhaps it is other residents who complain too little.

Another similar effect is the calls for easing regulations. In 2014, parliament proposed easing noise regulations, to allow for homes to be built in environments where noise from e.g. traffic exceeds national regulations; this is often cited as a way to build cheap homes for people who may not otherwise be able to afford an apartment (e.g. SVT 2015). More recently, the Centre Party of Stockholm proposes easing regulations concerning cultural- and natural values, such as shoreline protection preventing building close to waterfronts (Centre Party 2018), while both the Centre Party and the Moderate Party propose easing regulations to promote 'simpler' housing (Centre Party 2018; Moderate Party 2018).

The combination of these proposals might lead to the construction of houses providing lesser quality of life or which carry with them other issues or negative effects in relation to the surrounding areas. Limiting the right to appeal is in effect limiting granted citizen rights. Easing noise regulations means exposing more people to harmful noise, and also indicates that reducing noise in the city is not a priority. The National Board of Housing, Building and Planning (Boverket) stated in 2017 that "noise is no longer a hinder for the construction of housing" (Gunne 2017).

Some urbanites leave the cities for rural areas (e.g. Agö and Saberski 2016), either because the city becomes too expensive (Angvarson and Vennang 2019) or because they want a different kind of life. This trend is reported to be highest among families with children (Pirttisalo Sallinen and Videll 2019). A survey among 3,000 Swedes showed that one-third would like to live rurally, while another third would like to live in a small to medium-sized town (Bolander 2018; although the hard work of maintaining a house and garden may be discouraging; Bolander 2019). According to that survey, rural populations would be 50% larger if everyone who wanted to could live there. Further, given that the population growth in Stockholm is in large part due to births (SCB 2015; SLL 2018), a 'problem' could instead be a need to make the city more suitable for children, including play areas and a healthier environment.

10
'Sustainability' in Stockholm policy for transport

In Chapters 5–9, I discussed what kind of 'tool' was produced by Stockholm policy for transport, or what transport 'does' (both directly and as effects). Now I turn to my second research question to answer: how is sustainability constructed in policy for urban transport? In this chapter, I use my previous analysis from Chapters 5–9, as well as the explicit representations of sustainability from Stockholm policy, to discuss the problem representation regarding 'sustainability'. In this way, I map out how sustainability is constructed through policy.

10.1 Explicit representations of sustainability

Stockholm policy has no clearly set definition of what 'sustainability' is. *Walkable City* notes that, "concepts such as sustainable growth and sustainable development are problematic, because there are no set definitions and because they contain a number of inherent conflicts" (Walkable City, p. 11). This is perhaps due to the construction of 'sustainable development' as a process: "Social development and its long-term sustainability is largely a matter of a process, rather than a desirable future state" (Walkable City, p. 11). This is in reference to *Our Common Future*, the Brundtland Report, which states that, "sustainable development is not a fixed state of harmony, but rather a process of change in which the exploitation of resources, the direction of investments, the orientation of technological development, and institutional change are made consistent with future as well as present needs" (WCED 1987, p. 17). The same is cited in the *National Strategy for Sustainable Development* (Skr. 2001/02:172, p. 7), which goes on to posit humans and nature as "our most important resources" and the health of humans and natural and cultural environment as the limits for society of the future (Skr. 2001/02:172, p. 13).

Meanwhile, the 2012 budget for Stockholm states that "a sustainable urban development, and thereby a sustainable economic growth, cannot be regulated into existence" (Budget 2012, p. 3; my translation), and further asserts that "it's not about changing what we do, but how we do it" through cost-efficient technological innovation, in collaboration with business, academia, residents, organizations, and authorities (Budget 2012, p. 3; my translation). After the 2014 change in municipal government, budgets take a different tack, setting up four 'orientational aims' for "a Stockholm for everybody, where social, ecological, economic, and democratic sustainability are important components": A Stockholm which sticks together (Swedish: *håller samman*); A climate smart Stockholm; An economically sustainable Stockholm; A democratically sustainable Stockholm (Budget 2017, p. 4; my translation). Social sustainability here seems to have turned into "A Stockholm which sticks together", while ecological sustainability seems to have become 'climate smartness'.

'Sustainable development' is often replaced with 'sustainable growth'. For example, the *Walkable* City uses 'sustainable growth' (seventeen different uses) over 'sustainable development' (nine uses; five of those on the same page while presenting the national guidelines).[23] In *Walkable City*, the definition of sustainable development is presented with the following words:

> These types of goal-based documents [such as *Vision 2030* and the City Plan] all attempt to outline growth that is sustainable in the long term from an ecological, social and economic perspective (Walkable City, p. 11).

and,

> The proposed City Plan is based on Vision 2030 being the City of Stockholm's current definition of sustainable growth. When comparing this with the national strategy for sustainable growth, it is also clear that there is broad consensus between the documents. The proposals for planning aims and strategies in the City Plan also encompass the core areas and objectives for sustainable development as set out by the government (Walkable City, p. 11).

It is clear that the national strategy for "sustainable growth" is in fact Sweden's *National Strategy for Sustainable Development 2002* (Skr. 2001/02:172). The change might have been made simply as a matter of harmonizing the English text, but although the translation is likely to have little impact on decisions made, it is telling of the overall focus of municipal urban

---

[23] 'Sustainable/sustainability', with or without any suffix, is mentioned 61 times in the *Walkable City*; 18 times in the *Mobility Strategy*; six times in the *Roadmap*; five times in the *Action Plan for Climate and Energy 2012-2020*; 23 times in the *Action Plan for Climate and Energy 2012-2015*; 56 times in the *Environmental Programme 2012-2015*; and 36 times in the *Environmental Programme 2016-2019*. A search was made for in the Swedish document for the word *hållbar*, 'sustainable', which readily becomes *hållbarhet*, or 'sustainability', and so covers both phrases. All counts include headers and mentions of other documents.

policy. As for the *Vision 2030*, it has no delineated definition of 'sustainable growth', but under the header "An environmentally sustainable city" it states that by 2030,

Innovations have resolved many environmental problems, and the city is well on the way to achieving its goal of being fossil fuel-free by 2050. The actions that have been taken have reduced energy consumption significantly among both companies and residents. Almost exclusively, Stockholmers drive clean vehicles. Smart traffic solutions and information technology have increased accessibility and further reduced emissions. Many Stockholmers use public transport, when they do not choose to cycle instead. Environmentally sound methods and materials are used for all new buildings. Together with the City, Stockholm's companies have broadened the range of environmentally efficient housing. The region's population increase has had little or no effect on the local environment, making Stockholm an international role model (Vision 2030, p. 11).

And under the header "Urban policies for sustainable growth" one can read:

The Stockholm–Mälar region is of great importance for the whole of Sweden's economic growth. This requires that national policies have an urban perspective and consider the region's specific circumstances, with high costs for housing, premises and salaries, long travel times, complex decision-making processes and the risk of segregation. The municipal equalisation scheme must be modified, and the allocation of state funds for infrastructure must increase. It is also essential for state sector governance to become more flexible and harmonised, particularly for the application of planning and construction legislation and the Environmental Code (Vision 2030, p. 16).

From these two sections, 'sustainable growth' can be understood as a state of technological innovation, energy efficiency, economic growth, and an urban perspective in politics. What an "effect on the local environment" entails is uncertain, as it remains undefined; possibly it refers to the local traffic environment, or it is an umbrella term for effects left undiscussed. The last sentence of the second quote may refer to suggestions for easing legislation for new housing in Stockholm, in order to promote faster construction (e.g. Andersson 2016). In the *Walkable City*, 'sustainable growth' seems to be used interchangeably for both economic and urban growth and refer to growth which controls greenhouse gas emissions (Walkable City, e.g. p. 20) and promotes a 'good' living environment – preserving (or replacing) green areas (Walkable City, p. 20–21), spaces of cultural-historical importance, and other features considered part of the city's 'identity' and attraction

(Walkable City, p. 26 Swedish). As shown, preservation of green areas is granted lower priority than urban growth and cohesion (Walkable City, p. 45). The *Walkable City* (p. 22 Swedish) also states that a quick pace in construction of new homes is necessary for sustainable growth, suggesting a continuous fast-paced growth, in this case of population numbers. 'Sustainable growth' then seems to be a growth which can be met by urban development, such as construction of housing and new transport infrastructure.

Policy hinges environmental sustainability on technology and economic growth. For example, the *Vision 2030* (p. 6) asserts that, "technological development and economic growth provides good conditions for an environmentally sustainable society". This is an echo of the *National Strategy* (2001/02:172, p. 58), which states that economic growth which takes environpmental aspects into consideration creates resources to address environmental issues and can break the connection between economic development and environmental degradation.

In Stockholm policy related to transport (2007–2017), the process of sustainability is constructed as a process of growth and technological innovation, and the environmental concern largely focused on CO_2 emissions and efficienct land use. The aim of sustainability in the first case implies a condition of *un*sustainability as its starting point. The shift in focus from 'sustainable development' (implying a starting point of *un*sustainable development) to 'sustainable growth' implies that we currently have *un*sustainable growth. The focus in policy on measures believed to promote urban growth, an increase in transport use, and economic growth, implies that it is not the growth itself which is unsustainable, but rather that the conditions for growth are unable to 'keep up', yielding too little space (physical and metaphorical) for continued growth. In this way, Stockholm municipal policy constructs growth as crucial and underpromoted; there represented margins for error or reductions in economic growth are limited: commutes and construction of homes, both assumed to contribute to economic growth, are promoted through nearly all measures. The concepts 'sustainable growth' and 'climate smartness' reflect both this concern and the way that climate change concern is subsumed into the work to promote growth. Sustainability is explicitly described as contingent on economic growth (see e.g. the National Strategy for Sustainable Development), meaning that urban growth and an increase in transport work are held necessary for sustainable development. Within this conceptual framework, transport can be understood as a literal vehicle for progress and development, a means for an end too important to give up. A 'sustainable increase in transport' is, by this representation, any increase in transport. Sustainable transport is constructed to be that which enables more people to commute longer distances to work, creating more economic growth, on limited urban space and without significant increases in emissions. The contradiction between environmental sustainability and the commuter imperative, visible in for example CO_2 emissions, particle emissions, and noise, is to be addressed by collective transport, easiest provided in dense settlements.

That said, some increases in emissions are clearly acceptable. The contribution of the Stockholm Bypass to CO_2 emissions is written off as "under one percent" of total emissions from road transport (STA 2011; it is unclear which year this refers to). The emissions during construction of the Bypass and other roads, as well as of the new metro routes, are missing from policy and from the general discussion of these projects. The focus is on emissions from transport work, rather than the transport system as a whole. For the new metro, energy use and construction-related emissions of CO_2 equivalents are not estimated. They are expected to be "great" but offset by the increased possibility to travel by "energy efficient" public transport (SLL 2015, p. 32).

The National Strategy for Sustainable Development states that economic growth is a necessity for sustainable development, and the Planning and Building Law posits sustainable development and economic growth as equal requirements. This 'means to an end' status of economic growth will also naturally promote it over other benefits – if there can be no sustainability without economic growth, then lack of economic growth will be a threat to sustainability, and so economic growth will most likely be prioritized even if it involves unsustainable practices. These allowances construct margins for sustainability, implying that there is leeway for reaching climate targets and that they are not as challenging as explicitly stated.

Sustainability is explicitly and implicitly constructed to be an issue of technological development. It is represented to be a matter of climate change mitigation through emissions reductions, primarily through effectivization. The urban is represented as the solution to contradictions between social practices such as commutes or consumption, on the one hand, and environmental health on the other. While land use is explicitly represented as a sustainability concern, practice and policy text implicitly represent the preservation of green as less necessary for sustainability than extended urbanization. The possibility of compensating for the loss of green areas of ecological importance (Walkable City, p. 21) is one example of this. While it is outside the scope of this study, it is interesting to note that the 'quality' and importance of green areas are primarily assessed by human use (e.g. Walkable City, p. 20), disregarding other functions of urban green areas such as mitigation of climate impacts. The representation of sustainability in Stockholm policy for transport is, to sum up, a technocratic vision in which the aim is to find the right fuels, vehicles, and routes, while attention to social issues is limited. This depoliticizes sustainability, effectively cutting off alternative ways of structuring society.

11
Conclusions and discussion

In this chapter I first sum up and then discuss my findings in this study. I describe how I answered my research questions, and then expand on what implications the answers have for policy, transport, and sustainability in Stockholm. In this discussion I relate to previous research on how sustainable transport as a concept is understood, to modernization, and to the 'life puzzle'.

11.1 What kind of 'tool' is produced by policy for transport in Stockholm municipality?

I used the WPR framework to address my research questions: What kind of 'tool' is produced by policy for transport in Stockholm municipality? How is transport constructed, through proposed measures and discourse of policy concerning transport in Stockholm between 2007 and 2017? If transport is a 'solution', what is it a solution *to*? What forms of society and subject are produced by this construction of transport, and how does this relate to environmental issues?

To answer these questions, I used the WPR framework (Bacchi 2009; Bacchi and Goodwin 2016), starting with the question *What is the problem represented to be [in Stockholm municipal policy for personal transport between 2007 and 2017]?* In Chapter 5, I showed that the key problems represented in Stockholm policy for transport, through measures proposed, were 1) emissions caused by 'wrong' technology; 2) wrong choices made by individual transport users; 3) too little transport work; and 4) too little urban space. These are the main 'problems' the measures proposed combine to address. I reached these 'problems' by mapping the measures for transport proposed in policy, considering the directionality – or, in this case, directionalities – they formed together, and drawing out what these implied or represented as 'problems'.

Following this, I dug into the conceptual premises, the assumptions and preconceptions which 'made sense' of the main problem representations (the second question of the WPR framework). In Chapters 6–9, I showed that the conceptual premises related strongly to logics of modernization. The most prominent one was efficiency and technological development, with concepts such as 'smartness', 'green' technology to replace fossil fuels, capacity as a keyword, and space-saving modes of transport assumed to create the "walkable city". Another aspect was economic growth, as in the description of Stockholm as the "growth engine of Sweden", and the stress on a "sustainable increase" in transport held to promote economic growth. Lastly, policy stressed individual responsibility, for example, people making the 'right' choices in transport mode and time and avoiding "unnecessary" car use.

To analyse what what policy does *does* (after Foucault: "People know what they do; frequently they know why they do what they do; but what they don't know is what what they do does", in Dreyfus and Rabinow 1983, p. 187), I turned to the question of *effects* (question five of the WPR framework): which discursive effects, subjectification effects, and lived effects are produced by the problem representations in Stockholm municipal policy for personal transport?

My analysis showed that the problem representations were supported by discourses of modernization and efficiency, with a heavy focus on technological development and individual responsibility. This discursive frame draws attention from underlying factors behind mobility practices and disregards questions such as: how free are people to choose *if* they wish to commute? Within the discursive frame made by attention to *how* we travel and which technologies we use, and the construction of a 'crisis' on the roads and the housing market, it is meaningless to discuss alternatives to the commuter paradigm and the urban as the ideal. Thus, the discursive effect of the problem representations is to cover over or silence the possibility of other modes of society. Examples of families who have moved from cities to more rural areas to "step off the squirrel wheel" function to cement the individual's responsibility to choose and glossing over the barriers to such choices, such as workplace location or access to services outside urban areas.

Further, my analysis showed that the affirmation of the commuter paradigm, and the focus on individual responsibility in making the 'good' consumer choices, constitutes the subject as: 1) commuting labour, willing to go great distances for work, and valuable especially for this; 2) a consumer of transport modes, either 'responsible' or 'irresponsible'; and 3) ultimately responsible for the outcome of sustainability policies. This has the effect to downplay the role of the subject as a collective member. The subject is urban, a city dweller, but throughout policy, the *citizen* is missing. Subjects are transport users, or transport consumers – obtaining services to move them to work, to schools and afterschool activities, to *opportunities* – and pro-ducers of benefits in the form of economic growth through their labour which they perform thanks to commutes. But they are not constructed as democratic subjects who may participate in political life, or as people who may undertake a journey simply because there is pleasure in going some-where (although the 'necessary/unnecessary' binary strongly indicates journeys which are not useful to society). *Homo ludens* exists in the margins of transport policy, as someone who may journey from home to a sports facility, but not in the transport system itself. There is pressure on the indi-vidual to make the 'right' choice, at the same time as the pressure for long commutes will increase with the growing labour market. The subjectification of the subject as a consumer and ultimately responsible for the environment downplays the role of the state as a decisive environmental actor, and of societal change as a possible necessity, even as the conditions for commuter practices are set by the state and its partners in governance.

Finally, the discursive and subjectification effects, and the material impacts of the measures, combine to form several lived effects. First, the commuter paradigm (locked-in and expanded by measures for long-distance transport, such as the metro and the Bypass, as well as explicit aims for regional cohesion) and the construction of the subject as labour have proven effects on physical, social, and political health. Second, the con-struction of the urban 'crisis' as one of too little housing, as well as the subject as an urban resident, and of the urban as naturally preferable, combines with measures for densification to increase a crowding and overlap of functions: the city's recent growth has come with reductions in green areas and play areas (Ritzén 2018; KTH 2019), despite assertions to the contrary in policy. This means less space for children to play and develop necessary skills, and less space for recreation and exercise. It also means less greenery to shield from pollution, fewer trees to shelter from heat and bind water (both of which are likely to be even more important with climate change). A denser city will also, as with the cases of closing clubs, bring conflict between citi-zens. For new residents, clubs, church bells, and daycares may prove closer than convenient or comfortable, and for established residents the attractions of the city may seem to be 'sanitized'. Altogether, one might ask for whom the city is to grow, and for whose sake transport should increase.

The lived effects go beyond the experiences of us as individuals. They extend to effects on us as a collective, and to effects on the environment. As I touched upon, the 'housing crisis' discourse produces urban density, which reduces green areas. This means less space for local wildlife (such as birds, squirrels, or roe deer), and overall less CO_2 absorbed and less oxygen produced by greenery. The construction of the subject as a commuting worker, and the expansion of the commuter paradigm by both rail and road, increases energy use. Car use is expected to be higher after the Bypass is built (although emissions are expected to increase by less than one percent), which means more vehicles will be produced. Electricity for new metro and light rail must come from somewhere, while the south of Sweden has already seen energy shortages. The physical construction itself will impact on the environment both through land use and through use of materials and energy. The cohesion of the region, central to the commuter paradigm, rests not only on extending the transport system but on expanding the urban as well. This means more land used in regional cores to create 'urban qualities', and new exploitation along new routes for homes, services, and other buildings.

The modernization logic running through policy, coupled with the 'crisis mode' produced by the depiction of a housing shortage, obscures the possibility of other alternatives, in particular as relates to other modes of societal structure. As a 'solution' to not only CO_2e emissions but to congestion and the aim for a cohesive regional labour market as well, public transport has been entirely deproblematized. The demand for energy to run the new rail lines is briefly acknowledged in the Roadmap (p. 39), but the LCA supplement (that is, the additional CO_2e calculated for each sector based on a 'cradle to the grave' perspective on emissions) does not take into account vehicles nor roads (Roadmap, p. 48). The land use for the new rail lines is left entirely without discussion in policy. In addition, the city's growth is almost entirely deproblematized. The 'problems' raised in policy related to ensuring space for new residents – but the effects of that are not discussed. The 'housing shortage' and the 'growth engine' rhetoric set aside discussions of what a 'good' living environment is for residents.

All of this is not to deny the proposals for reducing emissions and increasing the use of other modes than private car. But I show, like others before me (e.g. Richardson et al. 2010; Dickinson et al. 2016; Hrelja 2019), that these proposals coexist with proposals to increase car use, which turns their directionality into a variation of the status quo rather than a cumulative directionality towards a new transport paradigm.

The focus on transport *work* over the transport *system* leads to a re-narrowing of the concept 'sustainable transport' (cf. Black and Sato) to focus primarily on climate aspects, which reduces attention to other sustainability aspects. Policy addresses the emission effects of transport work, but not the effects of the transport system on the environment nor society. Instead transport, or mobility, covers over the cracks and tensions produced by the contemporary social structure. The 'tool' constructed by transport policy is then a tool for both increased urbanization and continued commuting, and for upholding a wider social structure and diverting critique of this structure to discussions on how to make the structure function better. The increasing distances between home, work, and schools etc, and the pressures on especially women to carry out a housewife's daily tasks as well as a full-time job, are to be overcome by faster transport and a cohesive (that is, expanded) labour market, not by reducing the distances through localized social spheres or reducing hours spent at work. Policy does explicitly claim job cafés and internet services as a way to reduce 'unnecessary' journeys, and the tax deductions for domestic services are a way to remove (or outsource) some of the pieces of the 'life puzzle'. However, as stated in Chapter 7, there is no practical proposal for job cafés, and many jobs would not be possible to perform through these anyway. Outsourcing household work is simply another way to paper over the cracks in the 'life puzzle' and the stresses posed by the way that we live and work, instead of asking *why* apparently-integral parts of daily life are overly taxing and sometimes beyond us. A similar, and not too far removed, example is when a business brings in stress consultants to teach employees meditation or mindfulness, without asking why the whole staff is stressed. Expanding the transport system serves to help workers and consumers perform better, but does not serve to ease the stress of an expanded labour market and fragmented daily tasks.

The *Mobility Strategy* says it well: "A growing city with a healthy economy acquires the exact amount of traffic in peak hours for which the road capacity has been created" (Mobility Strategy, p. 30). But induced demand – that people use cars more the easier it is, often for journeys which were not previously made, which is both the basis for our contemporary car dependence and what is expected to come from the Bypass – should not only relate to individual roads. I argue that the entire transport system is one of induced demand, especially when coupled with centralization of production and other available workplaces. A city, or society, can expect to have the traffic for which the transport system and the economic system have been created.

Transport as a whole, with its strong shaping impact on mobility practices and human society, becomes a coercive force. Mobility, as noted by Söderström et al. (2013) is constitutive of bodies, subjectivities, materialities, economic resources, social positions, and organizational structures. Transport is not merely, and perhaps never truly was, a question of meeting expected demand according to the predict-and-provide model of planning. It is a strongly visionary project for society as a whole. This is very clear in both *Vision 2030* and *The Walkable City*, but also in other policy documents and in the overall discussion of transport in Stockholm. To say under these circumstances that the transport system merely operates to meet a 'need' (for mobility, for a place in the city, for 'opportunities'…) is to deny the strongly shaping effect it has on society and our lives – that is, to deny the political power that is inherent in transport planning. This political force does not just relate to questions of sustainable choices, but to how society should function. Transport and mobility both enable and coerce. As Shove notes on the impact of faster transport, being able to perform our tasks faster simply meant that the social norm became to perform *more* tasks. Faster connections are not built to shorten our daily commutes, but to allow (or require) us to travel longer distances.

11.2 How is sustainability constructed?

To answer my second research question, "how is sustainability constructed in Stockholm policy for transport 2007–2017?", I looked at what measures were proposed for transport and what these implied (Chapters 5–9) and how sustainability was explicitly discussed and described (Chapter 10). In Chapters 5–10 I showed that sustainability is constructed to be urban, largely a question of technology, and intrinsically tied with urban and economic growth. In Chapter 10 I confirmed these implicit representations. I found that the construction of sustainability in the material is strongly rooted in modernization: faith that urban, technical, and economic development will address social and environmental issues; favouring of economic and technical solutions; focus on the urban, as well as on economic growth; and dependency on individual choices as well as (seemingly paradoxically) large-scale solutions. As there are no recognized limits (explicit or implicit) to either transport increase, energy use, or urban growth, my conclusion is that the use of 'sustainable growth' for 'sustainable development' is very much representative of the construction of sustainability. Sustainability is explicitly described as contingent on economic growth. Urban growth and an increase in transport work – described as contributors to economic growth – are then constructed as necessary for sustainable development. This 'means to an end' status of economic growth will naturally promote it over other benefits – if there can be no sustainability without economic growth, then lack of economic growth will be a threat to sustainability, and so economic growth will be prioritized even if it involves unsustainable practices.

Figure 11.1: Homo ludens. Addition to a pavement symbol by unknown artist. Picture by author, 2019-07-07.

Sustainable transport by definition of this construction is then transport which enables more people to move over larger areas, but more efficiently in use of space and fuel. The focus in policy, when it comes to environmental effects, lies largely on the effects of transport work. This is first and foremost greenhouse gas emissions, but also other harmful emissions as well as congestion and noise (Walkable City, p. 22), and various kinds of runoff (Environment programme 2012–2015, p. 7). The environmental effects of roads and rail themselves, such as lower albedo, construction-related emissions, energy use, and disruption of plant and animal life are not discussed. These effects are of course discussed in strategic environmental assessments (barring albedo, as far as I have been able to find), but it is interesting and telling that they are not brought up as part of the more overarching discussion of what the sustainable city and sustainable transport should be and do, and it supports my analysis that focus is on transport *work* over the transport *system*. The only recognized negative effect of the transport system itself is physical barriers between areas, making movement between parts of the city difficult (Walkable City, pp. 19, 22). The environment, in policy, becomes limited to climate concerns and what affects humans. This limitation of focus implies that only transport work affects the environment, and that the effects of building new transport routes rests solely on the vehicles using them. Consider, for instance, that the Stockholm Environment Barometer (*Miljöbarometern*) states that to reach emissions targets by 2020, CO_2e emissions must be reduced with 533,000 tons annually (Stockholms stad 2018f). At the same time, the construction phase of the Stockholm Bypass is expected to emit 570,000 tons over ten years (STA 2015a), or just over 10% of the necessary annual CO_2e emissions reduction. Consider also that the *Roadmap* (p. 48) limits its life-cycle analysis to fuels.

There is a built-in contradiction in the construction of sustainability in Stockholm municipal policy measures for transport of people. The key focus is on climate issues, but at the same time increased car use outside city limits is not constructed as a 'problem' which policy needs to address (despite the fact that the atmosphere does not care where CO_2 emissions originated). This constructs climate issues as a secondary concern to urban space, and de facto subordinates the key sustainability issue explicitly addressed in policy to urban growth and congestion reductions. I cannot based on my material make statements about intention or conscious strategies, but the impression left by my analysis is that climate is used rhetorically to lend weight to policies founded on concerns about human health or congestion.

11.2.1 Sustainability as urban

Politicians, civil servants, and researchers agree that urban regions have great potential for sustainable transport, as the concentrations of people make possible for cost-effective and high-service supplies of public transport. The construction of 'sustainable transport' implies that since the negative environmental impacts of transport are clear and due to inefficient or [bad] use of technology; and these inefficiencies are easiest solved in cities, where a greater concentration of people makes it easier to replace the private car with large-scale solutions, primarily public transport; ergo, more people should live in urban environments, where they can be provided with public transport or convinced to use bicycles. This, however, assumes that we should continue to commute long (or longer) distances to work, which in turn assumes certain types of work (or, rather, disregards work done from or close to home, such as care work, small-scale production, or art) and a labour market where living close to work is either unattractive, too expensive, or unfeasible (as in sectors where one's place of work may change frequently).

The concept of the 'smart city' constructs sustainability as an urban affair. Even though the urban is typically described as a kind of testing ground for sustainability measures and a cost-effective site to reduce emissions by shifting a lot of people over to public transport or non-motorized modes (e.g. Börjesson in Dietl 2018), measures such as the Stockholm Bypass and the much-debated and currently paused Eastern link show that sustainable solutions are not to be perfected in the city for better or cheaper implementation outside the city, or even implemented to reduce emissions overall. Rather, the extra-urban is to maintain and extend business-as-usual car practices for the convenience of the city. The many references to the bypasses as a means to move urban traffic show that the extra-urban is to pick up undesirable urban traffic and act as a sink for transport work that is incompatible with a green, climate-smart city. In this way Stockholm municipal policy constructs the extra-urban as not only irrelevant to sustainability work (as suggested in Chapter 6) but also as less affected by negative effects of the transport system – and the emissions of greenhouse gasses as being contingent on *where* they occur, with car transport work outside the city being represented as contributing less to climate change.

Consider for example the Stockholm Bypass. The highway will make it easier to use a car to, from, and past suburbs, while other policies serve to make car use to, from, and through Stockholm city more difficult. This constructs the 'green' (meaning to a larger extent car-free) inner-city, while simultaneously constituting suburbs such as Hjulsta and Akalla (where incomes are lower and public transport use is higher than in nearby single-house suburbs, and where the Bypass will run some 250 meters from tenement buildings) as less 'green'. In particular the placement of the intersection between the highway E18 and the Stockholm Bypass (which is predicted to carry some 300,000 cars through the area daily) so close to such a densely populated area represents this suburb in stark contrast to the 'climate smart' city.

Dividing the city into inner city and outer city/region allows for a dual characterization of the city as modern and sustainable, as both green and a growth engine. Public transport investments inside the city borders, complete with car-free streets, allows Stockholm to portray itself as the green ideal, while leading cars around the city allows it to maintain the mobility necessary for economic growth and regional development, as well as expand city borders and labour market. This duality allows modernization and sustainable development to coexist, seemingly peacefully. From a justice perspective, however, it might be said that the city proper is made green at the expense of the recipients of ring roads and bypass traffic.

The construction of the climate smart city, which stresses the sustainability of the urban and the urbanity of sustainability, coupled with the explicit aim of drawing more people into urban areas, imply that the problem is to be solved by individuals moving in to urban areas where they can be provided with efficient transport systems. Reports of urban CO_2e emissions and resource use have long excluded the effects of long-distance travel and consumer goods produced beyond municipal borders, reinforcing the reading of the ex-urban as less relevant (e.g. Action Plan 2012–2015, p. 7; Roadmap, p. 9). I acknowledge the practical reasons for this, but as these numbers are available – e.g. from the Swedish Environmental Protection Agency – I argue that excluding them is a choice with real effects.

11.2.2 Sustainability as growth

The overarching 'problem' represented in policy – explicitly stated in some, implied by the measures proposed in others – is that the city in not big enough, does not hold a large enough number of citizens, and furthermore that the surrounding region is insufficiently urban, populated, and connected via infrastructure. The focus on growth as an aim – the stress on developing the urban region, on cohesion, on extending commuter services – implies its opposite, the presumed negative alternative: stagnation.

The represented problems and conceptual premises represent the main focus in Stockholm policy for transport as economic growth (through commutes, through mobility) and urban growth (through space-saving measures and extensions of the urban area). A great deal of the concern with space is more about making space for *more* residents than making life better for current ones – see, e.g., constructing new homes on green areas (or instating a nature reserve but set aside space for 1,000 homes, citing a "housing crisis")

The base assumption is that the region must grow. Not only that it will, but that it *should*. It is described both as inevitable and as something to encourage, as is the case in *Walkable City*. The concern for city planners and policy makers is how to reduce the harmful effects of that growth (e.g. from car use, p. 45). The tone of the *Mobility Strategy* suggests an end to the "car first" planning that started in the 1950s–1960s (when the political agenda was that every household should own a car, and policy-makers took in American examples as ideals). However, this impression wears off somewhat when one looks at plans for the Stockholm Bypass, the completed Norra länken, and the eastern bypass currently discussed. Then it becomes clear that the city has simply run out of space to host a car for every individual – but outside of city borders, or beneath the streets, the car is still to be made welcome. Under the auspices of the 'housing crisis', the densification of the city becomes impossible to question without accusations of nimbyism and "wishing to keep young people homeless" (pick a letter from readers).

Sustainability is both explicitly and implicitly hinged upon economic growth (e.g. National Strategy for Sustainable Development). Given the construction of sustainability and 'climate smartness' as urban, it is perhaps logical that urban growth is constructed as a necessity for sustainability. The equation of 'sustainable development' with 'sustainable growth' shows that 'development' is understood as 'growth', and that sustainability cannot in this context be understood as a need to halt or scale back urban- or economic growth. With the construction of the transport system and transport practices as something which can and should continue to expand for the sake of a growing labour market and economy, Stockholm municipal policy does not in practice recognize limits to the urban shape, to the economy, or to energy use. The construction of growth as necessary for sustainability means that undesirable effects of growth do not carry as much weight as they otherwise might. In a sense, the Kutznet's curve is still at play, assuring that a little damage now can be remedied later as the economy allows. One might ask, however, how the use of green areas for urban expansion is to be remedied in the future. It seems more plausible to expect a continued expansion as long as this is held to bring benefits that outweigh the environmental and human health costs, and that a reversal of this cost-benefit relation will bring other costs (such as health costs, floods, or fires) that make compensation for environmental losses prohibitively expensive.

11.2.3 Sustainability as a piece of your life puzzle

The focus on growth as the responsibility of the municipal government, and the stress on the need for individuals to 'make better choices', places the responsibility for environmental sustainability – including the efficacy of measures to reduce CO_2e emissions – with the individual. The subject here is a consumer, either 'conscious' or 'irresponsible'. This individualization of responsibility, together with the focus on the regionally cohesive labour market which constructs the subject as a worker, means that sustainability efforts become one of the tasks that the individual should fit in their private life puzzle. In one sense, this shifts some of the responsibility back onto the state: efficient transport to simplify people's lives is the task of the state, as are the subsidies for electric cars and bicycles.

For the individual, however, the life puzzle is a concept which rests on the political shift from shorter work days or -weeks as an issue on the agenda, to higher wages in compensation for labour as a political goal (Enoksson 2009; 2011). This cements the subject as a worker and a consumer: the individual gets not more leisure time for life but more money for labour. Work hours as a political question is off the agenda, like questions of other ultimate goals of society and other social structures/models. In the aim for growth, the life puzzle is much more politically palatable than re-politicizing work time. Within the life puzzle framework, the focus is on measures of modernization: tax deductions for those who can afford to employ domestic services (Swedish: *RUT-avdrag*) and infrastructure for faster journeys (not fewer or shorter). There is considerably less attention to the structures which make it difficult to balance work, children, family, interests, health, etc, as well as to the ability of people to partake in political life and establish social cohesion, which is often discussed as in problematic decline (e.g. Walkable City, pp. 8, 16). This means that sustainability – or more accurately, consumption of sustainable choices – is hinged upon personal income and competes with other puzzle pieces over the space left next to work. It also reduces the communal aspects of the Brundtland Report. Failure to produce sustainability rests with the individual, the irresponsible consumer, who did not walk the straight and narrow path laid out by subsidies and charges. Calls and mani-festations for political responsibility for environmental issues, most notably Greta Thunberg's long strike for the climate which has engaged people of all ages and spread globally, highlight that many people wish not only for more collective policy, but also for political involvement.

11.3 Approaching transport as a governing tool

The most pressing conclusion I draw from my work is the need to recognize the possibility of alternatives. The material represents as inevitable the development of ever-more urban growth and ever-more transport (that is, transport work and expansion of the transport system). This relates to the understanding of economic growth as a) necessary for welfare and well-being, and b) created through work, in turn represented to create higher value when combined with long commutes. The growing scales of produc-tion and consumption, which rely on commutes and global trade routes, make for systems less able to adapt to new circumstances (see e.g. Wells et al. 2012 on regime stability in the automotive industry). That is, the larger the system, the more vulnerable. This perspective is lacking in transport policy in Stockholm. In policy, climate mitigation (reducing emissions) is used as a motivation for intense urbanization, but climate adaptation is missing. There is a lock-in of practices to the high-mobility paradigm which makes change – whether for sustainability purposes or because people sim-ply do not want to commute that much – not only difficult but also unthink-able. The notion of a "sustainable increase in transport" is a strong example of this: a continuous increase in transport (work and system) is so en-trenched in the social system that when sustainability measures are addres-sed these must come with further growth.

The depoliticization of transport policy, a result of the technical-rational perspective on transport and the notion of policy as a neutral response to naturally existing problems, means that this lock-in happens outside of the democratic process. While the Stockholm Bypass and congestion tax have been debated as election issues, the question *should we continue to strive for an urbanized commuter society?* has so far not made election posters. The question has been *how* we should continue to strive for an urbanized com-muter society. This has significant effects on who we can be as people in this society, how we live and what we can do, and what state the environment (local and global) may be in. Yet transport, the "backbone" of society, remains largely depoliticized. There is a strong and urgent need to introduce a recognition of alternatives, not only in transport modes but in the way that we should collectively live our lives. By doing so, transport and transport policy can be more deeply politicized, and different forms and goals of sustainability can be recognized and brought onto the agenda. Hysing (2009) observes politicization of urban transport as key to the successful integration of sustainability aims into policy; I add that the form of sustainability and what is produced by it should also be treated as inherently political topics.

Through this study, I add to the field of sustainable transport studies the re-politicizing attention to policy as a creative process of the *What's the problem represented to be?* approach. In doing so, I build upon the work of Hysing (2009), Hilding-Rydevik et al. (2011), Henriksson (2014), Richardson et al. (2010), Hrelja (2009, 2019), Isaksson et al. (2017), and others to expand on the understanding of transport and transport policy as more than a technical-rational issue. I re-conceptualize transport – transport work and the transport system – as a governing tool, studied best as a unit (rather than in its separate parts). The WPR framework has permitted me to view transport as more deeply connected to society and social practices (borrowing from mobilities studies, e.g. Söderström et al. 2013, and Shove and Trentmann 2018), and consider a wide range of implications.

The observations of my analysis, which show that policy represents transport as an issue of efficiency and individual choices, and sustainability as urban and a matter of growth, correspond with previous findings. Studies by e.g. Isaksson (2006) and Hilding-Rydevik et al. (2011) show the prevalence of ecological modernization as the active form of sustainability in transport policy and planning. My study shows that this logic is echoed in problem representation and subjectification, and has real and significant lived effects on people, human society, and natural environments. The WPR framework has then shown useful for not only drawing out logics or representations in policy, but also for getting at what is produced by these. This addition of a more human-focused form of effects – primarily the subjectification and lived effects – is the most valuable contribution that using this framework makes to sustainable transport studies.

Continued research

In this dissertation I have identified the representations of problems in Stockholm policy for transport of people 2007–2017 and discussed the conceptual premises which make sense of them as well as some effects. Both the analytical model and the empirical field provide ample source for continued study.

What I have not addressed in this study is *why*. Drawing on Sheller's (2014) suggestion that the emotional attachments to the car ("automotive emotions") can form a barrier to personal change, I propose exploring the affective aspects of policy for transport. If, as I have shown, reducing mobility (i.e. transport use) is unthinkable, what about mobility and increase in transport is it that grips us? Throughout my study I have seen elements of these emotions, as when the Chamber of Commerce warned that "without the Stockholm Bypass, Stockholm will stop". One way of looking at it is that without elaborated alternatives for a future, these projects may seem like the only way forward. Alternatively, it would also be relevant to study what it is about sustainability that grips us – or fails to, based on my findings in this study that growth aspects are represented as carrying a stronger sense of urgency. This kind of work would not answer the policy process form of 'why', in which actors, networks, or interests are considered. Rather, it would consider the ways that we as humans are affected by our emotions, and how these emotions relate to our perception and understanding of the world. This, in turn, means that affective content can work to regulate our behaviour as well as our thoughts on issues. This angle would link to some of the WPR questions which were not relevant for this study, especially that of the ways that the current problem representation(s) could be disrupted or altered. Studies such as Hilding-Rydevik et al. (2011), Pettersson 2014, and Isaksson et al. 2017 have shown that we know better than we do – that is, the stated aims are not reflected in practice. Remling (2019, forthcoming) has explored the important role of affectively charged content in policy discourses to explain that 'gap'.

For a broader understanding of transport as a governing tool, I see a need to perform a similar analysis for transport of goods. Goods transport, as well as transport of waste, fuels, and other materials, have enabled a global economic system as well as a deep-running separation of operations which is cemented in distance.[24] We not only can, but frequently must, consume produce grown across the globe, or clothes sewn in factories we will never even glimpse. Transport of goods have also enabled an expectancy of near-instant satisfaction of material desires. In my material, the role of goods transport as a cornerstone of the economic system, i.e. economic growth, appears to render it exempt from critique. The space-craving/space-saving

---

[24] See for example industrial meat production: food for animals is produced in one location and shipped to the farm, from which animal waste is shipped for use in food production or for destruction, and from which animals are shipped for slaughter. This kind of broken nutrient cycle is possible only with our contemporary transport system.

binary, discussed in Chapter 9, applies only to people, not to goods transport, which are represented as 'necessary'. Goods transport cannot, by definition of the graph in *Mobility Strategy*, be space-craving (there is, however, some aims for more efficient distribution of goods in policy). If one goes into detail, this means that accessibility services and sick transport can be space-craving, but delivery of cheap goods from far away consumed via web shops is not (and web shops is one way to reduce 'unnecessary transport' in text; Mobility Strategy, p. 3). While the *Roadmap* proposes measures for making goods transport more efficient (primarily increasing joint loading, although this is indicated to conflict with just-in-time delivery), the *Mobility Strategy* (p. 62) proposes an aim to "satisfy" freight companies. An obvious and relevant continuation of this study would then be to study what 'problems' these measures represent and how they relate to the 'problems' represented by measures for transport of people. How has the transport system for goods impacted the structures of society and cities, as well as our daily lives and what subject positions are available to us? And on what premises does this transport system rest?

12
Populärvetenskaplig sammanfattning
(Summary in Swedish)

Den här avhandlingen i miljövetenskap handlar om policy för persontransporter i Stockholm, med fokus på hållbarhet. Forskning om transportpolicy är ofta tekniskt inriktad, fokuserad på att utvärdera olika verktyg utifrån satta mål eller på att utreda hur olika åtgärder bäst kan implementeras eller mål kan uppnås. Policy hanteras i den typen av studier som ett neutralt och rationellt medel för att lösa befintliga problem. I den här avhandlingen studerar jag istället transportsystemet som en sorts styrning som får effekter inte bara på hur vi rör oss, utan också på vilken sorts samhälle vi kan leva i och vilken sorts person vi kan vara i det samhället. Utifrån Carol Bacchi's ramverk What's the problem represented to be? (på svenska ungefär Vad representeras problemet vara?) ser jag policy som något som konstruerar, eller representerar, problem genom att föreslå åtgärder. Långt från att se en åtgärd som något neutralt, teknisk eller rationellt, ser jag förslag på åtgärder som förankrade i antaganden om hur världen är och hur världen borde vara. Jag har valt en diskursiv ansats. Det betyder att orden och bilderna i policy skapar mening, men också att själva åtgärderna som föreslås bär och skapar mening. I kapitel 4 beskriver jag mer ingående min syn på policy, diskurs och kritik och hur jag bygger upp mitt teoretiska och metodologiska ramverk.

I början av min studie ställer jag mig frågorna:

1. Vilken sorts 'verktyg' skapas genom policy för transporter i Stockholms stad?

   a) Hur konstrueras transporter, genom förslag på åtgärder och diskurser i policy för persontransporter i Stockholm 2007–17. Om transport är en lösning, vad är det en lösning på?

   b) Vilka former av samhälle och subjekt skapas av denna konstruktion av transporter och hur relaterar detta till miljöfrågor?

2. Hur konstrueras hållbarhet i Stockholm stads styrdokument för persontransporter 2007–2017?

   a) Vilken är den explicita konstruktionen av hållbarhet – hur beskrivs och diskuteras hållbarhet?

   b) Vilken är den implicita konstruktionen av hållbarhet, genom de åtgärder som föreslås för transporter medan 'hållbar utveckling' är ett erkänt mål och ideal?

I min analys har jag utgått från åtgärder för transporter som presenterats i elva olika styrdokument från Stockholms stad mellan 2007 och 2017. Var och en av dessa åtgärder representerar ett problem: varje 'lösning' antar en sorts problem, på samma sätt som svaret i Jeopardy antar en särskild fråga. Dessa representerade problem är inte nödvändigtvis desamma som de uttalade problem som diskuteras. I kombination med andra åtgärder kan också en åtgärd representera en annan sorts problem. I kapitel 5 går jag igenom de olika åtgärderna och vad de betyder för sig och i kombination. Till exempel representerar trängselskatten i Stockholm ett problem med för många bilar som inte betalar för sin närvaro innanför trängselskattens gränser. Tillsammans med att trängselskatten vigts åt att finansiera ny infrastruktur, först Förbifart Stockholm och sedan den nya tunnelbanan, representeras dock ett problem med otillräcklig finansiering av infrastruktur – och som en logisk följd ett problem med för lite infrastruktur, det vill säga för lite transportarbete. Den nya tunnelbanan i sig representerar ett problem med för lite kollektivt resande; i kombination med krav på tusentals bostäder där ny tunnelbana dras representeras också ett problem med för lite stadsbebyggelse.

Sammantaget representerar de åtgärder som föreslås i materialet fyra övergripande slags problem: Utsläpp orsakade av fel teknik; Fel beslut av enskilda trafikanter; För lite transportarbete; För lite stadsutrymme. Var och en av dessa problemrepresentationer stöttas av olika antaganden. Var och en av dessa problemrepresentationer bär också med sig olika effekter: diskursiva, subjektskapande och levda. I kapitel 6–9 går jag igenom antaganden och effekter för varje övergripande representerat problem, ett kapitel för varje problem.

Jag analyserar antaganden genom att leta efter hierarkier eller motsattsförhållanden (engelska: binaries), kategorier (categories) och koncept eller nyckelord (concepts, keywords). Dessa olika typer av begrepp bidrar på olika sätt till att stötta och ge mening åt problemrepresentationen genom att förenkla en fråga eller koppla ihop den med vissa typer av värden. I materialet är problemrepresentationerna starkt kopplade till en bild av teknik som både problem och lösning (kap. 6), individualisering av ansvaret för miljöfrågor (kap. 7), tilltro till ökande arbetspendling som motor för ekonomisk tillväxt (kap. 8) och en idealisering av staden som lösning.

I samma kapitel analyserar jag också effekterna av problemrepresentationerna. Diskursiva effekter handlar om vad som kan och vad som inte kan sägas (utan att låta som nonsens) inom ramarna de skapar. För att finna dessa börjar jag med att titta på de antaganden som stöttar representationerna. Jag undersöker också vad som inte problematiseras i problemrepresentationerna: vad som presenteras som oproblematiskt. I materialet bidrar fokuset på individens val och teknik som lösning och problem till att en utesluta en diskussion om strukturer och olika samhällsformer, som möjliga bidragande orsaker eller lösningar. Transporter i sig – särskilt arbetspendling – och kollektivtrafiken avproblematiseras genom fokus på bilars negativa effekter och kollektivtrafikens yteffektivitet. Även om den förra översiktsplanen heter Promenadstaden och möjligheten att bo, arbeta och sköta vardagen till fots ofta nämns, finns det så gott som inga reella förslag för att skapa detta.

Subjektskapande effekter (engelska, subjectification) handlar om vilka vi som personer – subjekt – kan vara. Vilka roller skapas för oss att fylla, vilken sorts person beskrivs i dokumenten och vem verkar åtgärderna vara till för att styra eller hjälpa? De övergripande problem som representeras i materialet skapar framförallt det arbetspendlande subjektet: vi som personer är framförallt pendlande arbetskraft. Vi kan också vara medvetna eller självviska konsumenter (av olika transportslag, fordon eller bränslen). Den sociala och politiska människan saknas i materialet. Nöjesåkning, lokalt deltagande, de

211

delar av livet som ofta krockar med 'livspusslet' – dessa aspekter saknas när åtgärder för transporter och staden är inriktade på snabbare men längre transporter.

Levda effekter är den sammantagna effekten av de praktiska åtgärderna, de diskursiva effekterna och de subjektskapande effekterna. Dessa effekter handlar ofta om människor och våra kroppar, men kan också handla om miljöeffekter. I Stockholm bidrar avproblematiseringen av 'gröna' bilar till ett ökat tryck på produktionen av 'gröna' bränslen, vilket bland annat bidrar till avskogning i Skellefteå för en ny batterifabrik. Fokus på ökande transportarbete, i kombination med trycket på nya bostäder, leder till brytning av skogs- och jordbruksmark kring Stockholm, som på Lovö och Järvafältet för Förbifart Stockholm, och i Nacka för nya stationer och bostäder. Skiftet från bevuxen mark till bebyggd mark, i kombination med själva byggarbetet och det ökande transportarbetet, bidrar till ökade koncentrationer av växthusgaser i atmosfären. Skapandet av subjektet som pendlande arbetskraft kommer troligen att förstärka de negativa effekter av pendling som tidigare forskning redan visat. Avsaknaden av förståelse för subjektet som social, politisk och lekande människa gör också att dessa aspekter av våra liv på ett verkligt och negativt sätt försvinner när 'livspusslet' ska läggas.

Sammantaget konstrueras transporter som ett verktyg för att försörja näringslivet med arbetskraft och för en ökande stadsbyggnad i och utanför Stockholm (se mer i kap. 11). Hållbarhet konstrueras explicit som beroende av (ibland synonymt med) ekonomisk tillväxt, ett medel som därmed konstrueras som ett överordnat och sårbart ändamål (kap. 10). Enligt denna konstruktion kan ingen hållbarhet skapas utan ekonomisk tillväxt; därför kan negativa effekter på hållbarhetsmarkörer godtas för att främja ekonomisk tillväxt. Implicit konstrueras hållbarhet som urban – se till exempel begreppet 'klimatsmart stad' (kap. 6) – och staden som särskilt relevant för hållbarhetsmålen. Detta konstruerar samtidigt det som inte är stad som mindre relevant för hållbarhetsmålen, vilket kan leda till att stadens intressen väger tyngre än andra behov. Hållbarhet konstrueras också som synonymt med tillväxt, såväl ekonomisk som urban. Detta leder till att hållbarheten frikopplas från gränser: vare sig det gäller energi- eller resursförbrukning, hur långt staden ska växa, eller hur långt den ekonomiska tillväxten kan upprätthållas. Slutligen konstrueras hållbarhet som en del av individens livspussel. Då hållbarhet görs till en fråga om 'bra' eller 'dålig' teknik och subjektet till arbetare och konsument blir hållbarheten en fråga att lösa parallellt med arbete, barnhämtning, mathandling och andra vardagssysslor. Hållbarheten är genom dessa konstruktioner avpolitiserad, gjord till en fråga om 'smarta val' som inte kräver någon större förändring i vårt sätt att leva. Samtidigt visar rörelsen Fridays for future / Skolstrejk för klimatet ett växande stöd för att göra klimatfrågan just politisk – en fråga för politiker.

Denna avhandling kommer inte med några svar på hur transporter borde vara för att bli hållbara. Det jag föreslår är ett annat sätt att se på transporter: som en starkt styrande kraft i samhället med konsekvenser inte bara för hur snabbt vi kan åka från punkt A till punkt B, utan för hur vi lever med oss själva, varandra och resten av planeten.

13

References

2001/02:172. *Regeringens skrivelse 2001/02:172. Nationell strategi för hållbar utveckling.*

2013/14:SkU24. *Skatteutskottets betänkande 2013/14:SkU24. Förändrad trängselskatt och infrastruktursatsningar i Stockholm.*

Agö, J. and E. Saberski, 2016. "Därför ratade vi storstaden för landet", *KIT*, 2016-01-22. Available at: <https://kit.se/2016/01/22/31900/darfor-ratade-vi-storstaden-for-landet/ > [accessed 2019-09-20].

Ahmed, S., 2006. *Queer Phenomenology. Orientations, objects, others.* Duke University Press, Durham and London.

Andersson, O., 2016. "M: Stockholm bör få undantag i byggregler", *Sveriges television*, 2016-04-14. Available at: <https://www.svt.se/nyheter/lokalt/stockholm/m-stockholm-bor-fa-undantag-i-byggregler> [accessed 2019-02-25].

Angvarson, E. and J. Vennang, 2019. "Barnfamiljerna flyr länet – "dyrt att bo här" tycker pappa Henrik", *Mitt i*, 2019-07-21. Available at: <https://mitti.se/nyheter/bostad/ barnfamiljerna-lamnar-lanet/?omrade=haninge> [accessed 2019-09-20].

Ankersjö, P., 2013. Panel talk. Stora Transportdagen, 2013-04-17.

Bacchi, C. and S. Goodwin, 2016. *Poststructural policy analysis. A guide to practice.* Palgrave Macmillan, New York.

Bacchi, C., 2009. *Analysing Policy: What's the Problem Represented to Be?* Pearson Australia.

Bacchi, C., 2014. *WPR Workshop.* Online resource, University of Adelaide. Available at https://www.adelaide.edu.au/carst/online-modules/wpr/ [accessed 2019-01-25].

Backman 2017. "Pendlingens pris är högt", *Göteborgs-Posten*, 2017-02-03. Available at: <http://www.gp.se/livsstil/h%C3%A4lsa/pendlingens-pris-%C3%A4r-h%C3%B6gt-1.4143579> [accessed 2019-09-19]

Bang, D. and C. D. Frith, 2017. "Making better decisions in groups", *Royal Society Open Science*, Vol 4(8): 170193.

Banister, D., 2000. "Sustainable urban development and transport – a Eurovision for 2020", *Transport Reviews*, Vol 20:1, pp. 113–130.

Banister, D., 2008. "The sustainable mobility paradigm", *Transport Policy*, Vol. 15, pp. 73–80.

Bartolini, L., F. le Clercq and L. Kapoen, 2005. "Sustainable accessibility: a conceptual framework to integrate transport and land use plan-making. Two test-applications in the Netherlands and a reflection on the way forward", *Transport Policy*, Vol. 12, pp. 207–220.

Bauman, Z., 2000. *Liquid Modernity.* Polity Press, Cambridge.

Bemelmans-Videc, M. L., R. C. Ris and E. O. Vedung (eds.), 2011. *Carrots, Sticks, and Sermons: policy instruments and their evaluation.* Transaction Publishers, New Jersey.

Berglund, L., 2016. "Stockholm tar ockerpris för parkering", *Dagens Nyheter*, 2016-10-28. Available at: <https://www.dn.se/asikt/stockholm-tar-ockerpris-for-boendeparkering/ > [accessed 2019-03-07].

Bjarnestam, J., 2011. *En hållbar trafiklösning för nya Slussen? Uppfattningar om hållbarhet och hållbar stadsutveckling i Slussenprojektet.* PhD thesis, Uppsala University.

Black, W. R. and N. Sato, 2007. "From global warming to sustainable transport 1989–2006", *International Journal of Sustainable Transportation*, Vol. 1:2, pp. 73–89.

Blomberg, H., 2016. "Stockholms stad JO-anmälda", *Sveriges Motorcyklister*. Available at: <https://www.svmc.se/smc/SMCs-arbete--fragor/Infrastruktur/MC-parkering/Rekordhojning-av-P-avgifter-for-MC-foreslas-i-Stockholm/Stockholms-stad-JO-anmalda/> [accessed 2019-03-07].

Bolander, H., 2018. "Så drömmer svenskarna om att bo", *Dagens industri*, 2018-01-01. Available at: https://www.di.se/nyheter/sa-drommer-svenskarna-om-att-bo/ [accessed 2019-09-20].

Bolander, H., 2019. "Färre svenskar sugna på villa – trädgårdsslit avskräcker", *Dagens industri*, 2019-03-18. Available at: <https://www.di.se/nyheter/farre-svenskar-sugna-pa-villa-tradgardsslit-avskracker/> [accessed 2019-09-20].

Boussaw, K. and Vanoutrive, T., 2017. "Transport policy in Belgium: translating sustainability discourses into unsustainable outcomes", *Transport Policy*, Vol. 53, pp. 11–19.

Bradley, K., U. Gunnarsson-Östling, K. Isaksson, 2008. "Exploring environmental justice in Sweden – how to improve planning for environmental sustainability and social equity in an "eco-friendly" context", *MIT Journal of Planning. Projections*, Vol. 8, pp. 68–81.

Brandt, P., 2017. "Bilister: Lättare att hitta parkering efter nya p-avgifterna", *Stockholm Direkt*, 2017-05-27. Available at: <https://www.stockholmdirekt.se/nyheter/bilister-lattare-att-hitta-parkering-efter-nya-p-avgifterna/repqez!aPo06H7KTKpMhGCf3WbugA/> [accessed 2019-09-20].

Brinck, C., 2018. "Hållbarhet och bilar inte varandras motsatser", *Expressen*. Available at: <https://www.expressen.se/debatt/hallbarhet-och-bilar-inte-varandras-motsatser/> [accessed 2019-09-20].

Bråstedt, M., 2017. "Fusket kostar SL hundratals miljoner", *Expressen*, 2017-01-15. Available at: <https://www.expressen.se/nyheter/fusket-kostar-sl-100-tals-miljoner/> [accessed 2019-03-05].

Börjesson, M., D. Jonsson and M. Lundberg, 2014. "An ex-post CBA for the Stockholm Metro", *Transportation Research Part A*, Vol. 70, pp. 135–148.

Cannervik, 2015. "Starka åsikter om jättebygget", *Mälaröarnas nyheter*, nr. 13 2015, pp. 4–5.

Caro, R., 1975. *The power broker – Robert Moses and the fall of New York.* Vintage.

Centre Party, 2018. "Fler bostäder för alla plånböcker", *Election platform 2018–2022*. Available at: <https://www.centerpartiet.se/lokal/stockholmsregionen/stockholms-stad/start sida/var-politik/valplattform-2018-2022/fler-bostader-for-alla-planbocker> [accessed 2019-03-07].

Chamber of Commerce, 2010. "Utan Förbifarten stannar Stockholm", *Stockholms Handelskammares analys*, 2010:7.

City Council, 2009. *Budget 2010 för Stockholms stad.* Dnr 111-859/2009.

City Council, 2010. *Budget 2011 för Stockholms stad.* Dnr 111-939/2010.

City Council, 2011. *Finansborgarrådets förslag till budget 2012 för Stockholms stad.* Dnr 111-892/2011.

City Council, 2012. *Kommunstyrelsens förslag till budget 2013 för Stockholms stad.* Dnr 111-636/2012.

City Council, 2013. *Kommunfullmäktiges förslag till budget 2014 för Stockholms stad.* Dnr 111-575/2013.

City Council, 2014. *Budget 2015. En jämlik och hållbar stad.* Dnr 111-459/2014.

City Council, 2015. *Budget 2016. Ett Stockholm för alla.* Dnr 180-529/2015.

City Council, 2016. *Budget 2017. Ett Stockholm för alla.* Dnr 180-612/2016.

City Planning Office, 1999. *Stockholms översiktsplan 1999.* SBK 2000:6.

City Planning Office, 2010. *Promenadstaden. Översiktsplan för Stockholm.* SBK 2010:1.

City Planning Office, 2010. *The Walkable City. Stockholm City Plan.* SBK 2011:1.

City Planning Office, 2018. *Översiktsplan för Stockholms stad.*

Cornwall, A .and K. Brock, 2005. "What do buzzwords do for development policy? a critical look at 'participation', 'empowerment' and 'poverty reduction'", *Third World Quarterly*, Vol. 26, No. 7, 1043–1060.

Coutard, O. and E. Shove, 2018. "Infrastructures, practices and the dynamics of demand" in E. Shove and F. Trentmann (eds.), *Infrastructures in practice: the dynamics of demand in networked societies.* Routledge.

Cox, P., 2015. "Så får EU gemensam ryggrad för transporter", *Dagens Samhälle*, 2015-05-06. Available at: <https://www.dagenssamhalle.se/debatt/sa-far-eu-gemensam-ryggrad-foer-transporter-15476> [accessed 2019-09-06].

Dahlin, L., 2015. "Parkeringsavgifter upprör bilägarna", *Mitt i*, 2015-02-02. Available at: <https://mitti.se/nyheter/parkeringsavgifter-uppror-bilagarna/?omrade=bromma> [accessed 2019-03-07].

Delling, H. and L. Hennel, 2013. "Forskare dömer ut ny t-baneplan", *Svenska Dagbladet*, 2013-11-11. Available at: <https://www.svd.se/forskare-domer-ut-ny-t-baneplan> [accessed 2018-03-05].

Delling, H., 2013. "SvD-läsare: "Bevara t-banan grön!", *Svenska Dagbladet*, 2013-11-12. <https://www.svd.se/svd-lasare-bevara-t-banan-gron> [accessed 2017-09-25].

Dickinson, J., K. Isaksson, A. Gullberg, 2016. *Hållbar transportplanering? Jämförande studie av policy och planering i storstadsregionerna Stockholm, Vancouver och Hamburg.* Report for Swedish Environmental Protection Agency, no. 6732.

Dietl, T., 2018. "Maria Börjesson: "Fördubblingsmålet kontraproduktivt"", *RT-Forum*, 2018-02-12. Available at: <https://www.rt-forum.se/article/view/585055/maria_borjesson_fordubblingsmalet_kontraproduktivt> [accessed 2019-03-05].

Dreyfus, H. L. and Rabinow P., 1983. *Michel Foucault: Beyond Structuralism and hermeneutics*, 2nd ed. University of Chicago Press, Chicago.

Duranton, G. and M. A. Turner, 2011. "The fundamental law of road congestion: evidence from US cities", *The American Economic Review*, Vol. 101, No. 6, pp. 2616–2652.

Duranton, G. and M. A. Turner, 2018. "Urban form and driving: Evidence from US cities", *Journal of Urban Economics*, Vol. 108, pp. 170–191.

EconTalk, 2018. *Charlan Nemeth on In Defense of Troublemakers*. Podcast. The Library of Economic and Liberty. Available at: <http://www.econtalk.org/charlan-nemeth-on-in-defense-of-troublemakers/> [accessed 2019-09-13].

Ejneberg, R., 2018. "Protester mot att Riddarfjärdslinjen läggs ner", *SVT Nyheter*, 2018-12-07. Available at: https://www.svt.se/nyheter/lokalt/stockholm/protester-mot-att-riddar fjardslinjen-laggs-ner-1 [accessed 2019-01-29].

Eliasson, J., 2015. "Problemstyrd planering: en förklaring till att effektivitet spelar så liten roll för valet av transportåtgärder" in J. Odeck and M. Welde (eds.), *Ressursbruk i transportsektoren – noen mulige forbedringer*. Concept rapport 44. NTNU, Trondheim, pp. 235–250.

Emanuel, M., 2010. "Understanding conditions for bicycle traffic through historical inquiry: the case of Stockholm", *Urban Transport Journal*, December 2010, pp. 1–16.

Emanuel, M., 2015. "Monuments of unsustainability. Planning, path dependence, and cycling in Stockholm" in Oldenziel and Trischler (eds.), *Cycling and recycling: histories of sustainable practices*. Berghahn Books.

Enoksson, U., 2009. *Livspusslet. Tid som välfärdsfaktor.* Doctoral thesis, Växjö university.

Enoksson, U., 2011. "Tid som välfärdsfaktor", *Sociologisk Forskning*, Vol. 48, No. 3, pp. 75–92.

Environment Department, 2007. *Stockholms miljöprogram 2008–2011. Övergripande mål och riktlinjer.*

Environment Department, 2009. *Stockholms åtgärdsplan för klimat och energi 2010–2020.*

Environment Department, 2011. *Stockholm action plan for climate and energy 2012–2015. With an outlook to 2030.*

Environment Department, 2011. *Stockholms miljöprogram 2012–2015.*

Environment Department, 2011. *Stockholms åtgärdsplan för klimat och energi 2012–2015. Med utblick till 2030.*

Environment Department, 2014. *Färdplan för ett fossilbränslefritt Stockholm 2050.*

Environment Department, 2014. *Roadmap for a fossil fuel-free Stockholm 2050.*

Environment Department, 2016. *Stockholms stads miljöprogram 2016 – 2019.*

European Commission, 2011. *Roadmap to a Single European Transport Area – Towards a competitive and resource efficient transport system.* White paper.

Executive Office, 2007. *Vision 2030. A guide to the future.*

Executive Office, 2007. *Vision 2030. Ett Stockholm i världsklass.*

Executive Office, 2014. *Förslag till reviderad Vision 2030.*

Executive Office, 2017. *Vision 2040. Ett Stockholm för alla.*

Fagerström, C., 2017a. "Fler lediga p-platser med avgifter", *Mitt i*, 2017-11-21. Available at: <https://mitti.se/nyheter/lediga-platser-avgifter/?omrade=bandhagenarsta> [accessed 2019-03-07].

Fagerström, C., 2017b. "Slutsnurrat efter p-plats i Björkhagen", *Mitt i*, 2017-11-21. Available at: <https://mitti.se/nyheter/slutsnurrat-plats-bjorkhagen/?omrade=hammarbyskarp nack> [accessed 2019-03-07].

Fagerström, C., 2017c. "Slutsnurrat efter p-plats i Midsommarkransen", *Mitt i*, 2017-11-21. Available at: <https://mitti.se/nyheter/slutsnurrat-plats-midsommarkransen/?omrade =liljeholmenalvsjo> [accessed 2019-03-07].

Falkirk, J., 2017. "Vanligast med grannklagomål i rika områden", *Dagens Nyheter*, 2017-02-04. Available at: <https://www.dn.se/arkiv/stockholm/vanligast-med-grannklagomal-i-rika-omraden/> [accessed 2019-03-07].

Fendert and Andersson, 2013. "Bilarna måste bort från Stockholms innerstad", *Svenska Dag bladet*, 2013-10-08. Available at: <https://www.svd.se/bilarna-maste-bort-fran-stock holms-innerstad> [accessed 2019-03-07].

Finnveden, G. and J. Åkerman, 2014. "Not planning a sustainable transport system", *Environmental Impact Assessment Review*, Vol 46, pp. 53–57.

Firth, D., 2012. *Framkomlighetsstrategin*. Traffic Department. Dnr T2008-310-02378.

Firth, D., 2012. *Urban Mobility strategy*. Traffic Department. Reg. No. T2008-310-02378.

Forssén, G. and P. Juth, 2013. "Höj trängselskatten för privatbilister", *Dagens samhälle*, 2013-05-06. Available at: <https://www.dagenssamhalle.se/debatt/hoej-traengselskat ten-brfoer-privatbilister-5349> [accessed 2019-03-07].

Foucault, M., 2000. *So is it important to think?* in J. Faubion (ed.), *Power*. New Press, New York, pp. 160–161.

Frankl, V., 1959. *Man's Search for Meaning*. Beacon Press.

Frenker, C., 2018a. "Daniel Helldén (MP): 'Vi vill både höja och utöka trängselskatten'", *Stockholm Direkt*, 2018-08-18. Available at: <https://www.stockholmdirekt.se/nyheter/ daniel-hellden-mp-vi-vill-bade-hoja-trangselskatten/reprgw!RpHkp4MfnpBx5GqCq WNKLg> [accessed 2019-03-06]

Frenker, C., 2018b. "Här ska SL köra fler bussar nästa år", *Stockholm Direkt*, 2018-11-08. Available at: <https://www.stockholmdirekt.se/nyheter/har-ska-sl-kora-fler-bussar-nasta-ar/reprkh!9UZCgvJEAyQbuJwFeym9DQ/> [accessed 2019-02-25].

Friman, M., 2017. "Så får vi fler att välja bilen", *Dagens samhälle*, 2017-05-12. Available at: <https://www.dagenssamhalle.se/debatt/sa-far-vi-fler-att-valja-bort-bilen-17153> [accessed 2019-03-07].

Fröberg, J., 2018. "Dieselbluffen – så förstörde politikerna värdet på din bil", *Svenska Dagbladet*, 2017-11-18. Available at: <https://www.svd.se/dieselbluffen--sa-forstorde-politikerna-vardet-pa-din-bil> [accessed 2019-09-20].

Gabrielsson, O., 2018. "Besinna dig, Daniel Helldén!", *Dagens Nyheter*, 2018-04-11. Available at: <https://www.dn.se/asikt/besinna-dig-daniel-hellden/> [accessed 2019-03-07].

Gardebring, A., 2015. "Promenadstaden är stendöd", *Yimby*, 2015-11-01. Available at: <https://www.yimby.se/2016/01/promenadstaden-ar-stendod_3736.html> [accessed 2019-08-08].

Givoni, M. and D. Banister (eds.), 2013. *Moving Towards Low Carbon Mobility*. Edward Elgar, Cheltenham.

Glynos, J., E. Speed and K. West, 2014. "Logics of marginalisation in health and social care reform: Integration, choice, and provider-blind provision", *Critical Social Policy* 35(1), pp. 45–68.

Gullberg, A., 2001a. *City: drömmen om ett nytt hjärta. 1*. Stockholmia förlag, Stockholm.

Gullberg, A., 2001b. *City: drömmen om ett nytt hjärta. 2*. Stockholmia förlag, Stockholm.

Gullberg, A., 2015. *Här finns den lediga kapaciteten i storstadstrafiken*. Report, KTH Centre for Sustainable Communications, Stockholm.

Gunder, M., 2014. "Fantasy in planning organisations and their agency: The promise of being at home in the world", *Urban Policy and Research* 32:1, p. 1–15.

Gunne, N., 2017. "Moderaterna sågar Boverkets bullerutredning", *Arkitekten*. Available at: <https://arkitekten.se/nyheter/moderaterna-sagar-boverkets-bullerutredning> [accessed 2019-03-03].

Gustafsson, A., 2014. "Forskare: utbyggd tunnelbana inte lönsam", *Sveriges Radio*, 2014-01-10. Available at: <http://sverigesradio.se/sida/artikel.aspx?programid=103&artikel=-5752473> [accessed 2018-03-05].

Gustavsson, S. and A. Niklasson, 2014. *Städers arbete med koldioxidneutralitet. En textanalytisk studie om problemframställningar*. Bachelors thesis, Linköping University.

Gössling, S., 2016. "Urban transport justice", *Journal of Transport Geography*, Vol. 54, pp. 1–9.

Hall, P., 1998. *Cities in Civilization*, Phoenix Giant, London.

Hall, T., 1985. "The Central Business District: Planning in Stockholm, 1928–1978", in Hall, T. (ed.), *"i nationell skala…" Studier kring cityplaneringen i Stockholm*. Svensk stadsmiljö, Stockholm.

Hansdotter, Å., 2017. "Därför mår vi dåligt av att pendla", *Vetenskap & hälsa*, 2017-05-16. Available at: <http://www.vetenskaphalsa.se/darfor-mar-vi-daligt-av-att-pendla/ > [accessed 2019-02-20].

Haque, M. M., H. C. Chin and A. K. Debnath, 2013. "Sustainable, safe, smart – three key elements of Singapore's evolving transport policies", *Transport Policy*, Vol. 27, pp. 20–31.

Harvey, D., 1989a. *The Condition of Postmodernity. An enquiry into the Origins of Cultural Change*. Basil Blackwell: Oxford.

Harvey, D., 1989b. "From managerialism to entrepreneurialism: the transformation in urban governance in late capitalism", *Geografiska Annaler. Series B, Human Geography*, Vol. 71, No. 1.

Helldén, D., Y. Blombäck, S. Bergström, 2013. "Förbifarten blir dubbelt så dyr", *Svenska Dagbladet*, 2013-06-09. Available at: <https://www.svd.se/forbifart-stockholm-blir-dubbelt-sa-dyr> [accessed 2019-09-20].

Hemnet, 2016. "Ett par minuter på t-banan kan spara miljoner i boendekostnad." Available at: <https://www.hemnet.se/artiklar/bostadsmarknaden/2016/11/01/ett-par-minuter-pa-t-banan-kan-spara-miljoner-i-boendekostnad> [accessed 2019-03-07].

Henrik, 2016. "Helldén (MP) tvingar oss att betala 600 procent mer i p-avgift än våra grannar", *StockholmDirekt*, 2016-06-28. Available at: <https://www.stockholmdirekt.se/debatt/insandare-hellden-mp-tvingar-oss-att-betala-600-procent-mer-i-p-avgift-an-vara-grannar/aRKpfB!aNqV0CY15qog8cES@H2A8w/> [accessed 2019-03-07].

Henriksson, M., 2014. *Att resa rätt är stort, att resa fritt är större. Kommunala planerares föreställningar om hållbara resor*. PhD thesis, Linköping University.

Herbert, T. T. and R. W. Estes, 1977. "Improving executive decisions by formalizing dissent: the corporate devil's advocate", *Academy of Management Review*, Vol. 2, No. 4, pp. 662-667.

Hilding-Rydevik, T., M. Håkansson and K. Isaksson, 2011. "The Swedish discourse on sustainable regional development: consolidating the post-political condition", *International Planning Studies*, Vol. 16(2), pp. 169-187.

Holman, N., A. Mace, A. Paccoud and J. Sundaresan, 2015. "Coordinating density; working through conviction, suspicion and pragmatism", *Progress in Planning*, Vol. 101, pp. 1-38.

Howlett, M. and B. Cashore, 2009. "The dependent variable problem in the study of policy change: understanding policy change as a methodological problem", Journal of Comparative Policy Analysis. Vol. 11, No. 1, pp. 33-46.

Howlett, M. and B. Cashore, 2014. "Conceptualizing public policy" in I Engeli and A Rothmayr Allison (eds.), *Comparative Policy Studies*, pp. 17-33.

Hrelja, R., 2011. "The tyranny of small decisions. Unsustainable cities and local day-to-day transport planning", *Planning Theory & Practice*, Vol. 12, No. 4, pp. 511-524.

Hrelja, R., 2019. "Cars. Problematisations, measures and blind spots in local transport and land use policy", *Land Use Policy*, Vol. 87, article 104014, pp. 1-9.

HumUs, 2013. *Katrin Larsson intervjuar Ylva Uggla.* Podcast. HumUs Media. Available at: <https://soundcloud.com/humus-media/katrin-larsson-ylva-uggla> [accessed 2015-02-26].

Hysing, E., 2009. "Greening transport—explaining urban transport policy change", *Journal of Environmental Policy & Planning*, Vol. 11, No. 3, pp. 243-261.

Høyer, K. G., 1999. *Sustainable Mobility - the Concept and its Implications.* PhD thesis, Roskilde University.

IPCC, 2019. "Summary for policymakers" in *Climate Change and Land. An IPCC Special Report on climate change, desertification, land degradation, sustainable land management, food security, and greenhouse gas fluxes in terrestrial ecosystems.*

Isaksson, K. and T. Richardson, 2009. "Building legitimacy for risky policies: the cost of avoiding conflict in Stockholm", *Transportation Research*, Vol. 43, No. 3, pp. 251-257.

Isaksson, K., 2001. *Framtidens trafiksystem? Maktutövningen i konflikterna om rummet och miljön i Dennispaketets vägfrågor.* PhD thesis, Linköping unversity.

Isaksson, K., 2006. "Fernissa eller förändring? - om hållbar utveckling i svensk planering" in Blücher G and G Graninger (eds.), *Planering med nya förutsättningar. Ny lagstiftning, nya värderingar.* Stiftelsen Vadstena forum för samhällsbyggande, pp. 107-124.

Isaksson, K., H. Antonson, and L. Eriksson, 2017. "Layering and parallell policy making – complementary concepts for understanding implementation challenges related to sustainable mobility", *Transport Policy*, Vol. 53, pp. 50-57.

IVA, 2019. *Så klarar Sveriges transporter klimatmålen. En delrapport från IVA-projektet Vägval för klimatet.* Report, June 2019.

Jansson, J. O., P. Cardebring and Junghard, O., 1986. *Personbilsinnehavet i Sverige 1950-2010.* VTI report 301.

Jenkins-Smith, H., C. L. Silva, K. Gupta and J. T. Ripberger, 2014. "Belief system continuity and change in policy advocacy coalitions: using cultural theory to specify belief systems, coalitions, and sources of change", *The Policy Studies Journal*, Vol. 42, No. 4, pp. 484–508.

Joelsson, F., 2018. "Här tystas kyrkklockorna – efter grannarnas klagomål", *Metro*, 2018-09-22. Available at: <https://www.metro.se/artikel/h%C3%A4r-tystas-kyrkklockorna-efter-grannarnas-klagom%C3%A5l> [accessed 2019-03-07].

Johansson, B., 2011. "The post-war destruction of Swedish cities", *Building Research & Information*, Vol. 39, No. 4, pp. 412–429.

Johansson, B., 2015. "Dyrt att gå till jobbet med boendeparkering", *Mitt i*, 2015-04-13. Available at: <https://mitti.se/debatt/dyrt-att-ga-till-jobbet-med-boendeparkering/?omrade=bromma> [accessed 2019-03-07].

Jonsson, C. R., 2016a. "Se YIMBY-musikerns nya skövlarvideo: "Asfaltera hela gärdet och skogen nu!"", *Stockholm Direkt*, 2016-06-15. Available at: <https://www.stockholm direkt.se/nyheter/yimby-musiker-asfaltera-hela-skogen/aRKpfo!1wJyyj8gL45IXD3ju RkY0A/> [accessed 2019-03-07].

Jonsson, C. R., 2016b. "L: Bagisskogen är otrygg, bygg bort den!", *Stockholm Direkt*, 2016-11-09. Available at: <https://www.stockholmdirekt.se/nyheter/l-bagisskogen-ar-otrygg-bygg-bort-den/reppki!HqtR37IRrSu42uKULm7Dww/> [accessed 2019-03-07].

Jonsson, E., 2018. "Grannar på Söder klagar på gråtande barn", *Stockholm Direkt*, 2018-11-07. Available at: <https://www.stockholmdirekt.se/nyheter/garnnar-pa-soder-klagar-pa-gratande-barn/reprka!IpTYpXxUnXhkic0hePu7SA> [accessed 2019-03-06].

Järfälla, 2019-04-16. *Statistik*. Available at: <https://www.jarfalla.se/kommun-och-politik/kommunfakta/statistik.html> [accessed 2019-09-05].

Jönköpings kommun, 2014. *Hållbara transporter – ryggraden i den hållbara staden*. Report on transport plan sponsored by National Board of Housing, Building and Planning (Boverket), Dnr 1394-942/2010.

Kallin, J., 2008. "Storstadsnaturen får det trängre", *Svenska Dagbladet*, 2008-12-28. Available at: <https://www.svd.se/storstadsnaturen-far-det-trangre> [accessed 2019-03-07].

Kębłowski, W., M. Van Criekingen, and D. Bassens, 2019. "Moving past the sustainable perspectives on transport: An attempt to mobilise critical urban transport studies with the right to the city", *Transport Policy*, Vol. 81, pp. 24–34.

Kemp, R., F. W. Geels and G. Dudley, 2012. "Sustainability transitions in the automobility regime and the need for a new perspective" in F W Geels, R Kemp, G Dudley and G Lyons (eds), *Automobility in Transition? A Socio-Technical Analysis of Sustainable Transport*. Routledge, New York, pp. 3–28.

Kingdon, J. W., 1995. *Agendas, alternatives and public policies*. HarperCollins College Publishers.

Kronsell, A., L. Smidfelt Rosqvist, and L. Winslott Hiselius, 2016 "Achieving climate objectives in transport policy by including women and challenging gender norms: The Swedish case", *International Journal of Sustainable Transportation*, Vol. 10, No. 8, pp. 703–711.

KTH, 2019. *Stockholm växer, grönområdena krymper*. Press release, 2019-05-22. Available at: <https://www.kth.se/forskning/artiklar/stockholm-vaxer-gronomradena-krymper-1.906139> [accessed 2019-09-19].

Kunzig, R., 2011. "The city solution: why cities are the best cure for our planet's growing pains". *National Geographic*, December 2011, pp. 124–147.

Laclau, E. and C. Mouffe, 1987. "Post-Marxism without apologies", *New Left Review*, Vol. 166, No. 1, p. 79–166.

Landreth, J., 2011. "China Bans Time Travel Films and Shows, Citing Disrespect of History", *The Hollywood Reporter*, 2011-04-13. Available at: <https://www.hollywood reporter.com/news/china-bans-time-travel-films-177801> [accessed 2019-09-13].

Larsson, M. J., 2014. "MP pressas för ett ja till förbifart", *Dagens Nyheter*, 2014-04-30, p. 5.

Law, R., 1999. "Beyond 'women and transport': towards new geographies of gender and daily mobility", *Progress in Human Geography*, Vol. 23, No. 4, pp. 567–588.

Lindblom, C., 1979. "Still muddling, not yet through", in S Theodoulou and M Cahn (eds.), *Public Policy. The Essential Readings*, 2nd ed. Pearson, pp. 30–41.

Lindelöw, D., 2018. *Running to stand still - the role of travel time in transport planning.* Urban Move report for Sweco.

Lindholm, A., 2019. "Oklart när Förbifart Stockholm blir färdig", *Dagens Nyheter*, 2019-06-25. Available at: <https://www.dn.se/sthlm/oklart-nar-forbifart-stockholm-blir-fardig/> [accessed 2019-09-20].

Lundberg, J., 2018. "3 300 fler reser genom vägtullarna - per dag", *Mitt i*, 2019-01-22. Available at: <https://mitti.se/nyheter/trafik/aker-genom-vagtullarna/> [accessed 2019-09-20].

Lundin, P., 2008. *Bilsamhället*. Stockholmia förlag, Stockholm.

Lutz, C. and A. Lutz Fernandez, 2010. *Carjacked: The Culture of the Automobile and its Effect on Our Lives*. New York: Palgrave Macmillan.

Lärarförbundet, 2019. "Nytt jobb - högre lön?", *Lärarförbundet*, 2019-01-11. Available at: <https://www.lararforbundet.se/artiklar/nytt-jobb-hogre-lon> [accessed 2019-02-25].

Mahovic, A., 2015. "Järvabor vill stoppa Förbifart Stockholm", *Sveriges Television*, 2015-11-15. Available at: <http://www.svt.se/nyheter/lokalt/stockholm/jarvabor-vill-stoppa-forbifart-stockholm> [accessed 2019-03-06].

Majlard, J., 2016. "MP om nya p-regler: Bilägarna ska stå för kostnaderna", *Svenska Dagbladet*, 2016-08-30. <https://www.svd.se/mp-om-nya-p-regler-bilagarna-ska-sta-for-kostnaderna> accessed 2017-09-21.

Marsden, G. and L. Reardon, 2017. "Questions of governance: rethinking the study of transportation policy", *Transportation Research Part A*, Vol. 101, pp. 238–251.

Mattisson, K., C. Håkansson and K. Jakobsson, 2017. "Relationships between commuting and social capital among men and women in southern Sweden", *Environment and Behavior*, Vol. 47, No. 7, 734–753.

May, R., 1991. *The Cry for Myth*. WW Norton & Company.

May, T., T. Jarvi-Nykanen, H. Minken, F. Ramjerdi, B. Matthews and A. Monzón, 2001. *Cities' Decision-Making Requirements*. Report from Procedures for Recommending Optimal Sustainable Planning of European City Transport Systems (PROSPECTS), March 2001.

Mellgren, F., 2015. "Nödbroms ger dyrare SL-kort och glesare trafik", *Svenska Dagbladet*, 2015-02-05. Available from <http://www.svd.se/nyheter/inrikes/nodbroms-ger-dyrare-sl-kort-och-glesare-trafik_4313113.svd>. [Accessed 2015-04-03.]

Metz D, 2008. "The myth of travel time saving", *Transport Reviews*, Vol. 28(3), pp. 321–336.

Moderate Party, 2018. "Bostäder", *Moderaterna* (website). Available at: <https://moderaterna.se/stockholm/bostader> [accessed 2019-03-07].

Motorcyklist på Söder, 2018. "Därför ställer vi motorcyklar på p-rutor för bilar", *StockholmDirekt*, 2018-09-24. Available at: <https://www.stockholmdirekt.se/debatt/insandare-darfor-staller-vi-motorcyklar-pa-p-rutor-for-bilar/reprix!7R@NM5YRFR FhRlhjqistg/> [accessed 2019-03-07].

MSB 2015. *Kostnader för störningar i infrastrukturen. Metodik och fallstudier på väg och järnväg*. Report MSB907.

Mukhtar-Landgren, D., 2016. "Problematisations of progress and diversity in visionary planning. The case of post-industrial Malmö", *Nordic Journal of Migration Research*, Vol. 6, No. 1, pp. 18–24.

Månsson, J., 2016. "Jättebyggen på Lovö får både ris och ros", *Stockholm Direkt*, 2016-12-09. Available at: <https://www.stockholmdirekt.se/nyheter/jattebyggen-pa-lovo-far-bade-ris-och-ros/repplh!@wFk8my4bN6z7sd4k8RA/> [accessed 2019-09-20].

Månsson, J., 2018. "Pendelbåtens nya tidtabell har släppts", *Stockholm Direkt*, 2018-08-07. Available at: <https://www.stockholmdirekt.se/nyheter/pendelbatens-nya-tidtabell-har-slappts/reprhg!4BxdgS9LgqDRiOrseo6gIw/> [accessed 2018-12-03].

Nacka, 2019-09-18. *Statistik om Nacka*. Available at: <https://www.nacka.se/kommun--politik/ekonomi-och-statistik/statistik/> [accessed 2019-09-21].

Næss P, L Hansson, T. Richardson and A. Tennøyc, 2013. "Knowledge-based land use and transport planning? Consistency and gap between "state-of-the-art" knowledge and knowledge claims in planning documents in three Scandinavian city regions", *Planning Practice & Theory*, Vol. 14, No. 4, pp. 479–491.

Nathanson Thulin, A., 2018. "Vi vill verka för en bilfri innerstad", *Stockholm Direkt*, 2018-07-25. Available at: <https://www.stockholmdirekt.se/debatt/vi-vill-verka-for-en-bilfri-innerstad/reprgy!T6OtYxkTOjE0JGn@DJszcQ/> [accessed 2019-09-20].

Newman, P., T. Beatley and H. Boyer, 2009. *Resilient Cities: Responding to Peak Oil and Climate Change*. Island Press.

Ney, S., 2006. *Messy Issues, Policy Conflict and the Differentiated Policy: Analysing Contemporary Policy Responses to Complex, Uncertain and Transversal Policy Problems*. PhD thesis, University of Bergen.

Nilsson, B. and A. S. Lundgren, 2015. "Logics of rurality: political rhetoric about the Swedish North", *Journal of Rural Studies* 37, pp. 85–95.

Nordin, S., 2013a. "Viktiga steg mot byggstart av Förbifart Stockholm", *Sten Nordin* (blog), 2013-04-11. Available at: <https://stennordin.se/2013/04/11/viktiga-steg-mot-byggstart-av-forbifart-stockholm> [accessed 2017-09-21].

Nordin, S., 2013b. "Sten Nordin (M): Moderat "JA" till Förbifarten står mot Socialdemokratiskt "kanske"", *Dagens Opinion*, 2013-05-17. Available at: http://dagensopinion.se/sten-nordin-m-moderat-ja-till-förbifarten-står-mot-socialdemokratiskt-kanske" [accessed 2017-09-21].

Nordin, S., 2014. "Nu kan det bli fler gågator i Stockholms innerstad", *Svenska Dagbladet*, 2014-04-15. Available from <http://www.svd.se/opinion/brannpunkt/nu-kan-det-bli-fler-gagator-i-stockholms-innerstad_3468786.svd>. [Accessed 2015-04-03.]

Norell Bergendahl, A., 2016. *Den ohållbara resan mot det hållbara resandet. En studie av institutionella förutsättningar för att bedriva planering för hållbart resande i Stockholmsregionen.* Licentiate thesis, KTH Royal Institute of Technology.

Numan, E., 2016. "Hur cykelvänligt är Norra Djurgårdsstaden egentligen?", *Stockholm Direkt*, 2016-12-12. Available at: <https://www.stockholmdirekt.se/nyheter/hur-cykel vanligt-ar-norra-djurgardsstaden-egentligen/repplg!WrnehbNF8sabazcq3sG1aw/>

Nyström, J., 2003. *Planeringens grunder: En översikt,* Studentlitteratur, Lund.

Offentliga affärer, 2013. "Så mycket tjänar bostadsägarna på tunnelbanan", *Offentliga affärer*, 2013-11-28. Available at: <https://www.offentligaaffarer.se/2013/11/28/sa-myc ket-tjaenar-bostadsaegarna-pa-tunnelbanan/> [accessed 2019-03-07].

Olsson, D., 2018. *Conditions of 'Sustainability'. The Case of Climate Change Adaptation in Sweden.* PhD thesis, Karlstad University.

Perman, K., 2008. *Från el till värme. En diskursanalytisk policystudie av energiomställning på statlig, kommunal och hushållsnivå.* PhD thesis, Örebro University.

Permell, C., 2013. "Förbifarten kan kosta 60 miljarder", *Sveriges television*, 2013-05-13 Available at: <https://www.svt.se/nyheter/lokalt/stockholm/forbifarten-kan-kosta-60-miljarder> [accessed 2019-09-20].

Pettersson, F., 2014. *Swedish infrastructure policy and planning. Conditions for sustainability.* PhD thesis, Lund University.

Pirttisalo Sallinen, J. and L. Widell, 2019. "Nu flyttar fler från Stockholm än till", *Svenska dagbladet*, 2019-07-10. Available at: <https://www.svd.se/trenden-bruten-fler-flyttar-bort-fran-stockholm-an-till> [accessed 2019-09-20].

Poulsen, H., 2006. *The elusive gender. The international labour organisation and the construction of gender equality.* PhD thesis, University of Copenhagen.

Public Health Agency of Sweden, 2019. *Stress.* Available at: <https://www.folkhalsomyn digheten.se/folkhalsorapportering-statistik/tolkad-rapportering/folkhalsans-utveck ling/halsa/psykisk-ohalsa/stress/> [accessed 2019-09-18].

Redman, L., M. Fridman, T. Gärling and T. Hartig, 2013. "Quality attributes of public transport that attract car users: A research review", *Transport Policy*, Vol. 25, pp. 119–127.

Regionplane- och trafikkontoret and SL, 2008. *Trafiken i Stockholms län 2007.* Available at: <http://miljobarometern.stockholm.se/content/docs/tema/trafik/trafik_stockholms_la n_2007.pdf> [accessed 2019-06-13].

Reinfeldt, F., J. Björklund, A. Lööf and G. Hägglund, 2012. "Alliansen öppnar för t-bana och vägtunnel under Saltsjön", *Dagens Nyheter*, 2012-09-19.

Remling, E., 2019 (forthcoming). *Adaptation now? Exploring the politics of climate change adaptation through poststructuralist discourse theory.* PhD thesis, Södertörn university.

Richardson, T., K. Isaksson and A. Gullberg, 2010. "Changing frames of mobility through radical policy interventions? The Stockholm congestion tax", *International Planning Studies*, Vol. 15, No. 1, p. 53–67.

Riihinen, J. J., 2007. "Tio år sedan motståndet knäckte Dennispaketet", *Stockholms Fria*, 2007-02-06. Available at: <http://www.fria.nu/artikel/18659> [accessed 2019-09-20].

Ritzén, J. and Mahmoud 2018. "Förskolegårdarna krymper i nya stadsdelarna", *Dagens Nyheter*, 2018-01-10, pp. 4–5.

Ritzén, J., 2017. "Var tredje bil i Stockholm måste bort", *Dagens Nyheter*, 2017-03-05. Available at: <https://www.dn.se/sthlm/var-tredje-bil-i-stockholm-maste-bort/> [accessed 2019-03-07].

Robért, M. and R. D. Jonsson, 2006. "Assessment of transport policies toward future emission targets. A backcasting approach for Stockholm 2030", *Journal of Environmental Assessment Policy and Management*, Vol. 8, No. 4, pp. 451–478.

Ronnle, E., 2018. *Justifying mega-projects. An analysis of the Swedish high-speed rail project.* PhD thesis, Lund University.

Roosmark, C., 2016. "Holländsk cykling gör Kungsholmen sämre", *Stockholm Direkt*, 2016-08-30. Available at: <https://www.stockholmdirekt.se/nyheter/insandare-hollandsk-cykling-gor-kungsholmen-samre/aRKphC!xLx9uDYnsKSrxQTUopJBkA/> [accessed 2019-03-07].

Rosenholm, M., 2013. "Sju av tio politiker vill minska möjligheten att överklaga bygglov", *Branschaktuellt*, 2013-02.26. Available at: <https://www.branschaktuellt.se/bygg industrin/senaste-nytt-bygg/1574-sju-av-tio-politiker-vill-minska-moejligheten-att-oeverklaga-bygglov> [accessed 2019-03-06].

Rothengatter, T. and R. D. Huguenin, 2004. *Traffic & Transport Psychology: Proceedings of the ICTTP 2000.* Elsevier.

Rudbeck, E., 2019. "Det är dags att mynta begreppet bilskam", *Dagens Nyheter*, 2019-03-05. Available at: <https://www.dn.se/asikt/det-ar-dags-att-mynta-begreppet-bilskam/> [accessed 2019-03-07].

Röshammar, C. K., 2013."Livspusslet blev en privatsak", *Arbetet* 2013-09-03. Available at: <https://arbetet.se/2013/09/06/livspusslet-blev-en-privatsak> [accessed 2018-04-04].

Sabatier, P. and C. M. Weible, 2007. "The advocacy coalition: innovations and clarifications" in P Sabatier (ed.), *Theories of the policy process*, 2nd ed. Westfield Press, pp. 189–220.

Sales, J. M., N. A. Merrill and R. Fivush, 2013. "Does making meaning make it better? Narrative meaning-making and well-being in at-risk African-American adolescent females", *Memory*, Vol. 21, No. 1, pp. 97–110.

Sandelin, M., 2013. "Friskolor väljer bort besvärliga elever", *Sveriges Television*, 2013-10-28. Available at: <https://www.svt.se/nyheter/granskning/ug/friskolor-valjer-bort-besvarliga-elever> [accessed 2019-09-20].

Santarius, T. and M. Soland, 2012. "How technological efficiency improvements change consumer preferences: towards a psychological theory of rebound effects", *Ecological Economics*, Vol. 146, pp. 414–424.

Schulz-Hardt, S., M. Jochims and D. Frey, 2002. "Productive conflict in group decision making: genuine and contrived dissent as strategies to counteract biased information seeking", *Organizational Behavior and Human Decision Processes*, Vol. 88, No. 2, pp. 563–586.

Schumacher, E. F., 1973a. "Small is beautiful", *The Radical Humanist,* Vol. 37, No. 5, pp. 18–22.

Schumacher, E. F., 1973b. *Small is Beautiful: A study of economics as if people mattered.* Blond & Briggs, London.

SFS 2006:227. *Vägtrafikskattelag.*

SFS 2010:900. *Plan- och bygglag.*

Sheller, M., 2004. "Automotive emotions: feeling the car", *Theory, Culture & Society,* Vol. 21, pp. 221–242.

Sheller, M., 2012. "The emergence of new cultures of mobility: stability, openings and prospects" in F W Geels, R Kemp, G Dudley and G Lyons (eds.), *Automobility in transition? A socio-technical analysis of sustainable transport.* Routledge, pp. 3–28.

Shove, E. and F. Trentmann, 2018. *Infrastructures in Practice: The Dynamics of Demand in Networked Societies.* Routledge.

Shove, E., F. Trentmann and M. Watson, 2018. "Introduction – infrastructures in practice. The evolution of demand in networked societies" in E Shove and F Trentmann (eds.), *Infrastructures in practice: the dynamics of demand in networked societies.* Routledge, pp. 3–9.

Sjövik, I., 2016. "Parkeringshöjningen drabbar låginkomsttagare", *Stadshusoppositionen,* 2016-09-21. Available at: <http://stadshusoppositionen.se/2016/09/21/parkeringshoj ningen-drabbar-laginkomsttagare/> [accessed 2018-10-12].

Sköld, J., 2013. "T-banebesked öppnar för boprisuppgång", *Metro,* 2013-11-11. Available at: <https://www.metro.se/artikel/t-banebesked-%C3%B6ppnar-f%C3%B6r-boprisuppg%C3%A5ng-xr> [accessed 2019-03-07].

Skövlarsyntharen, 2017. "Skövla skogen i Söderort och bygg stad", *Stockholm Direkt,* 2017-09-18. Available at: <https://www.stockholmdirekt.se/debatt/insandare-skovla-skogen-i-soderort-och-bygg-stad/repqir!x2LNDc50QCm16gb0jcwUTw/> [accessed 2019-03-07].

Solna, 2019-05-22. *Befolkning.* Available at: <https://www.solna.se/om-solna/solna-idag-statistik/befolkning/> [accessed: 2019-03-06].

Sommarskog, E., 2016. "Sälj bilen och hyr!", *Dagens Nyheter,* 2016-11-01. Available at: <https://www.dn.se/asikt/salj-bilen-och-hyr/> [accessed 2019-03-07].

Soneryd, L. and Y. Uggla, 2011. *(O)möjliga livsstilar: samhällsvetenskapliga perspektiv på individualiserat miljöansvar.* Studentlitteratur, Lund.

Soneryd, L. and Y. Uggla, 2015. "Green governmentality and responsibilization: new forms of governance and responses to 'consumer responsibility'", *Environmental Politics,* Vol. 24, No. 6, pp. 913–931.

SOU 2017:107. *Slutrapport från Sverigeförhandlingen. Infrastruktur och bostäder – ett gemensamt samhällsbygge.*

Stadsbyggnadskontoret, 2004. *Trafikanalyser för Stockholm 2030.* Report 2030:5.

Stadsledningskontoret, 2018. *Effekter av miljözoner i Stockholms stad.* Report. Dnr: KS 2019/7.

Statens institut för kommunikationsanalys, 2007. "Yttrande över Beredning inför regeringens tillåtlighetsprövning enligt 17 kap Miljöbalken: Vägutredning effektivare nord-sydliga förbindelser i Stockholmsregionen". Dnr 026-200-07.

Statistics Sweden, 2015. *Dagens urbanisering – inte på landsbygdens bekostnad.* Available at: <https://www.scb.se/hitta-statistik/artiklar/2015/Dagens-urbanisering--inte-pa-landsbygdens-bekostnad/> [accessed 2019-09-06].

Steg, L. and G. Tertoolen, 1999. "Sustainable Transport Policy: The Contribution from Behavioral Scientists", *Public Money & Management*, Vol. 19, No. 1, pp. 63–69.

Stockholm Negotiation, Ministry of Enterprise and Innovation, 2007. *Trafiklösning för Stockholmsregionen till 2020 med utblick mot 2030.*

Stockholm Negotiation, Ministry of Enterprise and Innovation, 2007. *Traffic Solution for Stockholm.*

Stockholms läns landsting, 2018. "Länets befolkning mökar med en miljon till 2060" *Region Stockholm, verksamhet.* Available at: <https://www.sll.se/verksamhet/Regional-utveckling/Nyheter/2018/11/lanets-befolkning-okar-med-en-miljon-till-2060/> [accessed 2019-09-13].

Stockholms stad, 2014. *Färdplan för ett fossilbränslefritt Stockholm 2050.* Adopted by Stockholm City Council March 24 2014.

Stockholms stad, 2015. *Bostäder. Bostadslägenheter efter storlek.* Available at: <http://statistik.stockholm.se/images/stories/excel/Tabell%2020.htm> [accessed 2019-01-25].

Stockholms stad, 2016a. *Enkät om miljö och miljövanor i Stockholm. Miljöbarometern.* Available   at: <http://miljobarometern.stockholm.se/stockholmarna/medborgarenkat/> [accessed 2019-09-07].

Stockholms stad, 2016b. *Förslag till plan för gatuparkering. Bilaga 3.*

Stockholms stad, 2017a. *Andel kollektiva resor, dygn.* Available at: http://miljobaro metern.stockholm.se/trafik/kollektivtrafik/andel-kollektiva-resor-dygn/ [accessed 2019-06-13].

Stockholms stad, 2017b. *Ny plan för gatuparkering.* Available at: http://www.stock holm.se/TrafikStadsplanering/Parkering/ny-plan-for-gatuparkering [accessed 2017-09-21].

Stockholms stad, 2018a. *Andel miljöbilar i nyförsäljningen. Miljöbarometern.* Available at: <http://miljobarometern.stockholm.se/trafik/miljobilar/andel-miljobilar-i-nybilsforsaljningen/> [accessed 2019-02-25].

Stockholms stad, 2018b. *Levande Stockholm.* Available at: <http://www.stockholm.se/levandestockholm> [accessed 2019-01-25].

Stockholms stad, 2018c. *Miljöbilar och förnyelsebara bränslen. Miljöbarometern.* Available from: <http://miljobarometern.stockholm.se/trafik/miljobilar/> [accessed 2019-02-25].

Stockholms stad, 2018d. *Motorcykel.* Available at: <http://www.stockholm.se/Trafik Stadsplanering/Parkering/Motorcykel/> [accessed 2019-03-07].

Stockholms stad, 2018e. *Utsläpp av växthusgaser. Miljöbarometern.* Available at: <http://miljobarometern.stockholm.se/klimat/utslapp-av-vaxthusgaser/utslapp-av-vaxthusgaser/> [accessed 2019-09-06].

Stockholms stad, 2018f. *Utsläpp av växthusgaser. Miljöbarometern.* Available from: <http://miljobarometern.stockholm.se/miljomal/miljoprogram-2016-2019/hallbar-energianvandning/utslapp-av-vaxthusgaser/info1/> [accessed 2019-01-19].

Stockholms stad, 2018g. *Vad är miljöbil? Miljöbarometern.* Available at: <http://www.stockholm.se/Fristaende-webbplatser/Fackforvaltningssajter/Miljofor valtningen/Miljobilar/Bilar--branslen/Vad-ar-miljobil/> [accessed 2019-02-25].

Stockholms stad, 2018h. *Nya parkeringsregler i Stockholms stad.* Leaflet. Available at: <https://www.stockholmparkering.se/SiteAssets/Byggprojekt/Plan%20gatuparkering%20(kortversion).pdf> [accessed 2019-08-21].

Stockholms stad, 2019a. *Antal kollektiva resor, dygn. Miljöbarometern.* Available at: <http://miljobarometern.stockholm.se/trafik/kollektivtrafik/andel-kollektiva-resor-dygn/> [accessed 2019-06-13].

Stockholms stad, 2019b. *Cykeltrafik. Miljöbarometern.* Available at: <http://miljo barometern.stockholm.se/trafik/cykeltrafik/> [accessed 2019-09-20].

Stockholms stad, 2019c. *Motorfordon och trängselskatt Miljöbarometern.* Available at: <http://miljobarometern.stockholm.se/trafik/motorfordon/> [accessed 2019-09-20].

Stockholmsförsöket, 2006. *Dennisöverenskommelsen.* Website for the Stockholm congestion tax trial run, no longer updated. Available at: <http://www.stockholmsforsoket.se/templates/page.aspx?id=12561> [accessed 2019-03-02].

Storbjörk, S., 2001. *Vägskäl. Miljöfrågan, subpolitiken och planeringsidealets praktik i fallet Riksväg 50.* PhD thesis. Linköpings universitet, Linköping.

Storstockholms lokaltrafik, 2016. *Fördel buss.* Available at: <http://www.sl.se/fordelbuss> [accessed 2019-09-20].

Storstockholms lokaltrafik, 2017. *Fakta om SL och länet 2016.* Annual report for 2016. Diarienummer: S-2016-0762.

Stradling, S. G., M. L. Meadows and S. Beatty, 2000. "Helping drivers out of their cars. Integrating transport policy and social psychology for sustainable change", *Transport Policy*, Vol. 7, pp. 207–215.

Ståhle, A., 2016. "Marknaden vill inte ha bilstaden", *Stockholm Direkt*, 2016-01-19. Available at: <https://www.stockholmdirekt.se/debatt/replik-stadsbyggnadsforskare-alexander-stahle-marknaden-vill-inte-ha-bilstaden/aRKpas!Yf@XVtLtAd30i@qHmJv33w/> [accessed 2019-03-07].

SvD, 2012. "Omstridd skatt har rekordstort stöd", *Svenska dagbladet*, 2012-01-12. Available at: <http://www.svd.se/nyheter/stockholm/omstridd-tull-har-rekordstort-stod_6763441.svd> [Accessed on 2013-12-02].

SvD, 2018. "Här är företagen som släpper ut mest koldioxid", *Svenska Dagbladet*, 2018-12-06. Available at: <https://www.svd.se/har-ar-foretagen-som-slapper-ut-mest-koldio xid> [accessed: 2019-03-04].

Swedish Association of Local Authorities and Regions, 2018. Öppna jämförelser. Kollek tivtrafik 2017. Report.

Swedish Environmental Protection Agency, 2007. *Yttrande över Vägverkets vägutredning effektivare Nord – Sydliga förbindelser i Stockholmsområdet. Beredning inför regeringens tillåtlighetsprövning enligt 17 kap miljöbalken.* Dnr 541-1701-07 Rv.

Swedish Environmental Protection Agency, 2019. *Underlag till regeringens klimatpolitiska handlingsplan. Redovisning av Naturvårdsverkets regeringsuppdrag.* Report 6879.

Swedish Road Administration, 2005. *Vägutredning för Nordsydliga förbindelser i Stock holmsområdet.* Publication nr. 48590.

Swedish Road Administration, 2006. *Ställningstagande till vägutredningen Effektivare nord sydliga förbindelser i Stockholmsområdet.* PP20A 2002:1395.

Swedish Social Insurance Agency, 2016. "Sjukskrivning för reaktioner på svår stress ökar mest", *Psykisk ohälsa,* report 116-4 for series *Korta analyser,* 2016:2, pp. 1–5.

Swedish Society for Nature Conservation, 2009. *Synpunkter från Naturskyddsföreningen i Stockholms län på Förslag till regional utvecklingsplan för Stockholmsregionen – RUFS 2010.*

Swedish Transport Administration, 2011a. *E4 Förbifart Stockholm.* Paper, publication 100 409.

Swedish Transport Administration, 2011b. *Uppdatering av förstudie Ekerövägen väg 261.* Available at: <https://www.trafikverket.se/contentassets/8490f85abc0c491e97954d7ec 3e3d639/arkiv/5_uppdatering_av_forstudievag261.pdf> [accessed 2018-12-03].

Swedish Transport Administration, 2013. *Så används trängselskatten i Stockholm.* Available from: <http://www.trafikverket.se/Aktuellt/Nyhetsarkiv/Nyhetsarkiv2/Lansvisa-ny heter/Stockholm/2013-05/Sa-anvands-trangselskatten/> [accessed 2015-03-20].

Swedish Transport Administration, 2014. *Förbifart Stockholm: Om projektet.* Available from: <http://www.trafikverket.se/Privat/Projekt/Stockholm/Forbifart-stockholm/ Om-projektet> [accessed 2014-04-20.]

Swedish Transport Administration, 2015a. *Energieffektivisering och luftkvalitet.* Available at: <https://www.trafikverket.se/contentassets/8ee802f438714e0da9d481dac339dc7d/ provningar/energieffektivisering_luftkvalitet.pdf?fbclid=IwAR3pzmob2aez4oMNNo GOv_PUFr_otsxUYqSaNqwRgt5eT83bPrd92Zl94Egg> [accessed 2019-02-21].

Swedish Transport Administration, 2015b. *Så blir det i Hjulsta.* Available at: <https:// www.trafikverket.se/nara-dig/Stockholm/projekt-i-stockholms-lan/Forbifart- stockholm/Vagstrackning/Hjulsta/Sa-blir-det-i-Hjulsta/> [accessed 2019-03-07].

Swedish Transport Administration, 2017. *Så blir det i Akalla.* Available at: <https:// www.trafikverket.se/nara-dig/Stockholm/projekt-i-stockholms-lan/Forbifart- stockholm/Vagstrackning/Akalla/Sa-blir-det-i-Akalla/ > [accessed 2019-03-07].

Swedish Transport Administration, 2018a. *Miljö och klimat E4 Förbifart Stockholm.* Avail- able at: <https://www.trafikverket.se/nara-dig/Stockholm/vi-bygger-och-forbattrar/ Forbifart-stockholm/Miljo/> [accessed 2019-09-20].

Swedish Transport Administration, 2018b. *Om E4 Förbifart Stockholm-projektet.* Available at: <https://www.trafikverket.se/nara-dig/Stockholm/vi-bygger-och-forbattrar/ Forbifart-stockholm/Om-projektet/> [accessed 2019-08-20].

Swedish Transport Agency and Swedish Transport Administration, 2015. *Allt större gap mellan utsläppsminskning och klimatmålen.* Press release, 2015-02-27. Available from: <http://www.trafikverket.se/Pressrum/Pressmeddelanden1/Nationellt/2015/2015-

13. REFERENCES

02/Pressmeddelande-fran-Transportstyrelsen-och-Trafikverket-Allt-storre-gap-mellan-utslappsminskning-och-klimatmalen> [accessed 2015-03-24].

Swedish Transport Agency, 2018a. *Bonus malus-system för personbilar, lätta lastbilar och lätta bussar.* Available at: <https://www.transportstyrelsen.se/bonusmalus> [accessed 2019-09-20].

Swedish Transport Agency, 2018b. *Statistik 2017.* Available at: <https://transportstyrelsen.se/sv/vagtrafik/statistik/trangselskatt11/stockholm/statistik-2017/> [accessed 2019-09-20].

Swedish Transport Agency, 2019. *Statistik trängselskatt Stockholm 2018.* Available at: <https://transportstyrelsen.se/sv/vagtrafik/statistik/trangselskatt11/stockholm/statistik-2018/> [accessed 2019-09-20].

SVT, 2015. "Riksdagen vill sänka bullerkrav", *Sveriges Television*, 2015-04-29. Available at: <https://www.svt.se/nyheter/inrikes/riksdagen-vill-sanka-bullerkrav> [accessed 2019-03-07].

SVT, 2018. "Här är klimatbovarna som är värre än flyget", *Sveriges Television,* 2018-07-29. Available at: <https://www.svt.se/nyheter/har-ar-klimatbovarna-som-ar-varre-an-flyget> [accessed 2019-03-04].

Säll, A., 2018. "Stockholms utmaning: fler bebisar och fler pensionärer", *Dagens Nyheter,* 2018-05-15. Available at: <https://www.dn.se/sthlm/stockholms-utmaning-fler-bebisar-och-fler-pensionarer/> [accessed 2019-09-20].

Söderström O, S Randeria, G D'Amato and F Panese, 2013. "Of mobilities and moorings: critical perspectives" in Söderström O, S Randeria, G D'Amato and F Panese (eds), *Critical Mobilities.* Routledge, London, pp. 1–21.

Tamsons K et al., 2016. "Sveriges tillväxtmotor har drabbats av växtvärk", *Dagens Samhälle,* 2016-04-16. Available at: <https://www.dagenssamhalle.se/debatt/svergies-tillvaext motor-har-drabbats-av-vaextvaerk-24186> [accessed 2019-03-06].

The Stockholm Negotiation, Ministry of Enterprise and Innovation, 2013. *Överens kommelse om finansiering och medfinansiering av utbyggnad av tunnelbanan samt ökad bostadsbebyggelse i Stockholms län enligt 2013 års Stockholmsförhandling.*

Stockholm Negotiation, 2013a. *Utbyggnad av tunnelbanan och ökad bostadsbebyggelse i stockholms län.* Available at: <http://stockholmsforhandlingen.se/> [accessed 2019-09-20].

Stockholm Negotiation, 2013b. *Utbyggd tunnelbana för fler bostäder. Delrapport från 2013 års Stockholmsförhandling.* N 2013:01.

Theodoulou S, 2013. "The contemporary language of public policy: starting to understand" in S Theodoulou and M Cahn (eds.), *Public Policy. The Essential Readings.* Pearson, pp. 1–11.

Thuresson Kämpe J, 2019. "SOFO bävar inför bilfri festsäsong", *Södermalmsnytt,* 2019-02-16, pp. 4–5.

Thörnqvist D, 2016. "Promenadstaden är stendöd. Igen." *Yimby,* 2016-03-23. Available at: <http://www.yimby.se/2016/03/promenadstaden-ar-stendod_3801.html> [accessed 2019-01-25].

Tonell, L., 1997. "Stockholms trafikplanering – värderingar och underlag för beslut" / "Stockholm's traffic planning – values and bases for decisions", *Bebyggelsehistorisk tidskrift*, Vol. 34, pp. 119–136.

Tottmar, M., 2018. "Stockholms befolkning växer – med en buss om dagen", *Dagens Nyheter* 2018-11-12.

Tovatt L and A Askeljung 2013. "Sluta bygg Sveriges städer efter bilen", *Sveriges Television*, 2013-10-28. Available at: <https://www.svt.se/opinion/sluta-bygg-sveriges-stader-efter-bilen> [accessed 2019-03-07].

Trafikanalys, 2012. *Lokal och regional kollektivtrafik 2012. Local and regional public transport 2012. Statistik 2013:20.* Report, June 2013.

Transek, 2006. "Kollektivtrafikens marknadsutveckling – tendenser och samband." Report for Transek AB, 2006-09-27.

Trivector, 2009. *Kollektivtrafik på Förbifart Stockholm. Spår eller buss?* Report for SL, 2009:09.

Trivector, 2018. *Drivkrafter resandeutveckling med bil.* Report 2018:7.

Trött på MP, 2017. "Boendeparkering – som en trisslott", *Mitt i*, 2017-05-12. Available at: <https://mitti.se/debatt/insandare/insandare-boendeparkering-trisslott/?omrade=kungsholmen> [accessed 2019-03-07].

Ulver, S., 2018. "Därför sätter långresenärerna klimatmedvetenheten på paus", *Dagens Nyheter (Kulturen)*, 2018-01-08, p. 10.

Ulver, S., 2018. "Därför sätter långresenärerna klimatmedvetenheten på paus", *Dagens Nyheter*, 2018-01-18, p. 10.

Unesco, 2016. *State of Conservation of World Heritage Properties in Europe.* Available at: <https://whc.unesco.org/document/163339> [accessed 2019-03-06].

United Nations, 2018. "Percentage of the Tot. Pop. Residing in Each Urban Aggl. with 300,000 or more in 2018." *World Urbanization Prospects 2018.* Available at: <https://population.un.org/wup/DataQuery/> [accessed 2019-09-13].

Urry, J., 2004. "The 'System' of Automobility", *Theory, Culture & Society*, Vol. 21, pp. 25–39.

Urry, J., 2012. "Changing transport and changing climates", *Journal of Transport Geography*, Vol. 24, pp. 533–535.

UT, 2010. "Bilen basen för stressade shoppare", *Ulricehamns Tidning*, 2010-09-02. Available at <http://www.ut.se/ulricehamn/bilen-basen-for-stressade-shoppare> [accessed 2019-02-14].

Van der Vleuten, E., R. Oldenziel and M. Davids, 2017. *Engineering the future, understanding the past.* Amsterdam University Press.

Vedung, E., 1997. *Public policy and program evaluation.* Transaction Publishers, New Jersey.

Vickerman, 2000. "Transport and Economic Growth", *Institute of Transport Studies Working Paper*, Issue ITS-WP-00-11, July 2000.

Virgin, K., 2018. "Byt jobb och höj din lön!", *Ingenjören*, 2018-03-29. Available at: <http://www.ingenjoren.se/2018/03/29/52050/> [accessed 2019-02-25].

WCED, 1987. *Our Common Future.* Oxford University Press, Oxford.

Wells, P., P. Nieuwenhuis, R. J. Orsato, 2012. "The nature and causes of inertia in the automotive industry: regime stability and non-change" in F. W. Geels, R. Kemp, G. Dudley and G. Lyons, 2012. *Automobility in transition? A socio-technical analysis of sustainable transport.* Routledge, pp. 123–139.

Wikesjö, M., 2015. "Cykelmotståndare förstår inte orsak och verkan", *Dagens Nyheter*, 2015-09-14. Available at: <https://www.dn.se/asikt/cykelmotstandare-forstar-inte-orsak-och-verkan/> [accessed 2019-03-07].

Winberg, J. Z., 2014. "Kraftiga prisökningar i kollektivtrafiken", *SVT Nyheter*, 2014-02-24. Available from: http://www.svt.se/nyheter/inrikes/kraftiga-prisokningar-i-kollektivtra fiken [accessed 2014-02-02].

Ydstedt, A., 2017. "En parkering per bostad borde gälla", *Tidningen Årsta/Enskede* (now part of *StockholmDirekt*), May 6–12 2017.

Zetterlund, H., 2015. *Rätten att gå till kungs. En genealogisk studie av besvärsrättens funktion och framtid i stadsplaneringens Sverige.* Master thesis, KTH Royal Institute of Technology.

Åkerman, J., 2011. *Transport systems meeting climate targets – a backcasting approach including international aviation.* PhD thesis, Royal Institute of Technology in Stockholm.

Öbrink, A., 2019. "Nu inleds fabriksbygget som kan ge 3000 jobb", *SVT Nyheter*. Available at: <https://www.svt.se/nyheter/lokalt/vasterbotten/nu-inleds-fabriksbygget-som-blir-storre-an-gamla-stan> [accessed 2019-08-14].

Önneby, A., 2015. "Vari ligger elitismen att tänka på framtiden?", *Svenska Dagbladet*, 2015-09-09. Available at: <https://www.dn.se/asikt/magnus-ahlden-vari-ligger-elitismen-i-att-tanka-pa-framtiden/> [accessed 2019-03-07].

Österberg, E., 2014. "Dyrare att resa kollektivt", *Dagens Nyheter*, 2014-02-24. Available at: <https://www.dn.se/nyheter/sverige/dyrare-att-resa-kollektivt/> [accessed 2019-09-20].

14
Appendix: Measures and the problems they represent

MEASURE	DETAIL	'PROBLEM'
Non-motorized transport		
More bicycle lanes and –parking	- Extended, wider, and new bicycle lanes - Extending the loan cycle system and adding more bicycles - Thirty new "bicycle projects" are connected to the metro and rail extensions in Stockholm - Shifting space from cars (parking) to bikes	- Insufficient infrastructure – people should cycle more, or longer - Insufficient access to cycles; it should be easier to cycle w/o owning - Cars take up space needed for bicycles - There needs to be more cycling; cycling is a 'solution' – insufficient cycle mobility - There needs to be fewer cars, cars are a 'problem'
More attractive and safer walkways for pedestrians	Possibly signal priority in high-traffic intersections	- Insufficient priority to pedestrians - Insufficient safety of pedestrians – they should be protected against cars etc
Promote teleworking	e.g. by good internet access, job cafés	- If people had better internet access, they wouldn't need to travel to work. Insufficient support for computer work. - Possibility that people travel to work even when they don't need to? This kind of 'unnecessary' journey is a strain on the transport system.

Information	- Traffic information to travellers - Information on laws and regulations for cyclists - Improve information on bicycle lanes	- People are insufficiently informed. - Making bad choices of route? - Making bad choices re: laws and rules? - Mis- or ill-informed on the possibilities, leading to fewer cyclists than desired?
Signal priority to bicycles, in some cases pedestrians		Insufficient mobility of cyclists, perhaps of pedestrians
Public transport		

Rail extensions	- Metro extensions
	  - Odenplan to KI and Solna
	  - To Älvsjö (from Hagsätra or from Fridhemsplan)
	  - Kungsträdgården to Nacka and Tyresö (or to Nacka and Gullmarsplan)
	- Extended light rail/tvärbanan (Hammarby to Slussen; Alvik to Solna and Kista)
	- Spårväg syd (new light rail)
	- Increased capacity on regional and commuter tracks
	- Citybanan (new commuter rail tracks through the city)
	- Rail to Barkarby (connecting with Hjulsta and Akalla)
		- Insufficient supply of rail transport
		- Insufficient connection between Nacka, Solna, and Barkarby to the city and the central public transport network
		- Insufficient connection between the southern end of the red metro line and commuter trains
		- Insufficient capacity of rail transport

More intensely used public transport	- Closer departures - More vehicles - Shorter stops (for example by more efficient ticket controls)	Inefficient use of public transport system = insufficient number of passengers

Information to promote public transport use	- To encourage businesses to promote public transport use for employees
	- Target people moving to or within the city with information on advantages of public transport
	- Targeted information and 'tester' campaigns, handled by SL
	- Information to travellers (to increase satisfaction)
	  - on the targets of the Mobility strategy
	  - on reasonable expectations on mobility
	  - on personal responsibility for the quality of the transport system
	  - on options, "making the right decision at the right time."
		- People are mis- or ill-informed, causing insufficient use of public transport
		- People may use cars out of habit
		- People may have unrealistic expectations of the transport system
		- People may neglect their personal responsibility for the quality of the transport system; people may negatively affect the quality of the transport system
		- People may make the 'wrong choices at the wrong time'

Supporting a change in the public transport fleet	This is strictly speaking beyond the control of the City, but the City can participate in demonstrations and work to secure infrastructure and fuel access.	Public transport carries some responsibility for emissions (this was achieved in 2018)
Signal priority to public transport or bicycles		Insufficient mobility of public transport or bicycles due to having to wait at signals
Public transport by water		- Insufficient land capacity? - Insufficient use of water as transport surface - Possible insufficient use of connections made possible by water

Cars to be purchased or discarded		
Promoting 'green' fuels and vehicles	- Information to prospective buyers of new vehicles; individuals and businesses o Participate in or run demonstrations on vehicles and fuel handling - Municipal procurement of 1000 electric cars as a way to push prices down - Procurement policy for municipal operations, e.g. home care services - Work for a long-term keeping and development of tax incentives for bio fuels - Harder environmental regulations for cars - Promote incentives to benefit and remove obstacles for 'green' vehicles and renewable fuels - Increased mix-in of alternative fuels in petroleum fuels; biogas in gas fuels	- People are mis- or ill-informed - People may not make the 'best' choices on their own - People may be wary of the 'best' technology due to insufficient information or familiarity - Too few cars bought might keep the prices too high (the City can help with this) - The vehicles used in municipal operations, through procurement as well, are the responsibility of the City; emissions from these vehicles are a problem - People need tax incentives to choose biofuels over fossil - suggests price is an obstacle for choosing biofuels - suggests people make 'wrong' choices for financial purposes - People will choose the 'wrong' cars until forced to do different - Regulations are too lenient for the 'wrong' cars (and the people choosing them) - There are obstacles for 'green' vehicles and fuels - The mix-in of alternative fuels is insufficient or sub-optimal
Junking bonus for older cars (this is, however, beyond		- People need to be encouraged to get rid of their older cars

the control of the City)		- Older cars are a problem - Without a junking bonus, people will not scrap their old cars, and they will remain on the streets - People will prefer one month's SL-ticket over money from selling their old car???
Parked cars		
Higher parking charges, charges where before parking was free	Higher costs as well as charges where before parking was free	- Parking was too cheap - People didn't pay for street space - Not paying encouraged people to use street space 'wrong'
Fewer parking spaces	- Removed entirely - Turned into public transport- or bicycle lanes or bicycle parking - Reconsider the parking norm (requiring minimum of cars for each new home)	• There are too many parking spaces – there are too many parked cars – there are too many cars • Cars use up space needed for public transport or cycling • Cars are habitually planned for in new areas; this is 'bad' and encourages unnecessary car use • People will use cars out of habit unless prompted to change
Tax on free or discount employee parking		- People will use cars out of habit unless prompted to change - People should pay for parking in all places, in some way
Allowing car pool cars to use residential parking (requires a change in law)		- Insufficient support for car pools – hard to find parking in the municipality

		- Car pool users should receive the same benefits as residents owning their cars - Possibly people owning their cars should be 'crowded out' by car pool users, to some degree?
Cars in motion		
Road extensions	- Stockholm Bypass and Eastern Link - Improvements to existing roads (tune-ups, widenings; re-routings; smaller extensions or new constructions of roads and bridges) - Extensions of existing roads	- Insufficient road capacity around the city - Insufficient transport work (by car) through/across the region

Fuels and vehicles	- Supporting infrastructure for biogas and electricity
	  - Increasing the collection of food waste in the municipality*
	  - Setting aside land for a biogas facility
	  - Constructing a new biogas facility*
	  - Parking spaces for car pool vehicles
	  - Parking space for electric cars, with chargers and possibly lower cost (requires a change in law, because it is currently not legal to differentiate parking charges based on type of car)
	  - Build a foundation for an infrastructure
		- Insufficient fueling infrastructure for biogas and electricity
		- Insufficient collection of food waste
		- Insufficient biogas production
		- Insufficient parking capacity for car pool vehicles and electric cars
		- Insufficient incentives, through parking, for a switch to electric vehicles OR prohibitively expensive to own and charge an electric vehicle, while electric vehicles are a service to society which should be promoted and/or rewarded

	for fuels and charging stations	
Congestion tax	- Differentiated, lower charge for 'green' cars - "Optimize" the use to reach targets - Extend the toll or time zone	- Unfair or suboptimal charge; 'green' cars are a service to society which should be promoted/rewarded; insufficient incentives to switch cars - Suboptimal use of the tax risks the targets not being reached = too lenient congestion tax risks too high emissions - The charge is not covering all the times and places it should (connected to the Negotiations, it doesn't rake in as much revenue as it should)
Information	- To travellers on current traffic for smoother traffic flow and 'smart' choices - To businesses on more efficient business journeys - Recommend economic driving to businesses; give subsidies to businesses to establish routines and follow-up - To businesses on economic (fuel-saving) driving - To businesses on how to promote change in travel behaviour among employees - On fuel use and economic driving - To encourage a shift from private car to car pool	- People are mis- or ill-informed – this leads to 'dumb' choices, congestion - People and businesses use inefficient journeys, or use vehicles inefficiently, due to mis- or ill-information - People's travel behaviour is inefficient or 'bad'; employers should encourage change - Private cars are a problem - People have unreasonable expectations on transport system, etc

	- Information to travellers (to increase satisfaction) - on the targets of the Mobility Strategy - on reasonable expectations on mobility - on personal responsibility for the quality of the transport system - on options, "making the right decision at the right time."	
City-wide ban on fossil fuel sale after 2050		Availability of fossil fuels is a problem (or, it's no use banning them until the city is fossil fuel-free)
Climate tax (in addition to the congestion tax, operating at all times of the day and differentiating between how much carbon dioxide cars emit)		Carbon dioxide is a problem, people should pay for their emissions = unpaid-for emissions are a problem
Spiked tire ban or tax, local or city-wide		- Spike tire use is a problem, at least in some places - Unpaid-for spike tire use is a problem
Signal priority to public transport and non-motorized transport, limiting mobility of cars		Signals hamper the mobility of public transport and non-motorized transport; these modes should be promoted (at the expense of cars)
Environmental zoning for private vehicles		Emissions are a problem; some cars should be banned from parts of the city – 'wrong' technology is a problem

Was ist ist
Was nicht ist, ist möglich
Nur was nicht ist, ist möglich
Einstürzende Neubauten (1996), *Was ist ist*

What is, is
What is not, is possible
Only what is not is possible

Södertörn Doctoral Dissertations

1. Jolanta Aidukaite, *The Emergence of the Post-Socialist Welfare State: The case of the Baltic States: Estonia, Latvia and Lithuania*, 2004

2. Xavier Fraudet, *Politique étrangère française en mer Baltique (1871–1914): de l'exclusion à l'affirmation*, 2005

3. Piotr Wawrzeniuk, *Confessional Civilising in Ukraine: The Bishop Iosyf Shumliansky and the Introduction of Reforms in the Diocese of Lviv 1668–1708*, 2005

4. Andrej Kotljarchuk, *In the Shadows of Poland and Russia: The Grand Duchy of Lithuania and Sweden in the European Crisis of the mid-17th Century*, 2006

5. Håkan Blomqvist, *Nation, ras och civilisation i svensk arbetarrörelse före nazismen*, 2006

6. Karin S Lindelöf, *Om vi nu ska bli som Europa: Könsskapande och normalitet bland unga kvinnor i transitionens Polen*, 2006

7. Andrew Stickley. *On Interpersonal Violence in Russia in the Present and the Past: A Sociological Study*, 2006

8. Arne Ek, *Att konstruera en uppslutning kring den enda vägen: Om folkrörelsers modernisering i skuggan av det Östeuropeiska systemskiftet*, 2006

9. Agnes Ers, *I mänsklighetens namn: En etnologisk studie av ett svenskt biståndsprojekt i Rumänien*, 2006

10. Johnny Rodin, *Rethinking Russian Federalism: The Politics of Intergovernmental Relations and Federal Reforms at the Turn of the Millennium*, 2006

11. Kristian Petrov, *Tillbaka till framtiden: Modernitet, postmodernitet och generationsidentitet i Gorbačevs glasnost' och perestrojka*, 2006

12. Sophie Söderholm Werkö, *Patient patients? Achieving Patient Empowerment through Active Participation, Increased Knowledge and Organisation*, 2008

13. Peter Bötker, *Leviatan i arkipelagen: Staten, förvaltningen och samhället. Fallet Estland*, 2007

14. Matilda Dahl, *States under scrutiny: International organizations, transformation and the construction of progress*, 2007

15. Margrethe B. Søvik, *Support, resistance and pragmatism: An examination of motivation in language policy in Kharkiv, Ukraine*, 2007

16. Yulia Gradskova, *Soviet People with female Bodies: Performing beauty and maternity in Soviet Russia in the mid 1930–1960s*, 2007

17. Renata Ingbrant, *From Her Point of View: Woman's Anti-World in the Poetry of Anna Świrszczyńska*, 2007

18. Johan Eellend, *Cultivating the Rural Citizen: Modernity, Agrarianism and Citizenship in Late Tsarist Estonia*, 2007

19. Petra Garberding, *Musik och politik i skuggan av nazismen: Kurt Atterberg och de svensk-tyska musikrelationerna*, 2007

20. Aleksei Semenenko, *Hamlet the Sign: Russian Translations of Hamlet and Literary Canon Formation*, 2007

21. Vytautas Petronis, *Constructing Lithuania: Ethnic Mapping in the Tsarist Russia, ca. 1800–1914*, 2007

22. Akvile Motiejunaite, *Female employment, gender roles, and attitudes: the Baltic countries in a broader context*, 2008

23. Tove Lindén, *Explaining Civil Society Core Activism in Post-Soviet Latvia*, 2008

24. Pelle Åberg, *Translating Popular Education: Civil Society Cooperation between Sweden and Estonia*, 2008

25. Anders Nordström, *The Interactive Dynamics of Regulation: Exploring the Council of Europe's monitoring of Ukraine*, 2008

26. Fredrik Doeser, *In Search of Security After the Collapse of the Soviet Union: Foreign Policy Change in Denmark, Finland and Sweden, 1988–1993*, 2008

27. Zhanna Kravchenko. *Family (versus) Policy: Combining Work and Care in Russia and Sweden*, 2008

28. Rein Jüriado, *Learning within and between public-private partnerships*, 2008

29. Elin Boalt, *Ecology and evolution of tolerance in two cruciferous species*, 2008

30. Lars Forsberg, *Genetic Aspects of Sexual Selection and Mate Choice in Salmonids*, 2008

31. Eglė Rindzevičiūtė, *Constructing Soviet Cultural Policy: Cybernetics and Governance in Lithuania after World War II*, 2008

32. Joakim Philipson, *The Purpose of Evolution: 'struggle for existence' in the Russian-Jewish press 1860–1900*, 2008

33. Sofie Bedford, *Islamic activism in Azerbaijan: Repression and mobilization in a post-Soviet context*, 2009

34. Tommy Larsson Segerlind, *Team Entrepreneurship: A process analysis of the venture team and the venture team roles in relation to the innovation process*, 2009

35. Jenny Svensson, *The Regulation of Rule-Following: Imitation and Soft Regulation in the European Union*, 2009

36. Stefan Hallgren, *Brain Aromatase in the guppy, Poecilia reticulate: Distribution, control and role in behavior*, 2009

37. Karin Ellencrona, *Functional characterization of interactions between the flavivirus NS5 protein and PDZ proteins of the mammalian host*, 2009

38. Makiko Kanematsu, *Saga och verklighet: Barnboksproduktion i det postsovjetiska Lettland*, 2009

39. Daniel Lindvall, *The Limits of the European Vision in Bosnia and Herzegovina: An Analysis of the Police Reform Negotiations*, 2009

40. Charlotta Hillerdal, *People in Between – Ethnicity and Material Identity: A New Approach to Deconstructed Concepts*, 2009

41. Jonna Bornemark, *Kunskapens gräns – gränsens vetande*, 2009

42. Adolphine G. Kateka, *Co-Management Challenges in the Lake Victoria Fisheries: A Context Approach*, 2010

43. René León Rosales, *Vid framtidens hitersta gräns: Om pojkar och elevpositioner i en multietnisk skola*, 2010

44. Simon Larsson, *Intelligensaristokrater och arkivmartyrer: Normerna för vetenskaplig skicklighet i svensk historieforskning 1900–1945*, 2010

45. Håkan Lättman, *Studies on spatial and temporal distributions of epiphytic lichens*, 2010

46. Alia Jaensson, *Pheromonal mediated behaviour and endocrine response in salmonids: The impact of cypermethrin, copper, and glyphosate*, 2010

47. Michael Wigerius, *Roles of mammalian Scribble in polarity signaling, virus offense and cellfate determination*, 2010

48. Anna Hedtjärn Wester, *Män i kostym: Prinsar, konstnärer och tegelbärare vid sekelskiftet 1900*, 2010

49. Magnus Linnarsson, *Postgång på växlande villkor: Det svenska postväsendets organisation under stormaktstiden*, 2010

50. Barbara Kunz, *Kind words, cruise missiles and everything in between: A neoclassical realist study of the use of power resources in U.S. policies towards Poland, Ukraine and Belarus 1989–2008*, 2010

51. Anders Bartonek, *Philosophie im Konjunktiv: Nichtidentität als Ort der Möglichkeit des Utopischen in der negativen Dialektik Theodor W. Adornos*, 2010

52. Carl Cederberg, *Resaying the Human: Levinas Beyond Humanism and Antihumanism*, 2010

53. Johanna Ringarp, *Professionens problematik: Lärarkårens kommunalisering och välfärdsstatens förvandling*, 2011

54. Sofi Gerber, *Öst är Väst men Väst är bäst: Östtysk identitetsformering i det förenade Tyskland*, 2011

55. Susanna Sjödin Lindenskoug, *Manlighetens bortre gräns: Tidelagsrättegångar i Livland åren 1685–1709*, 2011

56. Dominika Polanska, *The emergence of enclaves of wealth and poverty: A sociological study of residential differentiation in post-communist Poland*, 2011

57. Christina Douglas, *Kärlek per korrespondens: Två förlovade par under andra hälften av 1800-talet*, 2011

58. Fred Saunders, *The Politics of People – Not just Mangroves and Monkeys: A study of the theory and practice of community-based management of natural resources in Zanzibar*, 2011

59. Anna Rosengren, *Åldrandet och språket: En språkhistorisk analys av hög ålder och åldrande i Sverige cirka 1875–1975*, 2011

60. Emelie Lilliefeldt, *European Party Politics and Gender: Configuring Gender-Balanced Parliamentary Presence*, 2011

61. Ola Svenonius, *Sensitising Urban Transport Security: Surveillance and Policing in Berlin, Stockholm, and Warsaw*, 2011

62. Andreas Johansson, *Dissenting Democrats: Nation and Democracy in the Republic of Moldova*, 2011

63. Wessam Melik, *Molecular characterization of the Tick-borne encephalitis virus: Environments and replication*, 2012

64. Steffen Werther, *SS-Vision und Grenzland-Realität: Vom Umgang dänischer und „volksdeutscher" Nationalsozialisten in Sønderjylland mit der „großgermanischen" Ideologie der SS*, 2012

65. Peter Jakobsson, *Öppenhetsindustrin*, 2012

66. Kristin Ilves, *Seaward Landward: Investigations on the archaeological source value of the landing site category in the Baltic Sea region*, 2012

67. Anne Kaun, *Civic Experiences and Public Connection: Media and Young People in Estonia*, 2012

68. Anna Tessmann, *On the Good Faith: A Fourfold Discursive Construction of Zoroastripanism in Contemporary Russia*, 2012

69. Jonas Lindström, *Drömmen om den nya staden: stadsförnyelse i det postsovjetisk Riga*, 2012

70. Maria Wolrath Söderberg, *Topos som meningsskapare: retorikens topiska perspektiv på tänkande och lärande genom argumentation*, 2012

71. Linus Andersson, *Alternativ television: former av kritik i konstnärlig TV-produktion*, 2012

72. Håkan Lättman, *Studies on spatial and temporal distributions of epiphytic lichens*, 2012

73. Fredrik Stiernstedt, *Mediearbete i mediehuset: produktion i förändring på MTG-radio*, 2013

74. Jessica Moberg, *Piety, Intimacy and Mobility: A Case Study of Charismatic Christianity in Present-day Stockholm*, 2013

75. Elisabeth Hemby, *Historiemåleri och bilder av vardag: Tatjana Nazarenkos konstnärskap i 1970-talets Sovjet*, 2013

76. Tanya Jukkala, *Suicide in Russia: A macro-sociological study*, 2013

77. Maria Nyman, *Resandets gränser: svenska resenärers skildringar av Ryssland under 1700-talet*, 2013

78. Beate Feldmann Eellend, *Visionära planer och vardagliga praktiker: postmilitära landskap i Östersjöområdet,* 2013

79. Emma Lind, *Genetic response to pollution in sticklebacks: natural selection in the wild,* 2013

80. Anne Ross Solberg, *The Mahdi wears Armani: An analysis of the Harun Yahya enterprise,* 2013

81. Nikolay Zakharov, *Attaining Whiteness: A Sociological Study of Race and Racialization in Russia,* 2013

82. Anna Kharkina, *From Kinship to Global Brand: the Discourse on Culture in Nordic Cooperation after World War II,* 2013

83. Florence Fröhlig, *A painful legacy of World War II: Nazi forced enlistment: Alsatian/Mosellan Prisoners of war and the Soviet Prison Camp of Tambov,* 2013

84. Oskar Henriksson, *Genetic connectivity of fish in the Western Indian Ocean,* 2013

85. Hans Geir Aasmundsen, *Pentecostalism, Globalisation and Society in Contemporary Argentina,* 2013

86. Anna McWilliams, *An Archaeology of the Iron Curtain: Material and Metaphor,* 2013

87. Anna Danielsson, *On the power of informal economies and the informal economies of power: rethinking informality, resilience and violence in Kosovo,* 2014

88. Carina Guyard, *Kommunikationsarbete på distans,* 2014

89. Sofia Norling, *Mot "väst": om vetenskap, politik och transformation i Polen 1989–2011,* 2014

90. Markus Huss, *Motståndets akustik: språk och (o)ljud hos Peter Weiss 1946–1960,* 2014

91. Ann-Christin Randahl, *Strategiska skribenter: skrivprocesser i fysik och svenska,* 2014

92. Péter Balogh, *Perpetual borders: German-Polish cross-border contacts in the Szczecin area,* 2014

93. Erika Lundell, *Förkroppsligad fiktion och fiktionaliserade kroppar: levande rollspel i Östersjöregionen,* 2014

94. Henriette Cederlöf, *Alien Places in Late Soviet Science Fiction: The "Unexpected Encounters" of Arkady and Boris Strugatsky as Novels and Films,* 2014

95. Niklas Eriksson, *Urbanism Under Sail: An archaeology of fluit ships in early modern everyday life,* 2014

96. Signe Opermann, *Generational Use of News Media in Estonia: Media Access, Spatial Orientations and Discursive Characteristics of the News Media,* 2014

97. Liudmila Voronova, *Gendering in political journalism: A comparative study of Russia and Sweden,* 2014

98. Ekaterina Kalinina, *Mediated Post-Soviet Nostalgia,* 2014

99. Anders E. B. Blomqvist, *Economic Natonalizing in the Ethnic Borderlands of Hungary and Romania: Inclusion, Exclusion and Annihilation in Szatmár/Satu-Mare, 1867–1944,* 2014

100. Ann-Judith Rabenschlag, *Völkerfreundschaft nach Bedarf: Ausländische Arbeitskräfte in der Wahrnehmung von Staat und Bevölkerung der DDR,* 2014

101. Yuliya Yurchuck, *Ukrainian Nationalists and the Ukrainian Insurgent Army in Post-Soviet Ukraine,* 2014

102. Hanna Sofia Rehnberg, *Organisationer berättar: narrativitet som resurs i strategisk kommunikation,* 2014

103. Jaakko Turunen, *Semiotics of Politics: Dialogicality of Parliamentary Talk,* 2015

104. Iveta Jurkane-Hobein, *I Imagine You Here Now: Relationship Maintenance Strategies in Long-Distance Intimate Relationships,* 2015

105. Katharina Wesolowski, *Maybe baby? Reproductive behaviour, fertility intentions, and family policies in post-communist countries, with a special focus on Ukraine,* 2015

106. Ann af Burén, *Living Simultaneity: On religion among semi-secular Swedes,* 2015

107. Larissa Mickwitz, *En reformerad lärare: konstruktionen av en professionell och betygssättande lärare i skolpolitik och skolpraktik,* 2015

108. Daniel Wojahn, *Språkaktivism: diskussioner om feministiska språkförändringar i Sverige från 1960-talet till 2015,* 2015

109. Hélène Edberg, *Kreativt skrivande för kritiskt tänkande: en fallstudie av studenters arbete med kritisk metareflektion,* 2015

110. Kristina Volkova, *Fishy Behavior: Persistent effects of early-life exposure to 17α-ethinylestradiol,* 2015

111. Björn Sjöstrand, *Att tänka det tekniska: en studie i Derridas teknikfilosofi,* 2015

112. Håkan Forsberg, *Kampen om eleverna: gymnasiefältet och skolmarknadens framväxt i Stockholm, 1987–2011,* 2015

113. Johan Stake, *Essays on quality evaluation and bidding behavior in public procurement auctions,* 2015

114. Martin Gunnarson, *Please Be Patient: A Cultural Phenomenological Study of Haemodialysis and Kidney Transplantation Care,* 2016

115. Nasim Reyhanian Caspillo, *Studies of alterations in behavior and fertility in ethinyl estradiol-exposed zebrafish and search for related biomarkers,* 2016

116. Pernilla Andersson, *The Responsible Business Person: Studies of Business Education for Sustainability,* 2016

117. Kim Silow Kallenberg, *Gränsland: svensk ungdomsvård mellan vård och straff,* 2016

118. Sari Vuorenpää, *Literacitet genom interaction,* 2016

119. Francesco Zavatti, *Writing History in a Propaganda Institute: Political Power and Network Dynamics in Communist Romania,* 2016

120. Cecilia Annell, *Begärets politiska potential: Feministiska motståndsstrategier i Elin Wägners 'Pennskaftet', Gabriele Reuters 'Aus guter Familie', Hilma Angered-Strandbergs 'Lydia Vik' och Grete Meisel-Hess 'Die Intellektuellen',* 2016

121. Marco Nase, *Academics and Politics: Northern European Area Studies at Greifswald University, 1917–1992*, 2016

122. Jenni Rinne, *Searching for Authentic Living Through Native Faith – The Maausk movement in Estonia*, 2016

123. Petra Werner, *Ett medialt museum: lärandets estetik i svensk television 1956–1969*, 2016

124. Ramona Rat, *Un-common Sociality: Thinking sociality with Levinas*, 2016

125. Petter Thureborn, *Microbial ecosystem functions along the steep oxygen gradient of the Landsort Deep, Baltic Sea*, 2016

126. Kajsa-Stina Benulic, *A Beef with Meat Media and audience framings of environmentally unsustainable production and consumption*, 2016

127. Naveed Asghar, *Ticks and Tick-borne Encephalitis Virus – From nature to infection*, 2016

128. Linn Rabe, *Participation and legitimacy: Actor involvement for nature conservation*, 2017

129. Maryam Adjam, *Minnesspår: hågkomstens rum och rörelse i skuggan av en flykt*, 2017

130. Kim West, *The Exhibitionary Complex: Exhibition, Apparatus and Media from Kulturhuset to the Centre Pompidou, 1963–1977*, 2017

131. Ekaterina Tarasova, *Anti-nuclear Movements in Discursive and Political Contexts: Between expert voices and local protests*, 2017

132. Sanja Obrenović Johansson, *Från kombifeminism till rörelse: Kvinnlig serbisk organisering i förändring*, 2017

133. Michał Salamonik, *In Their Majesties' Service: The Career of Francesco De Gratta (1613–1676) as a Royal Servant and Trader in Gdańsk*, 2017

134. Jenny Ingridsdotter, *The Promises of the Free World: Postsocialist Experience in Argentina and the Making of Migrants, Race, and Coloniality*, 2017

135. Julia Malitska, *Negotiating Imperial Rule: Colonists and Marriage in the Nineteenth century Black Sea Steppe*, 2017

136. Natalya Yakusheva, *Parks, Policies and People: Nature Conservation Governance in Post-Socialist EU Countries*, 2017

137. Martin Kellner, *Selective Serotonin Re-uptake Inhibitors in the Environment: Effects of Citalopram on Fish Behaviour*, 2017

138. Krystof Kasprzak, *Vara – Framträdande – Värld: Fenomenets negativitet hos Martin Heidegger, Jan Patočka och Eugen Fink*, 2017

139. Alberto Frigo, *Life-stowing from a Digital Media Perspective: Past, Present and Future*, 2017

140. Maarja Saar, *The Answers You Seek Will Never Be Found At Home: Reflexivity, biographical narratives and lifestyle migration among highly-skilled Estonians*, 2017

141. Anh Mai, *Organizing for Efficiency: Essay on merger policies, independence of authorities, and technology diffusion*, 2017

142. Gustav Strandberg, *Politikens omskakning: Negativitet, samexistens och frihet i Jan Patočkas tänkande*, 2017

143. Lovisa Andén, *Litteratur och erfarenhet i Merleau-Pontys läsning av Proust, Valéry och Stendhal*, 2017

144. Fredrik Bertilsson, *Frihetstida policyskapande: uppfostringskommissionen och de akademiska konstitutionerna 1738–1766*, 2017

145. Börjeson, Natasja, *Toxic Textiles – towards responsibility in complex supply chains*, 2017

146. Julia Velkova, *Media Technologies in the Making – User-Driven Software and Infrastructures for computer Graphics Production*, 2017

147. Karin Jonsson, *Fångna i begreppen? Revolution, tid och politik i svensk socialistisk press 1917–1924*, 2017

148. Josefine Larsson, *Genetic Aspects of Environmental Disturbances in Marine Ecosystems – Studies of the Blue Mussel in the Baltic Sea*, 2017

149. Roman Horbyk, *Mediated Europes – Discourse and Power in Ukraine, Russia and Poland during Euromaidan*, 2017

150. Nadezda Petrusenko, *Creating the Revolutionary Heroines: The Case of Female Terrorists of the PSR (Russia, Beginning of the 20th Century)*, 2017

151. Rahel Kuflu, *Bröder emellan: Identitetsformering i det koloniserade Eritrea*, 2018

152. Karin Edberg, *Energilandskap i förändring: Inramningar av kontroversiella lokaliseringar på norra Gotland*, 2018

153. Rebecka Thor, *Beyond the Witness: Holocaust Representation and the Testimony of Images - Three films by Yael Hersonski, Harun Farocki, and Eyal Sivan*, 2018

154. Maria Lönn, *Bruten vithet: Om den ryska femininitetens sinnliga och temporala villkor*, 2018

155. Tove Porseryd, *Endocrine Disruption in Fish: Effects of 17α-ethinylestradiol exposure on non-reproductive behavior, fertility and brain and testis transcriptome*, 2018

156. Marcel Mangold, *Securing the working democracy: Inventive arrangements to guarantee circulation and the emergence of democracy policy*, 2018

157. Matilda Tudor, *Desire Lines: Towards a Queer Digital Media Phenomenology*, 2018

158. Martin Andersson, *Migration i 1600-talets Sverige: Älvsborgs lösen 1613–1618*, 2018

159. Johanna Pettersson, *What's in a Line? Making Sovereignty through Border Policy*, 2018

160. Irina Seits, *Architectures of Life-Building in the Twentieth Century: Russia, Germany, Sweden*, 2018

161. Alexander Stagnell, *The Ambassador's Letter: On the Less Than Nothing of Diplomacy*, 2019

162. Mari Zetterqvist Blokhuis, *Interaction Between Rider, Horse and Equestrian Trainer – A Challenging Puzzle*, 2019

163. Robin Samuelsson, *Play, Culture and Learning: Studies of Second-Language and Conceptual Development in Swedish Preschools*, 2019

164. Ralph Tafon, *Analyzing the "Dark Side" of Marine Spatial Planning – A study of domination, empowerment and freedom (or power in, of and on planning) through theories of discourse and power*, 2019

165. Ingela Visuri, *Varieties of Supernatural Experience: The case of high-functioning autism*, 2019

166. Mathilde Rehnlund, *Getting the transport right – for what? What transport policy can tell us about the construction of sustainability*, 2019

www.ingramcontent.com/pod-product-compliance
Lightning Source LLC
Chambersburg PA
CBHW050647270326
41927CB00012B/2914